AMC'S BEST DAY HIKES IN
THE CATSKILLS AND HUDSON VALLEY

Four-Season Guide to 60 of the Best Trails, from the Hudson Highlands to Albany

THIRD EDITION

PETER W. KICK

Appalachian Mountain Club Books
Boston, Massachusetts

AMC is a nonprofit organization, and sales of AMC Books fund our mission of protecting the Northeast outdoors. If you appreciate our efforts and would like to become a member or make a donation to AMC, visit outdoors.org, call 800-372-1758, or contact us at Appalachian Mountain Club, 5 Joy Street, Boston, MA 02108.

outdoors.org/publications/books

Distributed by National Book Network.

Front cover photograph photograph © Peter W. Kick
Back cover photographs © Dan Kong, Creative Commons on Flickr, and Eric Atkins, Creative Commons on Flickr
Interior photographs © Peter W. Kick, unless otherwise noted
Maps by Ken Dumas © Appalachian Mountain Club
Book design by Abigail Coyle

Library of Congress Cataloging-in-Publication Data
Names: Kick, Peter, 1951- author. | Appalachian Mountain Club.
Title: AMC's best day hikes in the Catskills and Hudson Valley : four-season guide to 60 of the best trails from New York City to Albany / Peter W. Kick.
Other titles: Best day hikes in the Catskills and Hudson Valley | Appalachian Mountain Club's best day hikes in the Catskills and Hudson Valley
Description: Third Edition. | Boston, Massachusetts : Appalachian Mountain Club Books, [2017] | "Distributed by National Book Network"--T.p. verso. | Second edition: 2011. | Includes index.
Identifiers: LCCN 2016052062| ISBN 9781628420548 (paperback : alk. paper) | ISBN 9781628420555 (Epub) | ISBN 9781628420562 (Mobi)
Subjects: LCSH: Hiking--New York (State)--Catskill Mountains--Guidebooks. | Hiking--Hudson River Valley (N.Y. and N.J.)--Guidebooks. | Trails--New York (State)--Catskill Mountains--Guidebooks. | Trails--Hudson River Valley (N.Y. and N.J.)--Guidebooks. | Catskill Mountains (N.Y.)--Guidebooks. | Hudson River Valley (N.Y. and N.J.)--Guidebooks.
Classification: LCC GV199.42.N652 C3736 2017 | DDC 796.5109747--dc23 LC record available at https://lccn.loc.gov/2016052062

The paper used in this publication meets the minimum requirements of the American National Standard for Information Sciences-Permanence of Paper for Printed Library Materials, ANSIZ39.48-1984.

Interior pages contain 30% post-consumer recycled fiber.
Cover contains 10% post-consumer recycled fiber.
Printed in the United States of America,
using vegetable-based inks.

21 20 19 18 17   1 2 3 4 5

MIX
Paper from responsible sources
FSC www.fsc.org FSC® C005010

For Lori Lee Dickson

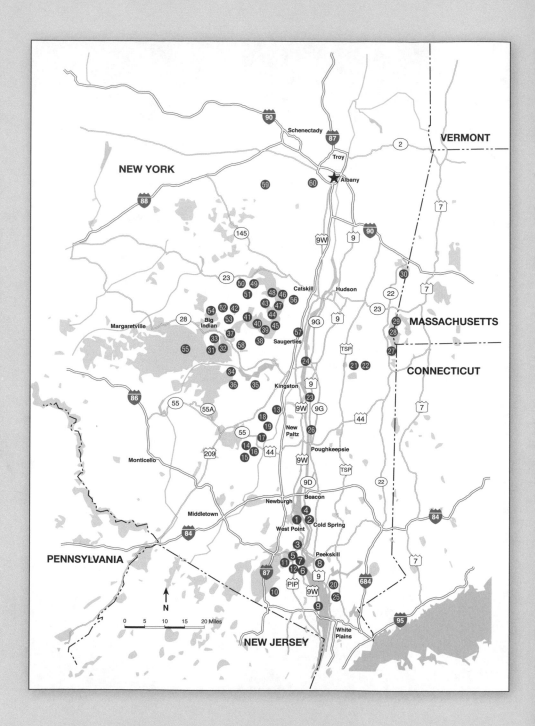

CONTENTS

AT-A-GLANCE TRIP PLANNER

TRIP NUMBER	TRIP NAME	LOCATION	DIFFICULTY	DISTANCE	ELEVATION GAIN
THE HUDSON HIGHLANDS					
1	Storm King Mountain	Cornwall-on-Hudson, NY	Moderate	6 mi	400 ft
2	Mount Taurus	Philipstown, NY	Moderate	6 mi	1,400 ft
3	Popolopen Gorge and the Torne	Fort Montgomery, NY	Moderate	4.5 mi	1,250 ft
4	Breakneck Ridge to South Beacon Mountain	Beacon, NY	Strenuous	9 mi	1,400 ft
5	Bear Mountain	Bear Mountain, NY	Strenuous	4 mi	1,000 ft
6	Dunderberg and the Timp	Stony Point, NY	Strenuous	0 mi	1,600 ft
7	Hessian Lake and Fort Montgomery State Historic Site	Fort Montgomery, NY	Easy	3.25 mi	350 ft
8	Anthony's Nose	Cortlandt, NY	Moderate	4 mi	700 ft
9	The Hook	Nyack, NY	Moderate	5.3 mi	1,200 ft
10	Diamond Mountain	Baileytown, NY	Moderate	4.8 mi	1,230 ft
11	Silvermine Lake and Black Mountain	Baileytown, NY	Moderate	4.5 mi	1,200 ft
12	West Mountain and Cat's Elbow	Bear Mountain, NY	Moderate	5 mi	1,467 ft
THE SHAWANGUNKS					
13	Bonticou Crag	New Paltz, NY	Moderate	3 mi	500 ft
14	Castle Point, Lake Awosting, and Margaret Cliff	New Paltz, NY	Moderate	10 mi	500 ft
15	Millbrook Mountain and Gertrude's Nose	New Paltz, NY	Strenuous	9.5 mi	850 ft
16	Lake Minnewaska	New Paltz, NY	Moderate	1.5 mi	230 ft
17	The Trapps	New Paltz, NY	Moderate	5 mi	400 ft
18	Sky Top	New Paltz, NY	Moderate	6 mi	650 ft
19	Eagle Cliff and Mohonk Lake	New Paltz, NY	Easy	6 mi (2 if you begin at the Mountain House)	625 ft

TIME	TRIP HIGHLIGHTS	FEE	GOOD FOR KIDS	DOG-FRIENDLY	PUBLIC TRANSIT	X-C SKIING	SNOWSHOEING
3 hrs	Signature Highlands hike with scenic views of the Hudson River			🐕			
5 hrs	A fairly relaxed outing with a few steep pitches through deep woods to a scenic viewpoint			🐕			🗹
3.5 hrs	360-degree views of the Hudson Valley			🐕	🚌		🗹
6 hrs	Quiet forests, views from open ridges, exposed scenic trail			🐕	🚌		
3.5 hrs	360-degree views	$		🐕	🚌		
4.5 hrs	A backcountry ramble through the interior Highlands' historic trails and remote forests			🐕		🎿	
2 hrs	Park, zoo, Revolutionary War site	$	🧒	🐕	🚌		
4 hrs	Memorable views of the Hudson River and Bear Mountain Bridge	$		🐕	🚌		
3.5 hrs	Scenic walk and climb of section of the northern Palisades	$		🐕	🚌		
4 hrs	High ridge hike with view of New York City skyline	$		🐕			🗹
3 hrs	Considered by many to be the best hike in Harriman State Park	$		🐕			🗹
4 hrs	Very scenic hike with views of the Hudson River, the Highlands, and New York City skyline	$		🐕			🗹
2.5 hrs	Vertical cliffs, excellent views	$					
6.5 hrs	Swimming in Lake Awosting, valley views from Castle Point	$		🐕		🎿	🗹
5.5 hrs	Glacial cobble fields, pitch-pine balds, sheer cliffs	$		🐕			🗹
2.5 hrs	Beautiful lake, far-reaching views	$		🐕		🎿	🗹
2 hrs	Easy hike, rock climbing	$	🧒	🐕		🎿	🗹
4 hrs	Crevice with interesting geology, ideal for young children	$					
3.5 hrs	View of nearby forests and mountains, benches along trail	$				🎿	🗹

TRIP NUMBER	TRIP NAME	LOCATION	DIFFICULTY	DISTANCE	ELEVATION GAIN
THE EASTERN MID-HUDSON REGION					
20	Old Croton Aqueduct	Croton-on-Hudson, NY	Moderate	4.75 mi	420 ft
21	Stissing Mountain	Pine Plains, NY	Moderate	3 mi	1,000 ft
22	Thompson Pond Preserve	Pine Plains, NY	Easy	3 mi	50 ft
23	Norrie Point	Staatsburg, NY	Moderate	5 mi	200 ft
24	Poets' Walk Romantic Landscape Park	Red Hook, NY	Easy	2 mi	200 ft
25	Teatown Lake Reservation	Ossining, NY	Easy-Moderate	Lakeside Trail: 1.5 mi Twin Lakes Trail: 2.3 mi Cliffdale Farm/ Catamount Hill Trail: 2.25 mi	Lakeside Trail: 187 ft Twin Lakes Trail: 450 ft Cliffdale Farm/ Catamount Hill Trail: 480 ft
26	Roosevelt Woods	Hyde Park, NY	Moderate	5 mi	200 ft
THE TACONICS					
27	Brace Mountain	Ancram, NY	Moderate	3.8 mi	1,300 ft
28	Alander Mountain	Mount Washington, MA	Moderate	8 mi	600 ft
29	Bash Bish Mountain	Mount Washington, MA	Moderate	3 mi	1,200 ft
30	Harvey Mountain	Austerlitz, NY	Moderate	3 mi	480 ft
THE CATSKILLS					
31	Slide Mountain	Shandaken, NY	Strenuous	7 mi	1,700 ft
32	Wittenberg and Cornell Mountains	Ulster, NY	Strenuous	9.4 mi	2,480 ft
33	Giant Ledge	Shandaken, NY	Moderate	3 mi	1,000 ft
34	Peekamoose and Table Mountains	Denning, NY	Strenuous	10 mi	2,200 ft
35	Ashokan Reservoir	Shokan, NY	Easy	4.5 mi	150 ft
36	Ashokan High Point	West Shokan, NY	Moderate	7.5 mi	1,980 ft
37	Mount Tremper	Mount Tremper, NY	Strenuous	5.6 mi	1,960 ft

TIME	TRIP HIGHLIGHTS	FEE	GOOD FOR KIDS	DOG-FRIENDLY	PUBLIC TRANSIT	X-C SKIING	SNOWSHOEING
3 hrs	Flat walk through deep woods, ideal for children, bicycles		✓	✓	✓	✓	✓
2 hrs	Views of Southern Taconic Plateau and Catskills		✓	✓			✓
2 hrs	Pond, wetlands, golden eagles, great for families		✓			✓	✓
3 hrs	Shoreline hike along Hudson River, great for families		✓	✓		✓	✓
1.5 hrs	Open fields, rustic gazebos, unforgettable views		✓	✓		✓	✓
Lakeside Trail: 45 min Twin Lakes Trail: 1.5 hrs Cliffdale Farm/ Catamount Hill Trail: 1.5 hrs	Ideal for families with young children, offers many variations of trips		✓	✓		✓	✓
2.5 hrs	FDR museum, library, and home		✓	✓	✓	✓	
4 hrs	Valley and mountain views			✓			✓
6 hrs	Gradual climb with generous views, free camping			✓			✓
3 hrs	Stream crossing, Bash Bish Falls			✓			✓
2.5 hrs	Blueberry knoll, free camping			✓			✓
5.5 hrs	Scenic day-long hike up Catskills' highest peak			✓			✓
7 hrs	Rustic area, a favorite of many Catskills hikers	$		✓			
2.5 hrs	Scenic cliffs of a glacial cirque, meteorite impact zone			✓			✓
5 hrs	Quiet boreal forests with southwesterly views		✓	✓			
2 hrs	Intimate views of the Catskills, accessible trail		✓			✓	✓
5.5 hrs	Blueberry heath, intimate views of the high peaks		✓	✓			✓
4 hrs	Quarry, lean-tos, summit fire tower			✓			✓

ACKNOWLEDGMENTS

The job of a guidebook writer (especially when the subject is hiking) is often a harsh, solitary, and tedious one. I am still of the mind, of course, that a "bad day hiking is better than a good day at work." During the creation of this book, there were many long days of travail and research; however, friends and acquaintances along the trail helped make this an entirely enjoyable and fascinating bipedal experience—from tip to toe.

In view of that, I'd like to recognize those who supported me. Foremost among them is the vibrant Inverna Lockpez of the Catskill Center for Conservation and Development (CCCD). For several successive summers, Inverna selected me as an artist-in-residence at the Platte Clove Preserve, a woodsy retreat of waterfalls and old-growth forest abutting the Indian Head Wilderness Area, where I worked on this book. Thanks also to the CCCD's former executive director, Tom Alworth. My appreciation also goes to the rest of the CCCD staff, who manage the Catskills' largest environmental watchdog agency.

My indebtedness extends to the many hiking companions who joined me on the trails, among them my good friends Barry Knight and Rita Berman, Dori O'Connell, Nick and Erika Minglis, and the Catskill Center's artist-in-residence, Susan Mayr. Thanks also go to Lori Lee Dickson, who helped to research this edition, and to Ingrid Strauch and Lee Ruelle.

I am indebted to the rangers and foresters who've helped me with this and other books, including the Rudges (Pat and Bill), Dennis Martin, Steve Preston, Stephen Scherry, Fred Dearstyne, Pete Evans, and George Profous. Thank you as well to Dr. John C. Dwyer, historian; and Dr. Mike Kudish, botanist, author of Catskill-related books and dissertations, and professor of forest history.

Gratitude goes to my woods-roving neighbors from the Hutterian Bruderhof's Catskill Community for their humble and lighthearted company on the trail and their sustained, cordial invitations to visit the community.

Of course, my endless appreciation goes to all of my readers. It's such a pleasure to find people carrying your book in the woods (especially if they're not lost).

Several current and former members of the AMC staff managed to push this project along through several hardships. Thanks go to Shannon Smith, Jennifer Wehunt, Sarah Jane Shangraw, Belinda Thresher, Laurie O'Reilly, Vanessa Torrado, and Abigail Coyle.

INTRODUCTION

I thank God I was born on the banks of the Hudson.
—Washington Irving

Welcome to the Hudson Valley and Catskill Region, birthplace of a nation. The Hudson River begins at the Adirondacks' Lake Tear of the Clouds at 4,300 feet in elevation, and makes its way 315 miles to New York City's Battery at sea level as it drains an area of more than 13,000 square miles. Except for the Saint Lawrence, it is the only river that provides such deep and cordial invitation into the North American continent—a fact that has had the largest single influence on the growth and development of the United States. Geologically, the Hudson River is a fjord, a long, narrow coastal inlet, its steep slopes formed by glacial action. It is one of only two water gaps that penetrate the Appalachian Mountain chain at a point that is below sea level (the other is Maine's Somes Sound). The Hudson River's deepest point is 216 feet, near West Point; its widest is 3.5 miles, at Haverstraw Bay; and its narrowest is at the Hudson Highlands, where it is constricted into the notorious throat of often rough and windy water dubbed the Devil's Horse Race by early mariners.

The history of the region is a study in change. After the Paleoindians left the Hudson Valley 12,000 years ago, when the glaciers retreated, the hunter-gatherer people of the Woodland Period arrived, leaving evidence of their existence in the form of oyster middens (mounds), fishing weirs (traps), camps, and villages. By 1,000 BCE, they began to cultivate crops, which required permanent villages and seasonal encampments, many positioned at the mouths of Hudson River tributaries. For crop rotation and soil revitalization, these villages were moved every eight to twelve years. This culture was altered permanently with the arrival of Europeans. Like its rival the English Hudson Bay Company, the Dutch East India Company (which employed Henry Hudson) was primarily interested in fur. American Indians, lured by the false promise of progress and prosperity, entered the business of commercial trapping and trade. This, along with broken treaties (particularly by the Dutch director-general Peter Stuyvesant), led to the destruction of a traditional lifestyle that was also subjected to conflict, disease, and ultimately, displacement.

Realizing that whoever controlled the Hudson River would also control the American frontier and its rich promise of trade, the British took control of New Amsterdam (now New York) from the Dutch by force in 1664. Stuyvesant had become so unpopular that he was unable to raise a militia. The French and the

English, using Mohawk and Algonquian mercenaries as their allies, then fought over the region, hoping to establish and maintain trade interests. The French and Indian Wars put an end to French aspirations south of the Great Lakes. The British focused on the Hudson Valley and were finally defeated by the Americans in the 1777 Saratoga campaign. The empire-building period was about to begin.

By this time, writers and artists had begun to praise the region's scenic character, part of an international Romantic movement that envisaged the world as a place both picturesque and sublime. This enhanced the valley's appeal as a place to live and also made it the first American tourist destination. For both Americans and Europeans by the early 1820s, the valley was a rural retreat, with a focus on the river and the Catskills in celebration of the aesthetic conventions of the time. Tremendous industrial growth was also taking place, spurred by the nationalistic pride created by the Revolution. During the nineteenth century, the valley was intensively developed for fishing, logging, agriculture, shipping, and power generation, while becoming widely settled residentially. Throughout the twentieth century, these conditions brought about habitat destruction, the depreciation of scenic resources, continual alterations of the natural shoreline of the river, and diminished public access. Major factors in the preservation of open space through this development period were the farms and patroonships, and, in the Catskills, the tenant farming system of the Hardenburgh Patent (a large land grant given by Queen Anne to a small group of investors).

Today, 70 percent of the Hudson's shore is inaccessible because of rail corridors and private property. The river is also home to a 35-foot-deep shipping channel maintained from New York Harbor to the Port of Albany; the Hudson drops only about 5 feet in this span, making it an ideal in-route for heavy shipping and a recreational route connecting the Atlantic to the Great Lakes. At the same time, improvements in the river's water quality, a heightened, positive public perception of the river, and increasing population have created demands for more public access and more open space. Of the 3.9 million acres in the Hudson River Valley National Heritage Area, only 5 percent (203,000 acres) is protected open space. Fortunately, early in its settlement history, sentiment was strong for the preservation of open space. This led to hard-fought battles by the environmental movement that resulted in the preservation of the Hudson Valley as we see it today.

Below Troy, the Hudson River is a rich and productive tidal estuary inhabited by ospreys, eagles, harbor seals, muskrats, beavers, herons, rails, deer, foxes, turkeys, coyotes, fishers, and even bears. Its diverse habitat is the result of a broad salinity gradient determined by the mixing of the Atlantic's sea water with the river's freshwater. The Hudson is home to 185 species of fish, and is the last estuary on the East Coast to retain self-sustaining spawning stocks of its original native fish species, such as the once commercially important shad and sturgeon and that very popular game fish, the striped bass. Under the federal Clean Water Act, the Environmental Protection Agency designated these resources the Hudson River National Estuarine Research Reserve. It contains 2,400 acres of tidal freshwater fish and wildlife habitat, with an additional 1,500 acres undesignated. All of the reserves in the Hudson River estuary are protected and managed as field laboratories for research and education.

Beyond the river is a seemingly endless assortment of mountains, lakes, ponds, valleys, and geological intrusions that give the Hudson Valley its character and appeal. The valley's historical development is almost as diverse as its habitat. The region is so striking in appearance that early German Palatine settlers from the County Palatine (a historic state of the Holy Roman Empire) of the Rhine Valley region called it the American Rhineland. The first European visitors, the members of Henry Hudson's crew (who were looking for China), called it "as fine a place as we have ever seen . . . so pleasant with grass and flowers, and goodly trees." Klara Sauer, the former director of Scenic Hudson, put the river's beauty into another perspective, remarking, "Had this continent been settled west-to-east, the Hudson Valley would be a national park today." It is interesting to reflect on Sauer's comment now that the National Park Service (NPS) has designated the Hudson Valley a National Heritage Area (1998). Because the Hudson River valley is so large and its resources so diffuse, and because it is so developed, the NPS realized it could not create a national park in the traditional sense, such as a Yellowstone or Yosemite, but it did recognize that the region's cultural and natural attributes were worthy of federal protection, preservation, and interpretation for the benefit of the nation. Congressman Maurice Hinchey drafted the legislation that created the Hudson River Valley National Heritage Area.

The designation is based on the region's Revolutionary War history, its role as a living canvas for the first American school of art (the Hudson River School of landscape painting, whose celebration of nature contributed to the creation of our national parks system), the river's function as the nation's principal artery of commerce, and the fact that the Hudson Valley was the birthplace of the modern environmental movement—the basis of environmental law was formed by a fight that took place here in the Hudson Valley.

This book will lead you to the Hudson's greatest scenic landscapes: the Highlands, the ancient Taconics, the white cliffs of the Shawangunks, and the recesses of the distant Catskills. It reaches west to the Delaware watershed, east to the Taconics, and north to the fortress of the Helderbergs. It penetrates the Southern and Northern Taconics and the Greylock Range. It brings you to the tops of this series of ranges, allowing you the best views of their succession and of the Hudson Valley. From the resistant limestone of the Helderberg Escarpment to the dissected plateau of the Catskills and into the crystalline Hudson Highlands lying beside the younger folded rocks of the Appalachians, you can see the parts of the puzzle that make up the region's geological history and that have earned the Hudson River its place as one of America's premier scenic and recreational assets.

AUTHOR'S NOTE

Guidebooks directly affect the use patterns and development of recreational resources. New York State's Department of Environmental Conservation (DEC) welcomes such publications from the private sector, which allow it to cut back substantially on costly in-house guide and map production. During the 35 years or so that I have written outdoor material about specific destinations, I have watched some areas change because of increased public use. The state has responded by designating trails and adding signage in such areas, and by including them on maps and pamphlets. Such "pressure" increases as more books are written and more trails are built, a fact that some people lament.

But I do not feel this pressure has brought harm, especially given that education fosters appreciation for the land and, thus, preservation. (With few exceptions, the region's trails have not exceeded their carrying capacity.) Nor do I offer apologies for divulging the whereabouts of these trails. Revealing what I feel are the most desirable hiking destinations is my promise to my readers.

The natural environment is our single largest human resource, and it's there to be used and enjoyed. It is my sincere wish that this book and its carefully selected inventory of special, scenic places helps you to do that. Just be prepared to rub up against the world a bit. Get wet, get dirty, get hungry, and get sore. And whatever you do, get out there and enjoy the trails!

HOW TO USE THIS BOOK

There are many ways to enjoy these walks. Social hikers will find many outdoor groups that offer regularly scheduled hikes and trips. The Appalachian Mountain Club (AMC) offers a variety of volunteer-led hikes in the Hudson Valley. The New York–New Jersey Trail Conference (NY–NJTC) will put you in touch with many other groups. Organizations such as the Catskill 3500 Club, the Sierra Club, the Catskill Mountain Club, and chapters of the Adirondack Mountain Club all offer outing schedules for a variety of hikers. Each organization also provides ways for hikers to return something to the land with programs of trail maintenance, conservation, and education to promote wise use. These organizations help protect our wild lands—and help acquire more of them.

Those who seek quiet in the wildlands can find ways to do that here. Some of these routes are never heavily used. Others are, and these trails may best be hiked in early spring, late fall, or on weekdays, when solitude can be mixed with expanded vistas in ways that are sure to please any wilderness seeker.

There are relatively few hikes on the east side of the Hudson Valley. Its gentler hills were settled early, and although the farms are shrinking, settlements have grown to fill most of the open land. In contrast, the forests on the west side of the Hudson have been protected as the valley's water source and as part of the New York State Forest Preserve, whose unique state constitutional protection ensures its land will remain "forever wild." Lands within the Blue Line (as it appears on many maps) of the Catskill Park make up the largest group of hikes in this guide.

Almost all the lands traversed by today's trails were once settled and used by soldiers, farmers, miners, loggers, and Romantics. Their presence inevitably is reflected in the lore that surrounds the trails. This guide serves as an invitation to the mountain ranges and valleys of the southern part of the state (as well as a few Hudson Valley watershed hikes in neighboring states), but it cannot begin to probe the vast history that enlivens each route.

With 60 hikes to choose from, you may wonder how to decide where to go. The locator map at the front of this book will help you narrow down the trips by location, and the At-a-Glance Trip Planner that follows the Table of Contents will provide more information to guide you toward a decision.

Once you settle on a destination and turn to a trip in this guide, you will find icons that indicate whether the hike is a good place for children, whether dogs are permitted, whether you can go snowshoeing or cross-country skiing there, and whether there are fees.

Information on the basics follows: location, difficulty rating, distance, elevation gain, estimated time, and available maps. The difficulty ratings are based on the author's perception and are estimates of what the average hiker will experience; you may find the hikes to be easier or more difficult than stated. Elevation gain (or vertical rise) is the total change in cumulative elevation for the hike. Hiking time is for walking the trail as described at a leisurely pace. The text often suggests that you allow more time for sightseeing.

Information is included about the relevant U.S. Geological Survey (USGS) maps, as well as about where you can find trail maps. You will find the trail map in the book helpful, but take the recommended maps, too. These maps give the larger picture, and you will have more fun on a mountaintop if you can identify the surrounding countryside.

A cautionary note on USGS Maps: although contours and elevations are by and large reliable, some of the manufactured features, including trails, are out of date. All of the supplementary maps mentioned in the hike headings are more convenient and up to date than the USGS quads, and I recommend acquiring them. In particular, I suggest the Appalachian Mountain Club Catskill Mountains map that was designed to accompany my book *Catskill Mountain Guide* (in its third edition at the time of this writing), published by AMC. That book is sold with a paper-printed map, but a waterproof version of the map can be purchased separately and will prove helpful for the Catskills-related trips in this book.

The trail maps that accompany each trip will help guide you along your hike. Additional resources include National Geographic's Trails Illustrated map of Catskill Park, NY-NJTC maps, AMC *Catskill Mountains Trail Map*, and various state park maps.

Following the trail description, a More Information section provides details about the locations of bathrooms and other amenities, the land ownership of the trail, and any fees. If you are interested in nearby campgrounds, stores, restaurants, etc., refer to the background information on the region at the beginning of each regional section.

The trail descriptions are grouped by geographic region within the Catskills and Hudson Valley. At the beginning of each regional section is a summary of local resources.

Also included in this book is an appendix with helpful information on land organizations in the areas mentioned in the book.

Before starting out, read the trail description to decide if the hike is right for you. Remember that the difficulty rating naturally involves some subjectivity. "Easy" means the terrain is relatively level and the hike is less than 3 miles long or that the hike is somewhat steep but very short. "Moderate" means the terrain may be rocky or that there is a steeper grade. The hike may be 2 to 5 miles long. "Strenuous" means the terrain can be difficult and generally inappropriate for young children, the elevation gain is greater than 2,000 feet, and the hike may be 5 to 10 miles long. The estimated times are for hiking and factor in some additional time for any stops to enjoy a vista or have lunch.

The directions explain how to reach the trailhead. Global Positioning System (GPS) coordinates for parking lots are also included. When you enter the coordinates into your vehicle's navigational GPS device, it will provide driving directions. (Set your device to the "degrees and decimal minutes" format. Please remember that trailheads can be obscured by foliage. Although the author and AMC have made every effort to ensure accuracy, GPS coordinates may direct you very near, but not directly to, the trailhead.) Whether or not you have a GPS device, bring an atlas or a county or state road map with you, such as the DeLorme Atlas and Gazetteer for New York State. Don't rely on finding small preserve maps and other handouts at kiosks. Often the supplies are exhausted. Try to find the map you need online, where many are available these days.

If you do not know how to read a map, you should learn to do so before hiking all but about a dozen of the simplest trails in this guide. Spend time walking with someone who does know how to read a map, such as the friendly hikers from your local AMC chapter. The same instructions are appropriate for the use of a compass. You may not need either on the easiest of this guide's trails, but walking the easier routes with map and compass will allow you to become comfortable with their use so you can extend your hikes beyond the ones described, or to the more difficult hikes in this book. Get the best compass you can afford. I've had the same Silva Ranger for 30 years and highly recommend a similar type of orienteering compass with a flip-up sight that will also be useful in identifying far-away peaks or triangulating your position from a set of known peaks.

Some of the trips are accessible by public transportation. For those that are, basic instructions are included in the Directions sections. However, remember to call ahead for schedules and to confirm routes. AMC's New York–North Jersey Chapter has helpful information on its website: amc-ny .org/transportation-codes. You can also find other resources online, such as the Metro-North website or the Coach USA website.

In the trail description, you will find instructions on where to hike, the trails on which to hike, and where to turn along the trail. You will also learn about natural and human history along your hike, along with information about flora, fauna, and any landmarks and objects you will encounter.

Each trip ends with a More Information section that provides details about the locations of bathrooms, access times and fees, the property's rules and regulations, and contact information for the place where you will be hiking.

TRIP PLANNING AND SAFETY

This guide contains a wide range of hikes—from easy walks to strenuous climbs. The information about distance, estimated time, and elevation gain should help you gauge the difficulty of each hike and prepare properly. Almost all hikes follow clearly marked trails, although this can change. The greatest source of confusion seems to be the constant revisions in trail designation for the more southerly trails, particularly in the Highlands region, where interconnecting routes can be confusing and color changes in the markings have been common.

Preparedness is key to your hiking enjoyment, and you should be well equipped before you start. If you are new to hiking, it is a good idea to join an AMC group and learn from those with experience. The more background you have in the woods, the greater will be your safety and your enjoyment. Even with the best of forecasts, you should know that you will face the unexpected. Elevations in and around the Hudson Valley are varied, and often steep and rugged. Some of the walks traverse moderately rugged terrain along rocky hills, but others lead to ponds and fields where you'll have a lot of sun exposure and to areas where walking is slow in soft soil or mud. Many parks in the Hudson Valley have complex trail networks based on old cart and carriage roads, some of which are unmarked. Always allow extra time in case you get lost. Before heading out for your hike, consider the following:

- Select a hike that everyone in your group is comfortable making. Match the hike to the abilities of the least capable person in the group. If anyone is uncomfortable with the weather or is tired, turn around and complete the hike another day.
- Plan to be back at the trailhead before dark. Before beginning your hike, determine a turnaround time even if you have not reached your intended destination.
- Check the weather. Whenever possible, wait for a sunny day. But even on sunny days you should be prepared for changes and extremes. It can be at least 20 degrees colder on the mountaintops of the Catskills than in the valley, close to the river. Storms can appear with little warning. Many prefer walking in southern New York State during fall and spring; just remember these are the most volatile times—extremes ranging from heat waves to snowstorms can occur. But the less populated trails and expanded distant vistas in the leafless season make hiking at such times worthwhile.

- If you are planning a ridge or summit hike, start early so you will be off the exposed area before the afternoon hours when thunderstorms most often strike, especially in summer. The weather in the Hudson Valley is highly variable. Significant storms—including heavy winter snowfalls, spring rainstorms, and tropical storms in late summer and fall—can cause flooding and other hazards.
- Bring a pack with the following items:
  - ✓ Water: Two quarts per person is usually adequate, depending on the weather and the length of the trip. These mountains are dry much of the year. It is becoming increasingly dangerous to trust open water sources because of the spread of the *Giardia* parasite.
  - ✓ Food: Even if you plan just a 1-hour hike, bring high-energy snacks such as nuts, dried fruit, or snack bars. Pack a lunch for longer trips.
  - ✓ Map and compass: Be sure you know how to use them. A handheld GPS device may also be helpful, but is not always reliable. Even if you plan to stay on marked trails in the Catskills, it is still advisable to carry a compass. A compass will help you verify directions, help you find your way back to a trail you have wandered from, and aid in your identification of landmarks, which adds to the fun of hiking. The best compass for the identification of peaks is an orienteering compass, the kind with a mirror and flip-up sight that enables you to take bearings with about a 2-degree error or less. In using the book's bearings, you will be able to identify points that are identified in the text. All bearings are given as magnetic. If you plan to navigate over land with your compass, be sure to correct for declination (13 degrees W).
  - ✓ Headlamp or flashlight with spare batteries.
  - ✓ Extra clothing: rain gear, a wool sweater or a fleece, a hat, and mittens. Experiment with layers of light, waterproof gear. In the mountains, you will want a layer of fleece or wool even in summer, so carry a sweater in your day pack.
  - ✓ Sunscreen
  - ✓ First-aid kit, including adhesive bandages, gauze, pain medicine, and moleskin
  - ✓ Pocketknife or multitool
  - ✓ Matches and a lighter
  - ✓ Trash bag
  - ✓ Toilet paper
  - ✓ Whistle
  - ✓ Insect repellent
  - ✓ Sunglasses

✓ Cell phone: Cell phones will work from most mountain summits and many upper-elevation areas in the Catskills, but seldom from valleys and hollows and generally will not work from main roads in the interior Catskill Forest Preserve. They will work from slopes only if there is no significant geology between the phone and the tower. It can be difficult or impossible to reach 911 even from secondary roads that are surrounded by ridges. It is possible that a caller will be able to connect with and listen to a 911 operator, even when that operator can't hear the caller, because 911 transmitters are more powerful than cell phones. Although the opposite is rarely the case, it is possible. If you think your call may be being monitored by someone, it is helpful to supply your exact location, ideally using GPS coordinates if you are carrying a GPS unit and can establish them.

   ○ If you or a member of your party are injured or incapacitated but someone is still able to walk to a higher elevation or open area (sometimes even moving a short distance will help), your chances for getting through could improve. If you are confident in leaving an injured party (with a companion), make sure to mark their location with a GPS if you have one. Also try calling local forest rangers' numbers or the number of the nearest state campsite. Under certain conditions it may be possible to reach information (845-555-1212) or any local land line that can relay a message for you. Hikers are advised never to rely on a cell phone for emergencies. The only fail-safe wireless communications from any remote area are provided by satellite telephones, and even these are subject to satellite positions and weather.

✓ PLBs and Satellite messengers: Most hikers are aware of the safety advantages of a Personal Locator Beacon (PLB), which, when activated, sends a signal via a system of military satellites (Cospas-Sarsat). These devices are considerably more powerful (and expensive) than the more recent group of satellite messenger devices (such as the SPOT and Delorme InReach), which communicate with commercial satellite networks (Iridium and Globalstar). Emergency calls using either network are routed to the privately run GEOS International Emergency Response Coordination Center headquartered near Houston. A messenger allows you to send emails and your location to any cell phone. The advantage of such devices is that they use satellites rather than cell towers and could provide you with an additional safety net. Satellite messengers in general are not considered to be good alternatives to the more powerful PLBs.

✓ Binoculars (suggested): Binoculars will add significantly to the enjoyment of your trips to the mountains and to many other places as well. There are many advantages to owning a good pair of binoculars—from identifying the elusive hermit thrush on Slide Mountain to finding important landmarks. The ability to locate many of the landscape features identified in the text, especially those that are not visible with the naked eye, will give you a much better sense for regional geography than you will experience without magnification. For hiking, you can see all you want with 8 x 21 mm to 10 x 25 mm magnification, still staying within the 6- to 10-ounce range.

✓ Trekking Poles: Hikers have been catching on to the advantages of trekking poles. They help you to travel faster, easier, safer, and with less fatigue. In icy conditions, they increase your stability. Descending, they'll help save your knees. During ascents, they'll give you a little extra push and will contribute to upper-body tone, making a hike more of a "total body" form of exercise. For traversing slopes, adjustable poles can be adapted to the angle of the slope. Poles are a great advantage during slippery stream crossings. They can be used as tent and tarp poles.

o Adjust your poles according to the slope and your comfort level. For climbing, use a shorter length. For descents, a longer adjustment will give you increased options for support points. For walking across a slope, make your downhill pole longer. For hiking on the level, adjust your poles so that your forearm is parallel (or a bit higher) to the ground when you're holding the grip. Once you get used to traveling with poles, you will want them on every hike, particularly in winter. A day pack with ski slits or compression straps will come in handy during times when you want your hands free. Bear in mind that trekking poles can contribute to environmental impact in sensitive areas with soft soils, moss, and various ground-cover types.

✓ Microspikes

✓ Camera (suggested)

Wear appropriate footwear and clothing. Wool or synthetic hiking socks will keep your feet dry and help prevent blisters. Comfortable, waterproof hiking boots will provide ankle support and good traction. Avoid wearing cotton clothing, which absorbs sweat and rain. Polypropylene, fleece, and wool all wick moisture away from your body and keep you warmer in wet or cold conditions.

A sturdy pair of broken-in, over-the-ankle boots is essential. Boots of lightweight Gore-Tex or a similar material are ideal; they will give you good traction and support, and they will be all the footwear you will need, except when you're hiking on the higher mountain trails in early spring or winter. In even the worst winter conditions, I have never needed crampons, even in the Catskills, but a pair of studded ice creepers is a good thing to bring along on winter or spring hikes. You will also be more sure-footed with a pair of trekking poles or a staff, which will take some weight off your knees, too.

If you see downed wood that appears to be purposely covering a trail, it probably means the trail is closed because of overuse or hazardous conditions.

If a trail is muddy, walk through the mud or on rocks, never on tree roots or plants. Waterproof boots will keep your feet comfortable. Staying in the center of the trail will keep it from eroding into a widening footway.

Poison ivy is always a threat when you're hiking. To identify the plant, look for clusters of three leaves that shine in the sun but are dull in the shade. If you do come into contact with poison ivy, wash the affected area with soap as soon as possible.

Wear blaze-orange items during hunting season. In New York, the peak hunting season for big game and birds generally runs from mid-October to the end of December, with high-powered rifles permitted in most counties from mid-November to mid-December. Seasons for small game extend into March. Turkey season is held in fall and spring. Yearly schedules are available at dec.ny.gov and in fliers and brochures available at town halls and in other public areas.

After you complete your hike, check for deer ticks, which carry dangerous diseases, such as Lyme disease. The deer ticks that transmit Lyme disease are now found far north and west of Westchester County, where the problem has reached epidemic proportions. Their range is expanding rapidly north and west, and you should take a few preventive measures: wear long, light-colored pants; wear socks; check yourself for ticks; keep to the trail; avoid high grass; and use repellent.

Biting insects are present during warm months, particularly in the vicinity of wetlands. They can be a minor or significant nuisance, depending on seasonal and daily conditions. One serious concern is the eastern equine encephalitis virus (commonly referred to as EEE), a rare but potentially fatal disease that can be transmitted to humans by infected mosquitoes. The Hudson Valley's many swamps and wetlands provide ideal mosquito habitats.

Many Hudson Valley hikers have expressed concern about the recent appearance of the West Nile Virus, a mosquito-borne infection that has been known to cause encephalitis. The chances of infection are small, but are greater in infants, the elderly, and people with weak or damaged immune systems. Symptoms include low-grade fevers and headaches, but more severe infections can result in high fever, headaches, and body aches. There is no cure for viral infections—only the symptoms can be treated. Of the 65 mosquito species in New York State, only the most common species, *Culex pipiens*, is associated with the virus. If you're concerned, you can protect yourself with insect repellent, long shirt sleeves and pant legs, and a hat or bug shirt during mornings and evenings, when mosquitoes are most active.

There are a variety of options for dealing with bugs, ranging from sprays that include the active ingredient N,N-diethyl-meta-toluamide (commonly known as DEET) to more skin-friendly products. Head nets, which often can be purchased more cheaply than a can of repellent, are useful during especially buggy conditions.

Remember, hiking should be fun. If you are uncomfortable with the weather or are tired, turn back and make the complete hike another day. Don't create a situation where you risk yourself or your companions. And, try not to walk alone. Be sure someone knows your intended route and expected return time. Always sign in at a trailhead register if one is available. The unexpected can occur. Weather can change, trail markings can become obscured, you can fall, and you can get lost. But you will not be in real danger if you have anticipated the unexpected.

LEAVE NO TRACE

The Appalachian Mountain Club is a national educational partner of Leave No Trace, a nonprofit organization dedicated to promoting and inspiring responsible outdoor recreation through education, research, and partnerships.  The Leave No Trace program seeks to develop wildland ethics—ways in which people think and act in the outdoors to minimize their impact on the areas they visit and to protect our natural resources for future enjoyment. Leave No Trace unites four federal land management agencies— the U.S. Forest Service, the National Park Service, the Bureau of Land Management, and the U.S. Fish and Wildlife Service—with manufacturers, outdoor retailers, user groups, educators, organizations such as AMC, and individuals.

The Leave No Trace ethic is guided by these seven principles:

1. *Plan Ahead and Prepare.* Know the terrain and any regulations applicable to the area you're planning to visit, and be prepared for extreme weather or other emergencies. This will enhance your enjoyment and ensure that you've chosen an appropriate destination. Small groups have less impact on resources and the experiences of other backcountry visitors.

2. *Travel and Camp on Durable Surfaces.* Travel and camp on established trails and campsites, rock, gravel, dry grasses, or snow. Good campsites are found, not made. Camp at least 200 feet from lakes and streams, and focus activities on areas where vegetation is absent. In pristine areas, disperse use to prevent the creation of campsites and trails.

3. *Dispose of Waste Properly.* Pack it in, pack it out. Inspect your camp for trash or food scraps. Deposit solid human waste in cat holes dug 6 to 8 inches deep, at least 200 feet from water, camps, and trails. Pack out toilet paper and hygiene products. To wash yourself or your dishes, carry water 200 feet from streams or lakes and use small amounts of biodegradable soap. Scatter strained dishwater.

4. *Leave What You Find.* Cultural or historic artifacts, as well as natural objects such as plants and rocks, should be left as found.

5. *Minimize Campfire Impacts.* Cook on a stove. Use established fire rings, fire pans, or mound fires. If you build a campfire, keep it small and use dead sticks found on the ground.

6. *Respect Wildlife.* Observe wildlife from a distance. Feeding animals alters their natural behavior. Protect wildlife from your food by storing rations and trash securely.

7. *Be Considerate of Other Visitors.* Be courteous, respect the quality of other visitors' backcountry experiences, and let nature's sounds prevail.

AMC is a national provider of the Leave No Trace Master Educator course. AMC offers this five-day course, designed especially for outdoor professionals and land managers, as well as the shorter two-day Leave No Trace Trainer course, at locations throughout the Northeast.

For Leave No Trace information and materials, contact the Leave No Trace Center for Outdoor Ethics, P.O. Box 997, Boulder, CO 80306. Phone: 800-332-4100 or 303-442-8222; fax: 303-442-8217; web: lnt.org. For information on the AMC Leave No Trace Master Educator training course schedule, see outdoors.org/education/lnt.

THE HUDSON HIGHLANDS

Perhaps no other landmark characterizes the Hudson Valley like its Highlands, the scenic and rugged group of Appalachian hills that rise between Dunderberg Mountain and the Fishkill Ridge in the southeastern part of the state. Here, where the river is deep and narrow and the mountains rise steeply from its shores, the topography has determined the military, cultural, and environmental history of the region.

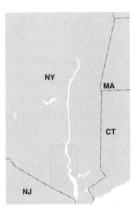

Geologically known as the Highlands Province, the area is home to rocks that are crystalline in structure, originating from Precambrian and early Paleozoic igneous and metamorphic action rather than from the sedimentation that created a great deal of the surrounding region's surface rock. Hikers will see marble, schist, and gneiss embedded, ribboned, and sprinkled throughout the open outcrops and exposed ridges. Surface scars of Pleistocene glacial activity are also visible, and visitors will walk across solidified, granitic magma chambers that were once buried deep in the earth, such as Bear Mountain. Stripped of their overburden of softer geology, the hard, weather-resistant crystalline rocks remain exposed. The upper-elevation ridges are dry and relatively open, with frequent sweeping views. Today's Highlands are geologically equivalent to and scenically comparable to the Blue Ridge Mountains of North Carolina and Virginia.

Beyond its significance as a commercial trade route, the Highlands' topography determined the settlement of the continent in other ways. Military leaders considered it the most important strategic location in the American colonies. Here, in 1778, the great Hudson River Chain—wrought in the forges of Sterling Forest at Sterling Iron Works and floated on log booms—was stretched across the river to stop the British from advancing northward. Already in control of Canada and the Atlantic coast, the British sought to control the Hudson, hindering military transport and travel between the north and south. Several chains spanned the river between New York City and Fort Montgomery, but the West Point Chain, built after the defeat of the north-lying forts Montgomery and Clinton, was the most notable in engineering: Its 2-foot-long links weighed in excess of 125 pounds each, and the entire 1,500-foot span weighed nearly 65 tons. Defended from both sides of the river, the chain was never challenged or penetrated. The treasonous Benedict Arnold attempted to help the British overcome it, but he was captured before he could put his plan into action. The chain changed the course of the war, shortening it substantially. Thirteen of the original links can still be seen at West Point, but the rest were re-smelted for armament at the West Point Foundry in Cold Spring, near the point where the east end of the chain was anchored on Constitution Island. Today the island is an Audubon nature preserve and popular canoeing destination.

A few decades after America gained independence, the picturesque and sublime landscapes of the Hudson Valley gave rise to the Hudson River School of landscape painting, which first focused on the Highlands area and northward. Most of the era's painters worked from New York City studios and painted to please European audiences until, in the early 1820s, Thomas Cole burst on the scene, including among his Catskill scenes several of the Highlands. Inspired by Cole's nearly instant fame and by a growing audience of prosperous patrons and admirers with widening tastes, other artists began to emulate and train under Cole. Among them were John Frederick Kensett, Sanford R. Gifford, George Inness, Jasper Cropsey, and Frederic Church, who was Cole's star student.

Developing alongside this artistic revolution were the New York literati known as the Knickerbockers, who shared the popularity and Romantic vision of their counterparts in the art world. The Knickerbockers included Washington Irving, Nathaniel Parker Willis, William Cullen Bryant, and James Fenimore Cooper (when his Tory sympathies could be overlooked), among others.

These artists and writers, inspired by the beauty and grandeur of the Highlands, celebrated an America that could stand on its own in the world of arts and letters, a young country with a fierce stamp of individuality. That pride would later be called into play to protect these same resources from ruin.

1

STORM KING MOUNTAIN

This signature Highlands hike begins with a steep ascent before easing up. It is among the shorter and more beginner-friendly hikes in the region, with a scenic destination providing views up and down the Hudson River.

DIRECTIONS

Getting to the scenic parking area where the yellow-blazed Stillman Trail begins is tricky because it's located on a "no turns" section of US 9W in the northbound lane. If you are traveling south from Cornwall, drive past the parking area and make a U-turn at the intersection of US 9W and NY 293/218, at the United States Military Academy at West Point, 3 miles south. As you are driving south from Cornwall on US 9W, you will see the parking turnout at the top of the pass, 1.5 miles beyond the Angola Road overpass. From the intersection of US 9W and NY 293/218 (the U-turn), you must turn around and drive the 3 miles back north, to the parking area. *GPS coordinates: 41° 25.390′ N, 74° 00.087′ W.*

TRAIL DESCRIPTION

Storm King Mountain (1,340 feet), among the most popular hiking destinations in the Hudson Highlands, has had a decisive influence on the national environmental movement. If there is one symbol of the struggle to preserve scenic open space, this is it. Dramatic views and open rock ledges characterize the trails in Storm King State Park, managed by the Palisades Interstate Park Commission. Until recently, some interesting destinations in the park were inaccessible, but proactive trail advocacy by the New York–New Jersey Trail Conference has provided more access, particularly in the southern area bordering the United States Military Academy at West Point.

LOCATION
Cornwall-on-Hudson, NY

RATING
Moderate

DISTANCE
6 miles

ELEVATION GAIN
400 feet

ESTIMATED TIME
3 hours

MAPS
USGS Cornwall, USGS West Point; NY-NJTC West Hudson Trails

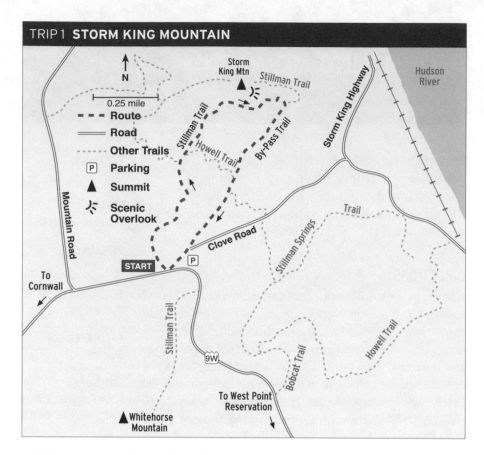

This prominent little mountain draws its name from its tendency to bottle-neck storms at the head of the Highland Gap.

It is one of the easiest scenic hikes in the region, ideal when a moderate, half-day's outing with a view is your goal. If you want to add distance and elevation, you have several choices. The Highlands may not be as lofty as surrounding mountain groups, but the trails are extensive and as steep as many others in the Catskills.

Butter Hill Trail to Stillman Trail is the most popular approach to Storm King with casual day-hikers, largely because the trailhead lies in the upper elevations west of the mountain, making for a fairly easy hike. Stillman Trail makes up most of the portion of Highlands Trail that runs from the Sutherland Pond area of adjacent Black Rock Forest to Cornwall.

Park at the turnout. Marking is inconspicuous from the parking lot but is consistent throughout the hike. There is no signage in the parking lot itself, aside from a plaque describing the return route of the hostages who were taken in Iran in 1979 and driven past this point en route to West Point for debriefing.

Walk to the extreme west edge of the parking area or you may not find the trail. At this point you will see the white-blazed By-Pass Trail to your right. This will be your return route, closing the loop. Look closely for the triple-orange paint blazes of Butter Hill Trail that lead uphill.

The large, round, rocky hill you see directly north of the parking area is your first objective. This is not Storm King but Butter Hill, translated from the early Dutch place-name, Boterberg.

After you make a few minutes' fairly steep climb up an open series of shrubby slabs, the terrain levels out at the ruins of the Spy Rock House, the summer cottage of Dr. Edward L. Partridge a park commissioner who served from 1913 to 1930. (There are open views of 1,461-foot Spy Rock to the south-southwest.) Next descend into a shady ravine full of talus that has fractured away from the upper ledges of Butter Hill. The trail rises sharply from here, turning northeast past several interesting south-facing vistas. As the trail levels, Butter Hill Trail joins the yellow-blazed Stillman Trail. The teal-colored diamond blazes of Highlands Trail also appear. Turn right and ascend to the small, open, grassy summit of Butter Hill. Take a moment to enjoy some of the sights you won't see from the east ledges of Storm King. The long, serpentine ridge to the west is the low-lying Schunemunk Mountain, over which Long Path travels for roughly 6 miles on its way to the southern Shawangunks. The long trestle to the north of Schunemunk is the Moodna Viaduct, the longest rail trestle east of the Mississippi; built between 1906 and 1908, it is 3,200 feet long. With binoculars, you can spot a few of the large, welded-steel sculptures at the Storm King Arts Center, in the far, low western foreground. See if you can identify bits of Andy Goldsworthy's 2,278-foot-long Storm King Wall at the south end.

As you look south toward the Black Rock Forest, you'll see Mount Misery (1,268 feet) and a fire tower beyond, and you can see from the West Point reservation lands and the Hudson River to Mount Taurus's lower slopes and the open quarry scar above the village of Cold Spring. The entire Shawangunk Ridge is visible in the west-northwest, all the way to Sky Top Tower in the Mohonk Preserve (5 degrees magnetic). Several major Catskill wilderness areas can also be seen, with Slide Mountain at magnetic north. There are three U.S. Geological Survey (USGS) triangulation benchmarks on Butter Hill (1,360 feet).

On a clear day, you will most likely encounter several hikers on Butter Hill. Beyond Butter Hill, continue to follow Stillman Trail's yellow paint blazes. Continue on the trail through an oak forest, dropping in elevation slightly. In five minutes, you'll reach a T intersection where the blue-and-red-blazed Bluebird Trail drops off to the left, heading northwest. Bear right (east), continuing on the yellow-blazed trail. In a minute or two, you'll come to a Y intersection where you should bear left, following yellow square and blue diamond blazes. (To the right is the northern end of the blue-blazed Howell Trail, which descends across the Clove.)

Soon you will encounter hemlock trees, mountain laurel, and little patches of pitch pine as the trail levels for a while, passing two vantage points looking north. The trail then dips once more into the woods and arrives at Storm King's summit, a northeast-facing promontory.

Views are spectacular. An ice sheet carved a deep gorge through the Highlands here, one of the few places where a river bisects the Appalachian chain almost to sea level, lending considerably to the savage look of the landscape. Below and to the east is Constitution Marsh. Mount Taurus is close across the river, and you might see hikers near the stunning vertical drops of Breakneck Ridge. In the northeast, with its many towers, is Mount Beacon. Views taper into the endless, verdant flatlands and the dimple hills and mountains to the northeast. To the southeast, you can see into Putnam and Westchester counties. An issue deserving attention here is the evidence of illegal camping taking place along the summit area.

In the river below is Bannerman's Castle, which you can see on Pollepel Island. Francis Bannerman was an arms dealer who bought the island in 1900 and built the castle to serve as an arsenal for surplus arms from the Spanish American War. The island is said to be haunted by horses, sea captains, goblins, witches, and spirits. American Indians and the Dutch genuinely feared the place, probably due to the strong tidal rips and high winds. A fire destroyed the rest of the buildings in the late 1960s. The island is owned by New York State, and the Bannerman Castle Trust, a preservation group, conducts a variety of special events there.

Views from the summit of Storm King reach beyond the Greylock Range of Western Massachusetts.

Continuing, descend to a T intersection where the yellow-blazed Stillman Trail joins the white-blazed By-Pass Trail that leads southwest and descends along a rock-strewn path, with several southerly lookouts. Leaving Stillman Trail you continue on the white-blazed By-Pass Trail, which sidehills easily along the southerly shoulder of the mountain and joins Clove Road, a dirt footpath, and begins climbing. Blazes are consistent. After a steep, final ascent, bear left as the trail joins the parking area turnout, and you're back at the trailhead.

For a more challenging hike, you can begin east of Storm King, at the lower elevations along the river, where trailheads can be reached from NY 218/Storm King Highway. This approach requires significant climbing to reach Storm King's summit. The southerly Howell Trail provides part of a very popular, longer loop hike that connects Pitching Point, on the eastern flank of the beautiful Crow's Nest, to Storm King via Bobcat Trail and Stillman Spring Trail. Stillman Spring Trail climbs through the steep valley of Mother Cronk's Clove, which is also known as Storm King Clove, beginning at 200 feet above sea level.

DID YOU KNOW

During the dry summer of 1999, fires on Storm King Mountain caused the detonation of century-old artillery shells that were test fired from canon produced at the West Point Foundry, across the Hudson River in Cold Spring. Fearing for the public's safety, authorities closed Storm King State Park to hiking until the remaining unexploded ordnance was removed. It opened again in 2003.

MORE INFORMATION

The park is open for day use year-round. It is undeveloped with limited parking and no restrooms: nysparks.state.ny.us/parks/152/details.aspx; 845-786-2701.

BIRTH OF THE ENVIRONMENTAL MOVEMENT

When development began in the Hudson Valley in the early twentieth century, the Highlands' valuable rocks—the building blocks of New York's skyline—were heavily quarried. The lack of public ownership and protection allowed private mining industries to dismantle the Highlands piecemeal.

In an effort to meet the energy needs of the Greater New York population, Consolidated Edison appealed to the Federal Power Commission in 1963 for permission to build a power-generating plant on Storm King Mountain. People who lived in the Highlands, with the support of hiking clubs and other groups, organized the Scenic Hudson Preservation Conference to fight the plan in court. The 1965 ruling in favor of Scenic Hudson was a legal landmark, the first time a conservation group had successfully sued both on behalf of the public and on the basis of the aesthetic value of a landmass.

The decision in favor of Scenic Hudson created important legal precedents, leading to the 1970 National Environmental Policy Act (NEPA) and other significant legislation, such as the Clean Air Act and the Clean Water Act. During this time, two environmental advocacy groups emerged: the Environmental Defense Fund and the National Resources Defense Council. As a direct result of the fight to save Storm King, the field of environmental law was born.

2

MOUNT TAURUS

This fairly relaxed outing follows a few steep pitches through deep woods to a scenic viewpoint then descends along a creek.

DIRECTIONS

From the intersection of NY 9D and NY 301 in the village of Cold Spring, drive north on NY 9D 0.7 mile to the Little Stony Point parking area. You can park on either side of NY 9D. This parking area is just under 8 miles south of I-84 at the City of Beacon. *GPS coordinates:* 41° 25.602' N, 73° 57.926' W.

TRAIL DESCRIPTION

Mount Taurus, formerly Bull Hill (1,400 feet), sits authoritatively in the eastern Highlands south of Breakneck Ridge, its ravaged frontcountry along the Hudson's shore the result of extensive quarrying in the early 1900s. If you've already climbed Storm King Mountain, you've seen the crumbled leftovers of Little Stony Point jutting into the river above Cold Spring, and you've marveled at the devastating crater on Taurus's lower western slopes. Throw in a few dioxin-belching industrial plants and a pumped storage project, and you have an idea of what the Highlands would look like if such extractive resource industries were left to their own devices. Fortunately, as a result of the sustained struggle for the protection of the Highlands and the Palisades, the lands involved were protected by the formation of the Hudson Highlands State Park Preserve in the late 1960s.

From the east side of NY 9D, follow the white-blazed Washburn Trail (the blue-blazed Cornish Trail, your return route, begins here also), heading uphill and passing the flat quarry entrance to your left as you circle around its southerly rim. You will see Storm King and

LOCATION
Philipstown, NY

RATING
Moderate

DISTANCE
6 miles

ELEVATION GAIN
1,400 feet

ESTIMATED TIME
5 hours

MAPS
USGS West Point; NY-NJTC East Hudson Trails

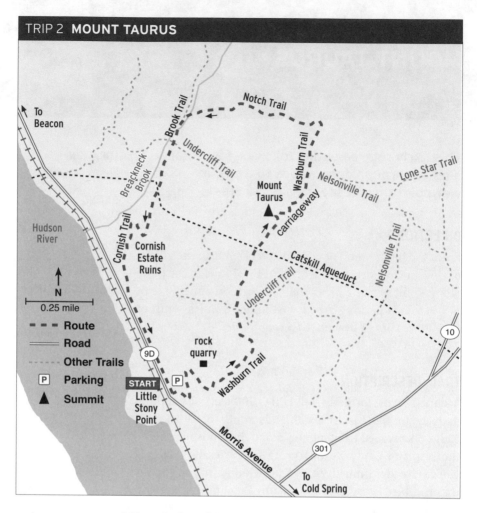

points west as you follow the lip of the mine and draw close to it here and there. The trail is confused with herd paths and shortcuts, some of them leading to southerly views over Constitution Island, others to the mine's edge, but the markers and blazes are consistent if somewhat sparse. Climbing sometimes strenuously up the southeasterly slopes through the dense hardwoods of looming locust and tulip trees, you will move generally north as you top a few bare rock lookouts, surveying West Point and the southerly hills. At 1,100 feet in elevation, you will intersect with and cross the yellow-blazed Undercliff Trail, a recently undertaken project of the NY–NJTC. Soon you cross a small, wet area and vernal brook home to laurel, where you will enjoy the first bit of descent since setting out. Several false summits cross open areas with southward views of the New York City skyline. Due to the impact of hikers, active habitat restoration measures have been taken throughout the area. And while many herd trails appear and can easily be confused with the main trail, and although it's easy to stray from the trail, marking is consistent and easily followed.

Hikers will encounter the haunting ruins of Northgate, once the retreat of Edward G. Cornish, a president of the National Lead Company.

An hour-plus into the hike, you arrive on Taurus, a flat, treed-in, and grassy summit that was once targeted for a hotel. At this elevation you'll encounter cherry trees, blueberry bushes, and mountain laurel. You'll find yourself on an old, reclaimed carriage road that came up the mountain from the east. Follow it to the mountain's eastern shoulder, where there are views of the flatlands toward Fahnestock State Park and points southeast. Continuing on, Washburn Trail switches into the north, where more interesting northward views include the Catskills and the Shawangunks. In the foreground is Breakneck Ridge, across the near vale of Breakneck Brook and the alluring and remote-looking Scofield Ridge. Soon the trail switches downhill and loops to the north in sweeping S curves, with limited views through the trees to the northeast. You arrive at a three-way intersection of Washburn Trail, the carriageway, the blue-blazed Notch Trail, and the green-blazed Nelsonville Trail. Washburn Trail ends here.

Follow north (left) and then west on the blue-blazed Notch Trail now, descending easily through a wet depression that forms a tributary of Breakneck Brook. Continue along the edge of a shallow ravine as the brook gains momentum, heading west. Beech, birch, and maple dominate the pretty surroundings as you enter an old settlement area in a pure sugar-maple forest. In early spring, hollows become marshy depressions rife with fragrant skunk cabbage, and purple trillium dot the trail. At the junction with the red-blazed Brook Trail, take a short detour to your right on Notch Trail (this is Old Lake Surprise Road, a.k.a. Dairy Road), passing a dilapidated concrete garage on your left, to look at the curious 1920s dairy-farm ruins of the Edward G. Cornish estate. Use caution in the ruins and go a bit farther to look at a bog that was once Notch Lake and the breached dam on its southwest end. An old silo and a large stone barn appear here.

Retrace your steps now to the red-blazed Brook Trail, and follow it a short distance south along Breakneck Brook; cross the yellow-blazed Undercliff Trail and bear left onto the blue-blazed Cornish Trail. Soon you will cross the Catskill Aqueduct that heads south under—or actually through—Mount Taurus. Pass a large, circular concrete cistern. Breakneck Ridge is up to your right (north). Blue blazes are less frequent along the road as it makes a long switchback downhill, soon coming on the gutted-by-fire (1958) ruins of Northgate (the Cornish estate) in silent grandeur, its old hand-laid foundations and greenhouse reclaimed now by mountain laurel, runaway ornamentals, and tangles of grape. Elegant specimens of cedar and Norway spruce stand in the dooryards; second-floor fireplaces suspended over nothing hint at the estate's rustic elegance. Continue on the road, now a poured concrete surface, descending still and passing enormous tulip trees south of the estate, then drawing close to NY 9D. At a gate near the road, look left and continue on the blue-blazed Cornish Trail, which you follow back to the parking area among tangles of triflora rose and brambles. Take 35 minutes to walk the short loop trail around Little Stony Point, along the scenic shore of the Hudson River, in full view of Storm King.

DID YOU KNOW

Edward G. Cornish (1861–1938) was the chairman of the National Lead Company (remember the Dutch Boy logo?) and among the first to point out the dangers of lead-based paints for residential use.

MORE INFORMATION

Hudson Highlands State Park Preserve, Taconic Region; 845-225-7207.

3
POPOLOPEN GORGE AND THE TORNE

An easier mountain hike than most in the Highlands, this route leads you through a scenic and rugged gorge to the summit of a low hill, or torne, with 360-degree views of the Hudson Valley and the United States Military Academy at West Point.

DIRECTIONS

Take I-87 (the New York State Thruway) to Exit 16. Exit right then take a left onto NY 17 south, then another left onto CR 6E, following signs for Bear Mountain State Park. At the first traffic circle, take the third exit, following signs for CR 6E. At the next traffic circle (Bear Mountain Bridge Circle), take the third right onto NY 9W north. In 0.5 mile, take a right into the Fort Montgomery visitor parking area. *GPS coordinates:* 41° 19.455' N, 73° 59.305' W.

An overflow parking area is located another 0.5 mile north on NY 9W. By train, take the Metro-North Hudson Line to Manitou station. Walk south on US 9D, then cross the bridge and walk north on US 9W (3 miles total).

TRAIL DESCRIPTION

Known simply as the Torne (from the Dutch *Torenberg*, for "tower" or "pinnacle"), this small, low-elevation peak (942 feet) provides hikers with unusual views across the eastern Hudson Valley and northwest into the lands of the United States Military Academy at West Point. Most of the vertical rise in this hike is concentrated into a short, steep ascent from the base of the hill. Although climbing the Torne is not as strenuous as navigating the neighboring Major Welch Trail to Bear Mountain's summit, the Torne is more remote and requires deliberate preparation for a half-day outing. To avoid descending the ledge-y and steep south face of the mountain, this hike is routed up

LOCATION
Fort Montgomery, NY

RATING
Moderate

DISTANCE
4.5 miles

ELEVATION GAIN
1,250 feet

ESTIMATED TIME
3.5 hours

MAPS
USGS Popolopen Lake, USGS Peekskill; NY-NJTC Harriman Bear Mountain Trails (Northern)

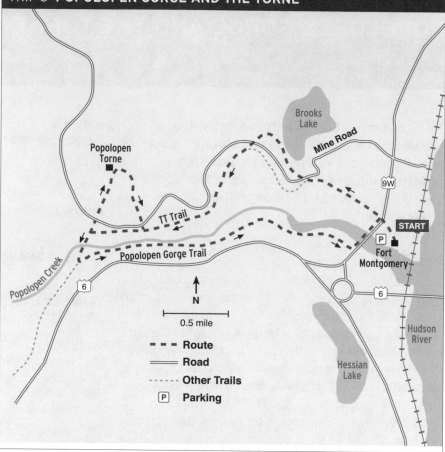

the steeper side first. The return follows alongside scenic Popolopen Gorge, also known as Hell Hole.

Your route is Timp–Torne Trail (TT), a blue-blazed loop leading west. TT climbs the Torne through open woodlands and returns to the Fort Montgomery parking area following the scenic, narrow gorge of Popolopen Creek. From the south side of the parking area, follow TT, the blue-blazed 1779, and the red-blazed 1777W trail signs up a small stone stairway, heading toward the west and the Round Hill redoubt area. This will lead you along the north side of Popolopen Creek (a.k.a. Popolopen Brook). Do not take the suspension bridge. Instead, go under NY 9W, heading west. You will see both the 1777W and 1779 trail disks and the blue blazes of TT. The trail is wide and self-guiding with interpretive signs. Continue straight ahead, following the red and blue trail blazes and the blue blazes of TT through dense hardwoods. Turn left on the single-lane road, entering the woods at the road's western end, a cul-de-sac. The trail continues in a westerly direction. A spur on the left leads to a view of Popolopen Bridge and the Bear Mountain area. Continue straight ahead.

The wilderness quality of the trail improves as you travel west, but first you have to hike through a few wooded residential areas. Soon you rise to meet Mine Torne Road (a.k.a. Mine Road), named for the many local iron mines that smelted ore for arms and ordnance during the Revolutionary War. Cross diagonally toward Brooks Lake. Bear left as you join the red-on-white-blazed Brooks Lake Trail, but don't take the trail around the lake, which is easy to do if you're not paying attention. As soon as you begin to walk along the lake's south shore (after crossing a pair of plank puncheons in a wet area next to the road), look left for the trail blazes, which lead you on a moderately steep uphill path, leaving the lake to your right. Passing through a maturing sugar-maple and oak forest, the trail turns again toward Mine Road, joining it and following it briefly. Pass the intersection of Mine and Wildwood Ridge roads, and follow the trail to the left back into Harriman State Park. On the steep banks of Popolopen Gorge, hemlocks appear in an area of early settlement, where the woods are strewn with glacial erratics. In high water, the creek runs audibly downhill to the left.

The roadbed, which once served the Forest of Dean Mine (1756), is also the route of the West Point Aqueduct (1906). It's wide and can be walked two abreast. Soon you will draw closer to the creek. Mine Road is still visible uphill to the right. You'll cross it ahead.

At a Y in the trail, the section of TT that forms a loop around the Torne begins. Take the right fork that heads uphill. The trail turns left and follows the Mine Road for a hundred feet or so, where a trailhead kiosk appears on your right. Now you begin the ascent to the Torne, following a gently rising switchback trail as it

Hikers take a break on Popolopen Torne, looking southeast over Bear Mountain Bridge and Anthony's Nose.

winds through hardwoods, heading north. Soon the ascent steepens, turns northwest, and climbs the northern flanks of the Torne. Now you are walking a series of upper-elevation, open ledges that provide scenic resting points en route to the summit, where an elaborate cairn, maintained by West Point cadets, commemorates fallen and wounded members of the U.S. military.

Along the north slope of Bear Mountain, you can see the exposed rock that Major Welch Trail traverses, as well as the road that climbs across the mountain's face to the Perkins Memorial Tower, but you can't see the tower itself. You can also see Hessian Lake directly below, to the southeast.

Continue across the open summit ledges. At the south end of the Torne ridge, the blue-blazed trail drops sharply downhill, with some ledges requiring the use of all-fours. The descent eases up through a series of switchbacks through the hardwoods. Cross Mine Road and enter the woods, descending to cross the unpaved Fort Montgomery Road. You will soon rejoin the 1777W and 1779 trails. Turn right, following the 1777W and 1779 trails as well as the TT. Within a few hundred feet, turn left and descend a series of stone steps and cross Popolopen Creek on the footbridge.

Once across the bridge, climb to the Bear Mountain Aqueduct (a dirt path), leaving the blue-blazed TT and both the 1777W and 1779 trails. Bear left following the red and white blazes of Popolopen Gorge Trail. This pretty woods road follows east along the creek, now to your left, and climbs away from it for a while. The trail switches back and forth down the ravine amid large oaks, tulip trees, locusts, and hemlocks that have been killed or damaged by hemlock woolly adelgid. The many pools of the gorge are visible down to the left. Trail blazes may vary in shape and size, but they appear frequently, and the trail is self-guiding.

Soon the trail returns to the creek's edge and climbs slightly uphill, passing above the former site of Roe Pond, where a bridge once spanned the brook over a steep-walled gorge at the site of a 1799 gristmill. The dam is now breached. Hikers will see references to the West Point Aqueduct. In fact, two aqueducts were built along the sides of the gorge in the early 1900s, one to bring water to West Point and the other (on the south side) to serve Bear Mountain. Remains of both are visible.

The trail continues slightly uphill on a wide dirt surface, rising gently to meet NY 9W. Marking becomes indefinite where herd trails make their way east to the nearby road. Trail blazes lead to the road beyond the first herd trail. Once at the road, turn north to cross the 600-foot-long bridge along the sidewalk, remaining on the west side without crossing the highway.

Turn left as you reach the north end of the bridge and, in lieu of crossing this dangerous section of the road, bear left until you reach the 1777W and 1779 trails you'll recognize from earlier in the hike. Look to your left, where a small sign reads, "Visitor Center," and go back under the bridge on the 1777W and 1779 trails. This will bring you back to the Fort Montgomery parking area.

DID YOU KNOW?

The center span of NY 9W's Popolopen Bridge is more than 150 feet high—high enough that in 2008, a parachutist was able to jump from it successfully. Police initially thought the stunt was a suicide and searched the waters below the bridge for some time without locating a body. The man was later arrested for disorderly conduct, unauthorized use of a parachute, and unauthorized swimming.

MORE INFORMATION

The Fort Montgomery visitor parking area is open mid-April to the end of October, sunrise to sunset. The visitor center is open Wednesday to Sunday, 9 A.M. to 5 P.M., but call ahead as times may vary; nysparks.com; 845-446-2134. Admission is free. Additional parking is available farther north on the east side (northbound) of NY 9W. From here, you can walk the site's foot trails back to the main parking area. The interpretive trails are not suited to people with limited mobility. Dogs are allowed on leashes in the park. Swimming is prohibited.

Palisades Interstate Park Commission
Bear Mountain, NY 10911
Phone: 845-351-2583
njpalisades.org

4

BREAKNECK RIDGE TO SOUTH BEACON MOUNTAIN

This demanding hike up the steepest and most exposed scenic trail in the Highlands offers sustained views from open ridges, with a return through quiet forests.

DIRECTIONS

From the intersection of Main Street and NY 9D in the village of Cold Spring, drive north on NY 9D, passing the Little Stony Point parking area at 0.8 mile and continuing north. Just as you pass under the tunnel at 2.1 miles, park immediately on the left (west) side of NY 9D, if possible. If this very small lot is full, continue north to find two more parking areas at 0.1 and 0.3 mile. This hike terminates at the parking area 0.3 mile ahead. *GPS coordinates:* 41° 26.584′ N, 73° 58.660′ W.

Breakneck Ridge Trail is easily reached via the Metro-North Hudson Line from Grand Central Station. On weekends and holidays, disembark at Breakneck Ridge, a popular hiker destination, situated just north of the trailhead. The trail is accessible from Cold Spring on weekdays. From Cold Spring, walk north on NY 9D to the trailhead.

TRAIL DESCRIPTION

The steep, windswept spine of Breakneck Ridge is considered the most difficult and rugged ascent in the Highlands. Rising from nearly sea level on the Hudson River at Breakneck Point to 1,100 feet on Breakneck's summit in less than 0.5 mile, it is a rock scramble, often requiring an all-fours approach. A light pair of gloves will be helpful, and proper footwear is vital. Because the sheer southerly face of Breakneck lies very close to the trail in spots, this hike is not advisable in wet or icy conditions, or in periods of high winds, nor is it recommended for those who fear heights. Likewise, it is not a good choice for unfit hikers

LOCATION
Beacon, NY

RATING
Strenuous

DISTANCE
9 miles

ELEVATION GAIN
1,400 feet

ESTIMATED TIME
6 hours

MAPS
USGS West Point; NY-NJTC East Hudson Trails; New York State Parks Recreation and Historic Preservation handout; Avenza PDF maps; Hudson Highlands State Park-North

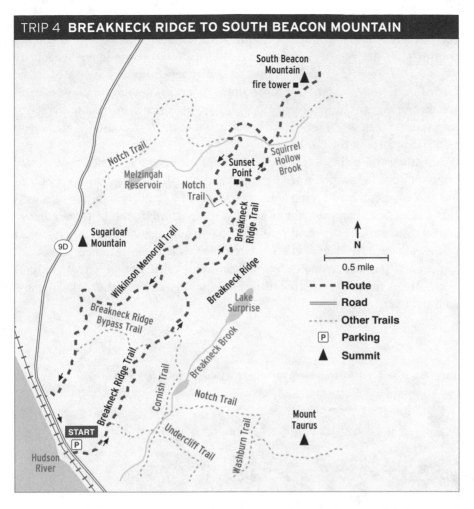

or those with bad knees. This is an intense aerobic workout, and hikers need to carry plenty of water. (In general, Appalachian Mountain Club trip leaders recommend participants carry a minimum of 2 quarts each on hikes of this nature.) The route described here is a long day hike, but there are several options for shortening the trip.

To begin, locate the white Taconic Region trail blazes and white paint blazes of Breakneck Ridge Trail (BR) immediately north of the tunnel on NY 9D. A trailhead kiosk is located here, and paper maps are provided. The maps are of relatively low quality and resolution, and can be difficult to read. Supplies are limited. Arrive at the trailhead with your own map! In a pinch, you can download the Avenza Systems geospatial PDF map application onto your iOS or Android device from the App Store, Google Play, or the Windows Phone Store. Downloadable maps from the NY–NJTC are available for purchase through this app. These maps are of high quality, but like many mobile applications, their frequent use can run your phone battery down faster than you might suspect.

Resuming the climb, follow along the southern cliffs of the ridge, enjoying increasingly good views north to south. If you're lucky, there will be a cooling southwest breeze pouring across the ridge top. You'll see military helicopters from West Point and C5 cargo planes on maneuvers from Stewart Air National Guard Base, and you can look down onto the decks of ships moving fuel and freight upriver and downriver from the Port of Albany. In fall, many of the large sailing craft you'll see will be heading out to the Intracoastal Waterway to wintering places in the Caribbean.

Sometimes the paint blazes may seem confusing, with alternate routes away from the rock ledges presented here and there. Older, disused sections of trail are also apparent, but keeping to the marked trail is important for the preservation of this heavily impacted footway. Continue climbing; the alternate markings tend to parallel the main trail. The sparse hardwood forest covering most of the ridge gives way to pockets of pitch pine, where sun-starched clutches of violet asters persist late into October. Hawks and vultures, their wingtips trembling, survey the ledges with the rising air. Pine needles make the rocks slippery, so mind your footholds.

Storm King is best seen from the steep northwestern flanks of Breakneck Mountain.

Once on top of Breakneck's main summit (the summit ridge is stretched out in a series of domes), you'll be ready for a break. The ground you've covered to this point is probably the most popular "weekend warrior" hike in the Highlands, and there is obvious impact. The trail would be in much worse condition if it weren't for the erosion- and impact-resistant rock surface. At this point, most day-hikers turn back, so chances are you will have the ridge to yourself from here.

Get a good look at the views again before you continue, descending to a point where the yellow-blazed Undercliff Trail departs to the south. Climb northeast on BR again to another scenic crest, where you look across the forests of Break-neck Brook at Mount Taurus. The trail continues through grassy oak woodlands. Nearly two hours into the hike, you will pass the red-on-white-blazed Breakneck Bypass Trail on your left. (You can shorten the hike by taking this trail north to the yellow-blazed Wilkinson Memorial Trail [WM] and turning southwest to NY 9D.) Continue straight ahead on BR. In fifteen minutes or so, the blue-blazed Notch Trail joins BR from the south and continues with it. Following blue and white blazes now, you're headed for Sunset Point. The trail surface is moderately rocky but soft; it is mostly self-guiding, and marking can be sparse in rocky areas. The trail goes through flat, shady woods for a spell.

Arrive at a T and bear left. Don't make the mistake of going off to the right, on the informal blue-blazed trails you'll see; stick to the white-blazed Breakneck Ridge Trail. You'll also see blue-and-white Taconic Region blazes. As you reach another T, bear right to follow the white blazes, as the blue-blazed Notch Trail goes left (northwest). (This is another place where you may want to turn around, following Notch Trail to WM, where you would turn left [southwest], with the option of climbing Sugarloaf Mountain on your return.)

Continue on BR, climbing slightly to Sunset Point. Once treeless and scenic, the point is now enclosed by vegetation. A well-built observation deck appears along the trail, but even it provides little in the way of views, although you can see South Beacon Mountain's fire tower, your ultimate turnaround point, if you look northeast. If it seems too far away, you can backtrack from here or bail out ahead. BR heads downhill now through an area crisscrossed with old trails and skid roads, to a point where it intersects with the yellow-blazed WM at a four-way intersection. (The unmarked trail to the right leads to private property.) This is your last bailout point. If it's late in the day or your energy is ebbing, consider the additional distance and elevation gain required to ascend South Beacon. (To stop here, bear left and follow WM out, as described earlier.)

Continue straight on a woods road now, following both white and yellow blazes for a few hundred feet, then turn left (north) to follow white blazes and begin the ascent of South Beacon. This is the steepest section of trail since Break-neck. Climb open rock ledges and east-facing flats as the woods turn grassy and sheltered again and the trail swings gradually into the east. After about 4 hours (total) of hiking, you will summit South Beacon at 1,650 feet, the highest point in the Highlands. North-lying Mount Beacon is 1,531 in elevation. (Your return route is much faster.) You won't see the fire tower until you're almost at its base. Mount Beacon Fire Tower, built in 1931 on the site of an earlier structure, was used by the State of New York to spot fires for five decades. On June 22, 2013, the Mount Beacon Fire Tower Restoration Committee reopened the historical structure. The 75-mile views are excellent from the tower as well as from the summit, revealing points north to the Catskills and the Shawangunks (you can pick out Sky Top Tower in Mohonk Preserve), south across the river into the Highlands, and east into the low hills of Dutchess and Putnam counties and Fahnestock State Park. Several towers identify North Beacon Mountain to the north. Newburgh–Beacon Bridge spans the Hudson 3 miles to the northwest.

Turn around now and retrace your steps to WM, following it to the right at both intersections. Proceed downhill to a point where it crosses Squirrel Hollow Brook, turns left (east, then south) and rises (with Notch Trail) along a pleasant old woods road. Watch carefully to the right as the easily missed, yellow-blazed WM parts company with Notch Trail. (You've gone too far if you encounter the white-and-blue-blazed intersection you crossed earlier.) Heading southwest, your route takes you through airy woods with a few herd trails to scenic overlooks, then climbs the northeastern shoulder of Sugarloaf Mountain. Views to the north and south from Sugarloaf are the last you'll get. The yellow WM blazes are complemented by white paint blazes here, so don't get confused. Drop down the south side of the mountain and pass Breakneck Ridge Bypass Trail on your left. The trail is now an old road with a good surface that takes you back to NY 9D. Be careful as you follow this busy stretch of road back to your car.

DID YOU KNOW?

Legend has it that in Colonial times, a farmer's bull escaped its confines and found its way to this steep ridge, where it plunged to its death, resulting in the odd place-name *Breakneck*. The dramatic cliffs of Breakneck Mountain that hikers see today were created by quarrying.

MORE INFORMATION

Breakneck Ridge is open daily from sunrise to sunset. Dogs are permitted, but must be on a leash of 10 feet or less; nysparks.state.ny.us/parks/9/details.aspx; 845-225-7207.

5

BEAR MOUNTAIN

This pretty hike departs from the famous Bear Mountain Inn on Hessian Lake en route to Perkins Memorial Tower and its 360-degree views then descends on the Appalachian Trail.

DIRECTIONS

Begin at Bear Mountain State Park, 0.4 mile south of the Bear Mountain traffic circle on US 9W. The traffic circle is located at the northern end of the Palisades Interstate Parkway, at the western entrance to the Bear Mountain Bridge. *GPS coordinates:* 41° 18.771′ N, 73° 59.335′ W.

By train, take the Metro-North Hudson Line to Manitou station. Walk south on US 9D, then cross the bridge and walk south on US 9W (3 miles total).

TRAIL DESCRIPTION

Since its creation in 1913, millions of people have visited Bear Mountain State Park to indulge in founder George Perkins's version of rest and relaxation, but only a fraction of them ever climb its namesake, the scenic "little" mountain lying west of Hessian Lake. Though Bear Mountain isn't especially formidable at 1,305 feet, the steep northerly ascent from near sea level to its summit via Major Welch Trail makes this hike feel longer than it is, and you should prepare accordingly.

There are several approaches to Bear Mountain, but Major Welch Trail is the most scenic and interesting, sharing its popularity among hikers with the somewhat easier southerly approach using the Appalachian Trail (AT). (It is also possible to drive to the summit on Perkins Memorial Drive, so expect to see cars and people at the summit picnic area.) Major William A. Welch was the general manager of Palisades Interstate Park from 1912 to 1940. He organized the completion of the first section of the AT

LOCATION
Bear Mountain, NY

RATING
Strenuous

DISTANCE
4 miles

ELEVATION GAIN
1,000 feet

ESTIMATED TIME
3.5 hours

MAPS
USGS Peekskill, USGS Popolopen Lake; NY-NJTC Harriman Bear Mountain (Northern); New York State Department of Parks, Recreation and Historic Preservation handout; Bear Mountain State Park

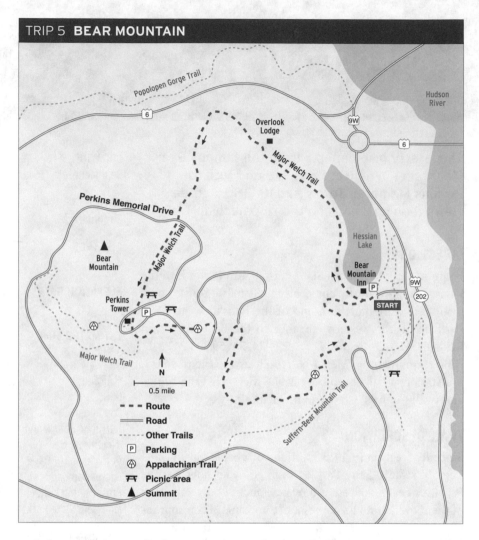

and designed the trail's distinctive logo. The Appalachian Trail Conservancy (ATC) believes the Bear Mountain section of the AT is the most heavily used portion of the 2,190-mile trail.

Despite the extremely high day-use figures Bear Mountain State Park sustains, it has been kept clean and orderly—a result of the park's careful planning, management, and supervision. You will appreciate this as you stroll through the inn complex, where you'll park. Try to plan your hike before the park's swimming pool opens for the season on the first day of summer or after it closes in early September, when parking is free and visitors are not present in great numbers.

Pass in front of Bear Mountain Inn and bear left toward the south end of Hessian Lake. Orient yourself at the southern shore, behind the inn on the paved path. Watch for the red circle on a white background as you follow the shore in the company of friendly geese and squirrels. Head toward the boat-rental concession to the west. In the vicinity of the children's playground on your left, the AT joins the paved lake path. (That's your return route.) Walk along the pretty western shore of Hessian Lake. In fifteen minutes or so, look left for a bench, where Major Welch Trail departs to the left (northwest). If you're daydreaming, you might miss it.

Major Welch Trail is slow in ascending. It takes a short jog around a water tank and continues, rising slightly. The tank supplies water for Overlook Lodge, which you can see downhill to the north. The first 0.5 mile is forgiving, as the trail rises gently and traverses along the northeasterly hardwood slopes, passing a water tower on the left and the park's Overlook Lodge downhill and north. By the time you're wondering where the vertical rise begins, you've turned south and the recently improved trail switches back upslope over a rocky surface. The Jolly Rovers, a volunteer trail crew of the NY-NJ Trail Conference, completed the trail improvement in 2013 with the aid of AmeriCorps interns and professional trail builders. You'll appreciate your trekking poles here. Most of the hike's vertical rise is packed into the next 0.5 mile.

The trail climbs through nearly pure oak and laurel woods among thick mats of blueberry bushes and dense mountain laurel. Underfoot is the bright limestone of the Greenville Series, which is of Precambrian origin and among the oldest surface bedrock of its kind. As you gain elevation, you'll come to a long, angled slab with northern exposure. Things get more interesting now as views of the valley open up. Here you will get a close look at the brown, exposed summit of Popolopen Torne. The scenery improves ahead, with views to the north, west, and east, encompassing a good deal of the northern Highlands and the river. You can identify Sugarloaf, Taurus, and Storm King mountains, the Black Rock Forest, the lands of Fahnestock State Park, and, down along the river, Garrison Landing. A few pitch pines appear.

The trail cuts across paved Perkins Memorial Drive and continues to climb, more easily now, flattening out after one more steep pitch. At a T intersection, a blue-blazed trail appears on the right. Bear left on Major Welch Trail. Completed by a professional trail crew, this beautiful, flat, garden-like, gravel section of trail was designed to be accessible by all users. At the next intersection, the AT joins Major Welch Trail. You will soon pass the true summit, with tower bolts visible in the large boulder to the left of the trail. Continue straight ahead, ascending slightly to Perkins Memorial Tower. Take a few minutes to view the tower, with its tiled, art deco pictorial history of the park and four walls detailed with panoramic locator maps of the 360-degree views. Note Anthony's Nose to the east and Dunderberg, Bald, and Timp mountains to the south. The tower commemorates George Perkins, of the banking firm J.P. Morgan, who envisioned a place where the people of New York City (visible to the south) could find "rest and relaxation." Perkins was instrumental in the long struggle to preserve the Palisades, which in turn led to the effort to protect the entire Hudson Valley from exploitation and development.

Major Welch Trail ends here. Just outside the front entrance of the tower and across the loop road and parking area to the south, your route continues on the AT. In the rocks at the trailside, you'll find the AT next to the bronze plaque honoring Joe Bartha, the NY-NJ Trail Conference trails chairman from 1940 to 1955. About 15 feet southeast of the plaque, search the rocks for a very vague, weathered carving indicating the AT's distance to the hamlet of Arden and to Vogel State Park in Georgia (1,260 miles; the southern terminus has since been relocated to Springer Mountain). Following the AT now, descend through open hardwoods.

In about ten minutes, you will cross Perkins Memorial Drive. Descending, you'll reach it at a point where a trail marker reads, "Tower, 30 Mins." The word *tower* is stenciled onto a rock to the left, next to the road. Pay close attention, as the trail turns right and follows the road. (It is evident from herd paths that many hikers unwittingly continue downhill into the woods after crossing the road.) Follow the road for ten minutes until you reach a dead end and loop. The AT leaves the loop on the right side, over a stretch of broken pavement; marking is good. Within 100 feet, it turns hard left (east) and descends. The AT switches and drops into the east, passing through a beautiful grove of white pine before continuing through hardwoods and crossing the road again.

Hikers enjoy sweeping views of the Hudson Highlands from the Appalachian Trail, atop Bear Mountain.

The AT has been improved throughout this section, all the way back to Hessian Lake. The Bear Mountain Trails Project (BMTP) is a major trail-building and rehabilitation effort managed by the NY–NJTC in cooperation with its partners: the Appalachian Trail Conservancy; National Park Service Appalachian Trail Park Office; New York State Parks, Recreation and Historic Preservation; and the Palisades Interstate Park Commission. The project is designed to rehabilitate and rebuild the trails on Bear Mountain, as well as to educate the public. The project includes the major relocation of the AT and the restoration of Major Welch Trail that you've witnessed on this hike. *Backpacker* magazine called this section of the rebuilt trail a "masterpiece."

At the head of a gully, the trail crosses a wooden bridge and swings hard to the right, continuing its descent and flattening out at a point where the park complex comes into view. Avoid the trail to the right, instead continuing on the AT.

Now the trail follows part of the old service road that went to the ski jump and arrives back at Hessian Lake, at which point the AT passes through the Bear Mountain Zoo and across the Hudson River toward Maine's Katahdin. You may ponder, for a moment, the vision of Mary Averell Harriman, who donated 10,000 acres of land with the condition that the state discontinue plans for the construction of Sing Sing prison at the base of Bear Mountain. The prison was eventually built downriver, in Ossining, north of New York City, giving rise to the expression "Sent up the river."

From here, follow the short trail back to your car.

DID YOU KNOW?

Perkins Memorial Tower on the summit of Bear Mountain was constructed to take advantage of the scenic Hudson Highlands views. It was such a hit with the touring public that in September and October of 1935, the year after it was inaugurated, it attracted 9,869 cars from 36 states and two Canadian provinces.

MORE INFORMATION

Bear Mountain State Park features a large playing field, shaded picnic groves, lake and river fishing access, a swimming pool, trailside museums and a zoo, and hiking, biking, and cross-country ski trails. An outdoor rink is open to ice skaters from late October through mid-March. The Perkins Memorial Tower atop Bear Mountain affords spectacular views of the park, the Hudson Highlands, and Harriman State Park. Perkins Memorial Drive and Tower are open from April through late November, weather permitting. For general information contact the Bear Mountain Office at 845-786-2701.

Palisades Interstate Park Commission
Bear Mountain, NY 10911
Phone: 845-351-2583
njpalisades.org

DUNDERBERG AND THE TIMP

This backcountry ramble through the interior Highlands' historical trails and remote forests offers many scenic lookouts.

DIRECTIONS

The trailhead is located on US 9W/202, 3.8 miles south of the Bear Mountain Bridge Circle. The trailhead parking area lies on the west side of US 9W/202 at its intersection with Jones Point Road, a.k.a. Old Route 9W. (If you go south as far as the anchor monument, you've gone too far. Backtrack 0.2 mile.) The trailhead parking area, while sanctioned, is not clearly identified by state park signs. Park in the gravel turnout and use caution as you walk about 200 feet south along US 9W/202. Look carefully to the right for the trail, as it is easy to walk past. *GPS coordinates* 41° 16.863' N, 73° 57.772' W.

TRAIL DESCRIPTION

Ravaged by fire, mining, and failed human ambition, the landscape of Dunderberg Mountain may at first strike you as raw and unappealing. The standing dead snags of bleached, barkless oaks project hauntingly above ravenous pioneer growth. Gaping pits and talus piles indent and litter the hillsides. Vast handmade berms, dark dead-end tunnels, and an embroidery of lost and forgotten roads are the haunting remains of an abandoned spiral railway to a hotel that was never built. Through here, in 1777, the British army marched on Fort Clinton and Fort Montgomery, destroying both and killing hundreds of American soldiers in the process.

In addition to the troubled history and visible scars of the mountain itself, the trailhead parking area may raise your suspicion that this area has everything going against it. Across the Hudson River, too close for comfort, you

LOCATION
Stony Point, NY

RATING
Strenuous

DISTANCE
6 miles

ELEVATION GAIN
1,600 feet

ESTIMATED TIME
4.5 hours

MAPS
USGS Peekskill, USGS Popolopen Lake; NY-NJTC Northern Harriman Bear Mountain Trails; National Geographic; Harriman, Bear Mountain, Sterling Forest State Parks

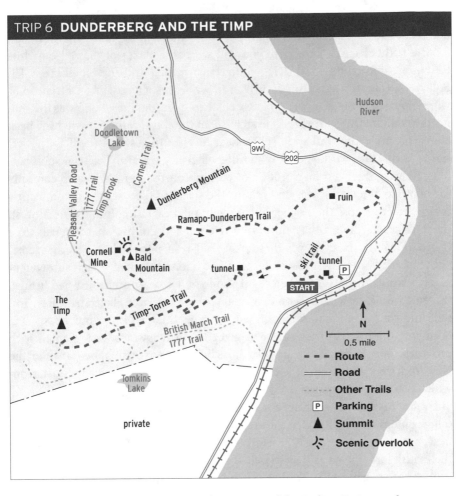

Hudson
River

Doodletown
Lake

Cornell Trail

Pleasant Valley Road

1777 Trail

Timp Brook

9W

202

Dunderberg Mountain

■ ruin

Ramapo-Dunderberg Trail

Cornell ■
Mine

▲ Bald
Mountain

tunnel ■

Ski trail

tunnel
■

P

tunnel ■

START

The
Timp

▲

Timp-Torne Trail

British March Trail

1777 Trail

N

0.5 mile

- - - Route
——— Road
········· Other Trails
P Parking
▲ Summit
⅄ Scenic Overlook

Tomkins
Lake

private

look directly at the reactors and cooling tower of the Indian Point nuclear power plant that has enjoyed the dubious distinction of being one of the Federal Energy Regulatory Commission's most-watched facilities. Traffic is fast and often heavy on this stretch of highway, and the road's wooded margins may be heavily littered. By the time you wend your way through the tangled margin of undergrowth below Dunderberg's easterly slopes, you'll breathe a deep sigh of relief as you witness the powers of Mother Nature at work in the slow but inexorable process of healing and reclamation.

This collection of three peaks and the attractions surrounding them, including West Mountain and the ghost town called Doodletown, have long been popular with hikers from the Appalachian Mountain Club (AMC). Although the trails have been rerouted time and again, AMC member Bob Marshall in 1987 pioneered Timp–Torne Trail (TT), which is used today. Many variations of this hike exist, but the classic approach is the one described here.

Walk just south of the sanctioned trailhead parking area along US 9W, perhaps 200 feet or about one minute, looking hard to the right beyond a highway sign for the fairly obscure trail. Here you will see paint blazes of the red-on-white Ramapo-Dunderberg Trail (RD), your return route, and the blue-blazed TT. Follow the trail through a thick and overgrown wood of locust and cottonwoods, where some of the trees are completely cloaked in grapevines. Follow as the trail heads uphill easily, passing a stone archway of the spiral railway. Switching back above the arch, the trail soon splits. Bear left (southwest) on the TT (the RD heads north) and work your way uphill over rocky terrain. The trail soon flattens, heading due west on a section of built-up railroad grade. Watch carefully for blazes as the trail leaves and rejoins the series of old roads and connecting paths that crisscross the slope as it climbs in pitches, rising into the northwest. In many places the trail is neither intuitive nor self-guiding, but you can trust the marking. (In the event you do step off-trail, return to the last blaze and reorient yourself. Trail markers work together, positioned to ensure each subsequent blaze is visible from the one before it.) Soon you will pass an unfinished tunnel, thereafter walking a berm with marginal views south over Haverstraw Bay. You will find yourself in a grassy, open oak wood as the trail turns northeast. One hour into the hike, at the point where the trail turns southwest, a small rock provides good views to the southeast, including a surprise appearance of the New York City skyline and the close knob of Dunderberg in the northeast, from which you will descend later.

The trail is rocky, winding, and heads up and down, over and around rock outcroppings through pretty, parklike forests as it makes its way southwest. It descends sharply to cross 1777 Trail (red numerals on a white disk), the route the British forces used as they marched north from Stony Point. Within twenty minutes of crossing 1777 Trail, you will intersect with RD. Take a left onto the blue-blazed TT here for the five- to ten-minute hike up Timp (1,080 feet), an airy, open cliff with excellent views south to New York City; west across the unbroken forests of Harriman State Park; and north, upriver, past Bear Mountain and the Perkins Memorial Tower, beyond the Bear Mountain Bridge and into the Highlands. (You can see the West Mountain Shelter from here, lying just east of the Appalachian Trail, if you know where to look carefully.)

Resume the hike, backtracking to RD (don't turn right onto RD), and following it straight ahead (northeast) and downhill, soon crossing 1777 Trail a very short distance north of where you crossed it earlier on TT. RD climbs and levels through open oak woods followed by a laurel tunnel, crosses a stream, and courts an old roadbed as it rises steeply now, up the southeasterly shoulder of Bald Mountain. Continue north; the southern summit offers marginal views to a point in the north, but just off the trail there are excellent views to the north. From this vantage, hikers can easily relate to the Hudson Valley's alternate identity as the "American Rhineland." The river bends north and west behind the Highlands, and the hills roll away into the fertile valley beyond. The

Dunderberg, Dutch for "thunder hill," stands at the southerly gate of the Hudson Highlands.

viewshed includes Bear Mountain Bridge and Bear Mountain (easily identified by means of Perkins Memorial Tower at its summit), Anthony's Nose rising above the eastern terminus of the bridge, Mount Taurus and Breakneck Ridge to the north, and Mount Beacon with its towers. The remains of the Cornell mines lie below the cliff face to the north and in other nearby sites on the mountain. (Thomas Cornell was a U.S. senator, as well as president of the Cornell Steamship Company and the Ulster and Delaware railroad. Cornell Mountain, the central peak in the Catskills' Burroughs Range, bears his name.) This vantage point is the scenic highlight of the hike. Return to RD, as it hairpins around and descends to the blue-blazed Cornell Mine Trail departing to the north. Bearing right on RD, follow through high, airy woods and climb the rolling ridge of Dunderberg. Soon you will cross the recovering ridges of long-dead oak, where wildflowers and sedges grow in moist pockets of moss amid vernal pools and wet swales. Ragweed, thistle, milkweed, wild rose, cattails, and speckled alder frame views to the south.

Just when you think Dunderberg's extended ridge will never end, the trail drops off the eastern knob (930 feet) and gradually turns south, leaving the fire-damaged, recovering young forest for the lush lowlands. A white spur trail leads east to the last of the viewpoints; the trail shares the old rail bed along a flat segment and descends over a long section of loose rubble to a stone wall ruin, dropping down on the large, built-up berm of the cable incline. Beyond, it rejoins the blue-blazed TT and backtracks past the archway and back to the parking area.

DID YOU KNOW?

In 1890, following his invention of a method by which electromagnets were used to separate and refine iron ore, Thomas Edison purchased 200 acres on the north slopes of Dunderberg, where he established an iron mine.

MORE INFORMATION

Nearby Bear Mountain State Park features a large playing field, shaded picnic groves, lake and river fishing access, a swimming pool, trailside museums and a zoo, as well as hiking, biking, and cross-country ski trails. An outdoor rink is open to ice skaters from late October through mid-March. Perkins Memorial Drive and Tower are open from April through late November, weather permitting. For general information contact the Bear Mountain Office at 845-786-2701.

Palisades Interstate Park Commission
Bear Mountain, NY 10911
Phone: 845-351-2583
njpalisades.org

7

HESSIAN LAKE AND FORT MONTGOMERY STATE HISTORIC SITE

This easy hike winds amid a park and a zoo, around a lake, and through a Revolutionary War site adjacent to the Hudson River.

DIRECTIONS

To reach Bear Mountain from the Bear Mountain Bridge Circle, which is located on CR 6 immediately on the west side of the Bear Mountain Bridge, take NY 9W south. At the first traffic light, bear right and go up the hill. The parking area is on your right. For directions to the Fort Montgomery State Historic Site, see Trip 3. *GPS coordinates:* 41° 18.771′ N, 73° 59.335′ W.

By train, take the Metro-North Hudson Line to Manitou station. Walk south on US 9D, then cross the bridge and walk south on US 9W (3 miles total).

TRAIL DESCRIPTION

This scenic, historical, and zoological hike gives you the opportunity to walk around Hessian Lake, through Bear Mountain Zoo (on the route of the Appalachian Trail, or AT), and across CR 6 to the Fort Montgomery State Historic Site. Although the trails in this hike are interconnected and the hiking time is fairly brief, put aside at least a half-day to wander among these interesting places, especially if you are with children, who will be fascinated by the zoo. Like most of the popular trails in the Bear Mountain vicinity, this one is best taken before the Bear Mountain complex opens for the season in June, when it is often congested with day users. Hiking in the off-season will provide you with more privacy on the trail, and you will not be charged the parking fee. If you have children with you and want to use the full services of the park, such

LOCATION
Fort Montgomery, NY

RATING
Easy

DISTANCE
3.25 miles

ELEVATION GAIN
350 feet

ESTIMATED TIME
2 hours

MAPS
USGS Peekskill; Bear Mountain and Harriman State Parks, Palisades Interstate Park Commission; New York State Parks Recreation and Historic Preservation handout

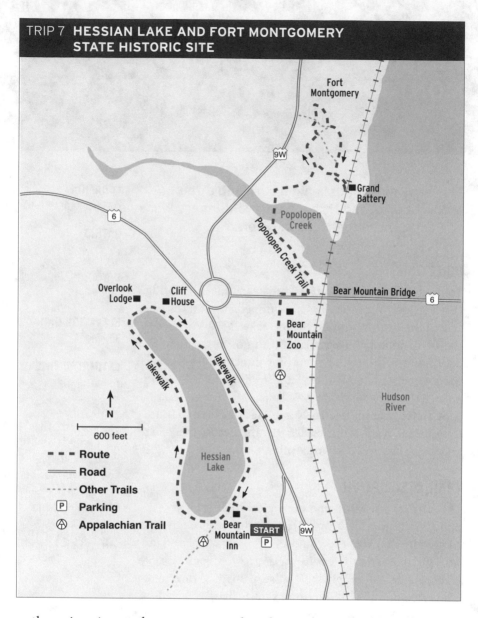

Fort Montgomery

9W

Grand Battery

Popolopen Creek

Popolopen Creek Trail

Bear Mountain Bridge

6

Overlook Lodge

Cliff House

Bear Mountain Zoo

lakewalk

lakewalk

lakewalk

Hudson River

N

600 feet

- - - Route
—— Road
----- Other Trails
P Parking
⊕ Appalachian Trail

Hessian Lake

Bear Mountain Inn

START
P

9W

as the swimming pool, merry-go-round, and picnic area, the fee is well worth these amenities.

Leave the Bear Mountain complex parking lot and head north, crossing in front of the Bear Mountain Inn and heading left toward Hessian Lake. The conspicuous mountain visible across the river east of the parking lot is Anthony's Nose, one of the Hudson Valley's most scenic hiking destinations. Immediately to the west, across the lake, the slopes of Bear Mountain rise sharply. The 1.25-mile loop around Hessian Lake makes for a pleasant walk. Follow the paved walk along the water's edge, bearing left toward the western shore.

Pass the boat-rental dock and follow the lake around the south end and into the north. Along the walk, you will see the Major Welch Trail blazes, red dots on white, and nearing the lake's north end you'll see where that trail leaves the lake to head for Bear Mountain's summit. Leave Major Welch Trail to your left and continue around the north end of the lake. Uphill to the north you will see Overlook Lodge and the Cliff House, along with the little cottages of the Bear Mountain lodge system. Walk south, remaining on the walkway until you enter the picnic groves. When you see the picnic shelter, leave the walkway and bear left onto a path that goes east toward the underpass in the direction of the zoo. Now you're following the AT. (Look for white paint blazes on the trees.)

Continue past the pool house and go through the gate into the zoo. (Entry is free for AT hikers; for others, a $1 donation is suggested.) The zoo features mostly species indigenous to the region, many of which are rescues. The zoo trail is very wooded and attractive as it winds its way north, past the Walt Whitman statue and into the area of the former Fort Clinton, which was razed so badly by the British during the Revolutionary War that not much of it is recognizable. A short diversion to the west takes you through the redoubt, or walled fortification area. Continue north, heading toward the museums, which feature rare collections of American Revolution artifacts, many of them excavated from forts Clinton and Montgomery.

On the zoo's north side, next to the history museum building, the AT leaves for Bear Mountain Bridge and points northwest. The trail you want is Popolopen Gorge Trail, which also leaves from here—blue stripes on gray; marking is sparse—and follows the AT a bit farther. Both trails cross the pedestrian crosswalk next to the tollbooth. (An alternate trail leaves the zoo to the east, goes under the highway, and joins Popolopen Creek Trail, but the zoo end of the trail is gated when the zoo is closed.) Cross on the pedestrian crosswalk and turn right (east), as if you intend to cross the Bear Mountain Bridge. If you have time, walk to the center span for a sweeping view of the river. Watch very carefully as you walk along the sidewalk; immediately before the bridge guardrail begins, bear left (north) onto Popolopen Creek Trail; the AT continues across the bridge. At this point, the trail is not marked and there is no signage. Follow the trail downhill on a natural stone stairway and bear left at the Y intersection.

Follow the trail downhill into the ravine toward Popolopen Creek, where it crosses the footbridge, a pedestrian suspension model that was dedicated in 2002 by Governor George Pataki. Bear right and uphill into Fort Montgomery State Historic Site. Here you will find the visitor center, along with many outdoor interpretive signs and maps. The site's trail system begins on the north side of the visitor center. A stroll through the redoubts and associated fortifications will take about a half hour, allowing time to read the interpretive information that's posted in each area of this extensive excavation. Here you

Once called Bloody Pond because it served as a dumping ground for Revolutionary War casualties, Hessian Lake today offers peaceful respite.

will see the foundations of several buildings, among them barracks, redoubts, bunkers, artillery placements, and yet-to-be-identified relics. Follow the interpretive trail past the site of the storehouse, the enlisted men's barracks, the officers' barracks and commissary, the north redoubt, the guardhouse, and the magazine, finishing with the cannon battery before returning to the visitor center. The Western and Round Hill redoubts on the west side of NY 9W can be examined by following 1777 and 1779 trails. Go west under the NY 9W bridge, a short detour on your return to the suspension bridge.

Early in the American Revolution, the Continental Congress recognized the need to defend the Hudson River from the British, who sought to take the river and divide the New England colonies from New York. It was believed the best location for such a defense was at the site of what's now called Bear Mountain, where the river narrowed and the current made navigation slow and difficult. Advancing ships would be easy prey for the cannon battery that was set atop the hill between Fort Clinton and Fort Montgomery. Construction of both forts began in 1776, despite difficulties in procuring supplies and manpower, and the combined fortifications were completed in 1777. After realizing Fort Montgomery was vulnerable to attack by land (revolutionaries originally felt the Hudson Highlands' rugged topography would protect it from a land-based assault), colonists fortified it by placing redoubts along its western line of defense. These were essentially earthworks behind which infantrymen could snipe at the advancing enemy.

Retrace your steps now, back to the zoo and the lake walk. If you return after closing time, you will not be able to follow the trail through the zoo and will instead have to walk along the grass strip next to NY 9W, crossing the highway at the paved spur on the north end of Hessian Lake, just south of the entrance road to the Bear Mountain Inn complex. (This is also the recommended route of the AT when the zoo is closed.) Try to avoid doing this, however, as traffic coming off the Bear Mountain Circle moves very fast.

DID YOU KNOW?

During the British attacks on forts Clinton and Montgomery, both the British and American forces suffered heavy losses. Bodies were disposed of in what was originally called Bloody Pond, later renamed Hessian Lake.

MORE INFORMATION

The trailside zoo and museum are open daily from 10 A.M. to 4:30 P.M.; Fort Montgomery is open April through October, sunrise to sunset; visitor center hours vary Wednesday to Sunday, 9 A.M. to 5 P.M. Admission is free.

Palisades Interstate Park Commission
Bear Mountain, NY 10911
Phone: 845-351-2583
njpalisades.org

8

ANTHONY'S NOSE

A fairly steep ascent to an easy woods road leads to Engagement Rock, which looks straight down on the Hudson River and Bear Mountain Bridge.

DIRECTIONS

Bear Mountain State Park is 0.4 mile south of the Bear Mountain traffic circle on US 9W. The traffic circle is located at the northern end of the Palisades Interstate Parkway, at the western entrance to Bear Mountain Bridge. Park in the Bear Mountain Inn parking lot (fee), or along NY 9D on the east side of the Hudson River, where parking along the road's narrow shoulder is legal. (Note: This option cuts out Bear Mountain Zoo and Bridge.) *GPS coordinates:* 41° 18.771′ N, 73° 59.335′ W.

By train, take the Metro-North Hudson Line to Manitou station. Walk south for 2 miles on US 9D. (This options also cuts out the zoo and bridge.)

TRAIL DESCRIPTION

How about a hike that takes you past a crystalline lake, through a zoo, along the lowest-elevation stretch of the Appalachian Trail (AT), and across Bear Mountain Bridge to one of the most dramatic scenic destinations in the Hudson Valley? This unforgettable outing begins at Bear Mountain State Park's inn complex, where you join the AT as it makes its way across the Hudson River. There are other ways to reach Anthony's Nose (900 feet), but this is the shortest, the most interesting, and easily the most exciting.

From the Bear Mountain Inn parking area, walk toward the inn, keeping the main entrance to your left. To the right, beyond the flagpole and cannon, you will see Anthony's Nose, rising 0.7 mile to the east. The highest reach of exposed rock, Engagement Rock on the western face, is your destination.

LOCATION
Cortlandt, NY; trail begins in Bear Mountain State Park

RATING
Moderate

DISTANCE
4 miles

ELEVATION GAIN
700 feet

ESTIMATED TIME
4 hours

MAPS
USGS Peekskill; NY-NJTC East Hudson Trails

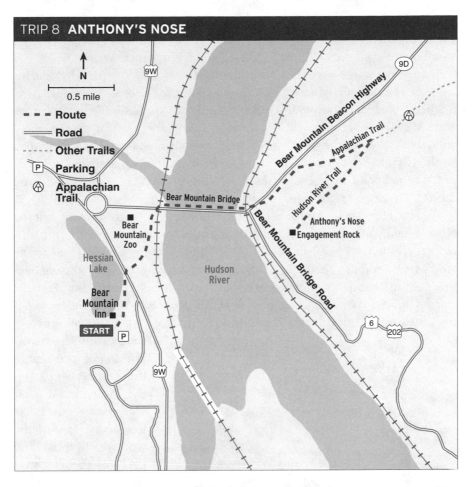

Two paved paths diverge in the picnic area to the north, within 100 feet of the inn. Stay to the left, walking with Hessian Lake to your left, and in a few minutes you will intersect with the white-blazed AT (near the restrooms). Be alert, as the AT bears right (east) and tunnels under US 9W/202, passing the pool and entering the wooded paths of the zoo. (There is a $1 fee for adults, but no charge for AT hikers. Accessible parking is available.)

The zoo marks the lowest elevation on the AT between Maine and Georgia (124 feet above sea level). The AT is consistently well-marked and will bring you to the northern exit at the Bear Mountain Bridge administration building. Bear left as you reach the toll plaza and stay left, following blazes to the pedestrian crossing just west of the tollbooths. Cross carefully here and walk along the north side of the bridge on the protected pedestrian path. As you reach the east side of the river, bear left onto the shoulder of NY 9D and follow the AT a short distance to where the white-blazed trail enters the woods on the right (east) side of the road. Be careful here. Although you have a very brief walk, traffic moves briskly along this roadside stretch of the AT. From the trailhead kiosk, follow the trail uphill as it swings northeast to begin a 700-foot vertical rise. Most of this gain is experienced in the first 0.6 mile of the AT, as it climbs a good footway on a well-maintained trail with makeshift steps and heavy rock water bars.

At an obvious, well-marked T, the trail relaxes and the AT departs left (northeast) to the Hudson Highlands State Park's Osborne Preserve. Turn right here, following the blue-blazed Hudson River Trail onto the lands of the New York State Military Reservation (also known as Camp Smith). This gentler, more enjoyable section of the trail follows an old woods road that rises briefly then levels at 700 feet of elevation, where it passes through open hardwoods, winds past a vernal pond, and gently rises to a T. This point is not signed, and if you didn't know to turn right here, you'd miss the Nose completely.

The blue blazes lead southeast on a foot trail to a southerly lookout, but the old roadbed you've been walking on continues to the right (west), immediately reaching the open ledges of Anthony's Nose at Engagement Rock. The views are startling, as is the breathless sensation you get from standing over the Hudson River, which lies beneath your toes, nearly 900 feet below. Freighters, plying the river's channel, pass beneath you, their turbid wakes twisting a half-mile behind them. The hills of Harriman State Park roll north to

south, from the northern Popolopen Torne to Dunderberg and the Timp. From here, Haverstraw Bay looks like a vast arm of the sea, which it is, and upriver the Central Highlands lie in a pastel haze of multiple horizons beyond World's End. This section of the Hudson is called the Devil's Horse Race, so named for the high winds and strong tides that funnel through its narrowest point. According to one legend, the Nose is named for the

From Bear Mountain State Park, you can see Anthony's Nose rising above the Hudson River.

proboscis of a sea captain, one Anthony Hogans, whose crew thought the captain's face and the geological phenomenon had a great deal in common.

You can see Perkins Memorial Tower on Bear Mountain and Iona Island, nudged against the western shore of the river. This is a popular spot, and you're likely to share it with other hikers. A less spectacular outcropping is nearby, just a few feet south on the blue-blazed trail from the junction where you turned east to the Nose. There you can find more privacy among the burnished summit rocks facing the southern valley. Directly below is Bear Mountain Bridge, privately built by the Harriman family in 1923.

Retrace your steps to return to your car.

DID YOU KNOW?

When Earl Shaffer in 1948 became the first AT hiker to cross Bear Mountain Bridge, it cost a nickel. Today passage is free for hikers.

MORE INFORMATION

Bear Mountain Inn parking lot is open year-round, 10 A.M. to 6 P.M. The zoo is open 10 A.M. to 4:30 P.M. A parking fee applies from late June through Labor Day (when the zoo and inn are closed, the official route of the AT becomes the shoulder of US 9W); nysparks.state.ny.us/parks/9/details.aspx; 845-225-7207.

This very scenic loop begins with a flat walk along the river then climbs a high section of the northern Palisades.

DIRECTIONS

To reach Nyack Beach State Park from west of the Hudson River on I-87 (a.k.a. I-287, the New York State Thruway), take Exit 11 for Nyack. At the traffic light, turn left onto CR 59 East. This leads you straight onto Main Street. Go under the I-87 underpass and through the intersection of NY 9W. Continue 1 mile straight through town on Main Street to its intersection with North Broadway in the center of the village. Turn left (north) and go another 2 miles to Nyack Beach State Park.

Coming from east of the Hudson River, take I-87 to Exit 10. This is a large circular interchange. Pass the turnoff to NY 9W and continue to the next right. This is South Nyack. At the stop sign, turn right onto Clinton Avenue, then left onto South Broadway. Go straight onto North Broadway and continue to the park entrance, 2.5 miles from the exit. *GPS coordinates:* 41° 7.235′ N, 73° 54.685′ W.

By bus, take Coach USA from Port Authority to Broadway and Cedar Hill in Nyack (call 201-263-1254). Walk north for 2 miles on Broadway to trailhead.

TRAIL DESCRIPTION

The Hook has long been a favorite of Hudson Valley hiking enthusiasts, who enjoy the very high scenic vistas from this easily accessible, although somewhat difficult trail. The trail is named for Hook Mountain, which at 728 feet is the trail's highest landscape feature and the second-highest point on the Palisades ridge, after High Tor. The long, flat approach along the river's edge and

LOCATION
Nyack, NY

RATING
Moderate

DISTANCE
5.3 miles

ELEVATION GAIN
1,200 feet

ESTIMATED TIME
3.5 hours

MAPS
USGS Sloatsburg; NY-NJTC Hudson Palisades Trail Map

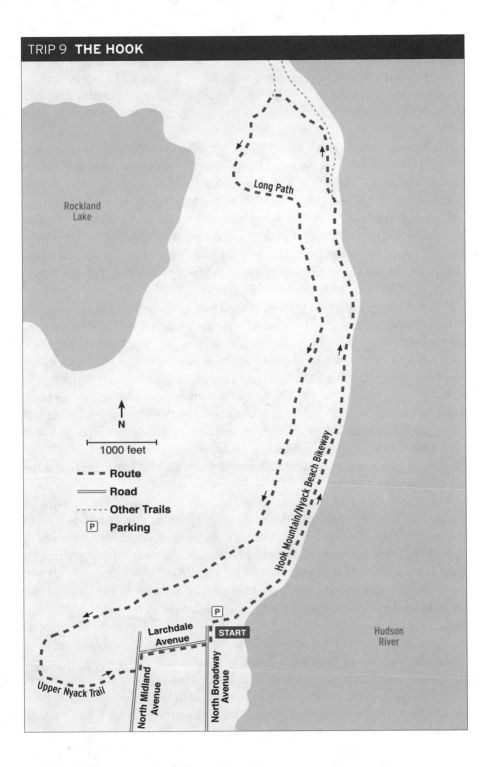

Rockland
Lake

N
1000 feet

Route
Road
Other Trails
P **Parking**

Long Path

Hook Mountain/Nyack Beach Bikeway

Hudson
River

Larchdale
Avenue

P

START

North Midland Avenue

North Broadway Avenue

Upper Nyack Trail

the high-country feel of the Palisades' vertical cliffs make this a satisfying hike of contrasts.

The Hook is a loop hike, beginning and ending at Nyack Beach State Park, a 76-acre parcel managed by the Palisades Interstate Park Commission. This is a part of Hudson River Valley Greenway Trail, a linear park development project that connects the scenic areas along the western shore of the Hudson River. Hook Mountain and Nyack Beach State Park have been designated a National Natural Landmark by the National Park Service; together, they possess exceptional value as an illustration of the nation's natural heritage.

From the entry kiosk, drive downhill to the parking lot, which has become a destination in itself for its scenic appeal. Walk to the north with the river on your right and follow the dirt path along the river's edge. This is a multiuse trail. The path continues along the river for more than a mile, to a point where it rises gently, passing small stone ruins on the left. Just ahead, you'll arrive at a fork. This is the 1.5-mile point. Bear left here.

Proceed along this paved section of road toward Rockland Lake. The forest is dense, consisting of sycamore, maple, locust, and mulberry. Passing a park administrative building on your right, continue uphill. At the point where the road levels out, walk through a barrier of large concrete blocks and look to your left for the Long Path trailhead (aqua blazes), which will take you in a southerly direction over the Hook. There is an interpretive sign at the trailhead describing the ice industry that began here in 1930. Ice was shipped from spring-fed Rockland Lake to the Hudson River via a long conveyor belt and onto barges at Slaughter's Landing, a settlement that dates from 1711. It was then shipped to New York City. The best restaurants and hotels preferred the ice for its purity and clarity.

You will not be walking as far as Rockland Lake, nor will you see much of it except for a brief glimpse looking west from this point or during leaf-out. From the trailhead, the foot trail now avoids a direct and steep ascent up the north side of the Hook and instead swings around into the west, where you'll see a herd trail. Avoid this trail and bear to the right (west), passing a foundation on your right, and climb along a switchback before turning east again to rise steadily to the ridge. Sumac and cherry trees dot the cliff's edge. From various outcroppings along the trail, you can look across the river at the ominous visage of Sing Sing Correctional Facility, the maximum-security state prison, and up to the town of Cortlandt. You can see south as far as the Tappan Zee Bridge and north into the Hudson Highlands. Directly west is Croton Point. Beneath and all along the eastern face of the escarpment, this area of the Palisades was subject to heavy quarrying, which, as you will observe, has claimed a good part of the mountain nearly to ridge elevation.

Long Path continues along near the edge of the cliffs as it enters and exits the hardwoods. You'll see old stone walls made of large talus blocks defining abandoned roads through here. You may see deer foraging in the dense underbrush. The terrain is rolling but never very steep at this point. Marking is sparse but adequate (the low-impact presence was the intention of the Long Path's originators, who didn't want a defined, physical trail, only a system of waypoints between which hikers would navigate using map and compass), but the trail is self-guiding and fairly smooth underfoot.

You will never stray far from the river, and although you will not always see it, you will sense the abyssal cliffs to the east. You will soon drop behind a low ridge and descend for a while before rising again to your original elevation. Soon you will reach a point above the parking area where you will look directly down at the beautiful Marydell Faith and Life Center, run by the Sisters of Our Lady of Christian Doctrine. This is the most spectacular cliff on the hike. Don't try to shortcut this hike by descending the cliffs on any herd trails you might see. The only safe way down the mountain is Long Path.

Continue, avoiding the yellow-blazed trail that leaves to the right. The trail becomes rocky now. A long, viewless ascent up to the summit of Hook Mountain follows, and soon you will hear the traffic on NY 9W. Following an old

High above the Hudson River, Hook Mountain is one of the Palisades' most popular and scenic hikes.

road lined with boulders (an abandoned attempt to create a road to the Hook's summit), look left for the white-blazed Upper Nyack Trail, which winds through a residential area, passing beneath a lovely young stand of vigorous tulip poplars.

Upper Nyack Trail ends on Midland Avenue, 500 feet south of the Marydell Center. Turn left toward the center, passing another residential street on your left, then bear right onto Larchdale Avenue and go down the hill. Up to your left are the high cliffs of Hook Mountain. Bear left onto North Broadway Avenue and join the park access road, descending toward the parking area. Look to the right just before the small stone office building for a stone staircase that shortcuts the road, taking you through a quiet woods with a few picnic tables along the river. In March 1898, more than three tons of dynamite was used to demolish Washington Head and Indian Head in Fort Lee, New Jersey, yielding several million cubic yards of traprock. The following year, work by the New Jersey Federation of Women's Clubs led to the creation of the Palisades Interstate Park Commission, which was authorized to acquire land between Fort Lee and Piermont, New York. Its jurisdiction was extended to Stony Point, New York, in 1906, thus preserving the area around Hook Mountain.

DID YOU KNOW?

Quarrying began as early as 1811 for the highly valued volcanic traprock that surfaces through an upper layer of Triassic sandstone in this location. The rock was used in road building as well as for concrete, most of which went to Manhattan. This industry helped wipe out the bluestone quarrying industry in the Catskills, which ended very suddenly with the invention of Portland cement. In the late 1800s, dynamite and steam-driven equipment were used here. The rapid deterioration of the landscape created public outcry, resulting in the formation of advocacy groups, including the Palisades Interstate Park Commission. By 1915, preservation of lands including the Palisades and the Hook Mountain area was accomplished using public funds and private funds donated by the Perkins family (George Perkins was the head of the Park Commission), the Rockefellers, and the Harrimans.

MORE INFORMATION

Nyack Beach State Park is open year-round for day use. A parking fee is charged on weekends, April through September. A restroom and telephone are located at the park building in the parking area.

Palisades Interstate Park Commission
Bear Mountain, NY 10911
Phone: 845-351-2583
njpalisades.org

10
DIAMOND MOUNTAIN

This hike along a high ridge delivers many scenic views, including the Hudson River, the Hudson Highlands, and the New York City skyline.

DIRECTIONS

From the south, take NJ 17 north to the New York State Thruway, then take Exit 15A into Sloatsburg. Turn left at the bottom of the ramp onto NY 17 north, continuing through the Village of Sloatsburg. At the traffic light intersection of NY 17 and NY 17A, turn right onto CR 106 (Seven Lakes Drive) and set your odometer to zero. Take Seven Lakes Drive 1.5 miles to the Reeves Meadow Visitor Center on the right side of the road. Park here. *GPS coordinates:* 41° 10.440′ N, 74° 10.080′ W.

Public Transportation: Take the NJ Transit/Metro-North Port Jervis Line to the Sloatsburg station. Leave the station, cross the railroad tracks, and turn right (north) onto Ballard Avenue. At the end of Ballard Avenue, go right onto Academy Avenue and continue to Seven Lakes Drive. Turn right (east) onto Seven Lakes Drive, go under the New York State Thruway, and leave Greenway Road and Laurel Road on the right. A short distance beyond, about 1.1 miles from the train station, you arrive at a bridge over Stony Brook, where you will see a triple red-square-on-white blaze and a directional arrow that marks the trailhead of Pine Meadow Trail. Turn right, leaving the road, and follow this trail for another mile to the Reeves Meadow Visitor Center.

TRAIL DESCRIPTION

Begin behind the visitor center and bear left, following the flat, well-used Pine Meadow Trail (red-on-white blazes). The trail travels next to Stony Brook, which appears on the left. You hike very close to the brook for some time.

LOCATION
Baileytown, NY

RATING
Moderate

DISTANCE
4.8 miles

ELEVATION GAIN
1,230 feet

ESTIMATED TIME
4 hours

MAPS
USGS Popolopen Lake; NY-NJTC Trail Map 118 16th Edition (2015) Southern Harriman Bear Mountain Trails; National Geographic Harriman, Bear Mountain, Sterling Forest State Parks

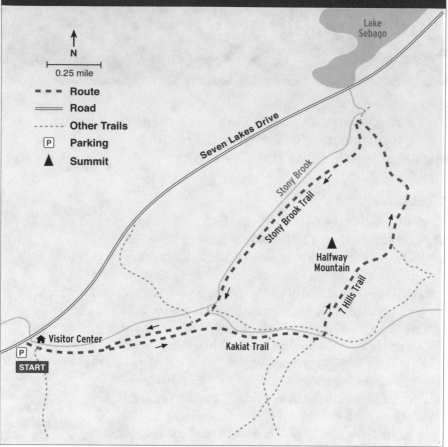

Legend:
- N — 0.25 mile
- – – – Route
- ——— Road
- - - - Other Trails
- P Parking
- ▲ Summit

Lake Sebago

Seven Lakes Drive

Stony Brook

Stony Brook Trail

▲ Halfway Mountain

7 Hills Trail

🚩 Visitor Center

P

START

Kakiat Trail

During winter, the trail is tamped down by heavy use and the compressed snow turns to ice, so it is a good idea to bring your microspikes. The brook can be boisterous at times, and sections of the trail have been inundated here and there, in which case the trail detours alongside a bit.

After ten minutes or so afoot, the yellow-blazed Stony Brook Trail comes in from the left (your return route). Pine Meadow Trail bears to the right and rises on an old roadbed, climbing steadily but easily, soon crossing a footbridge over Quartz Brook. Walk across a wide gas-line right of way and continue hiking east.

The trail gets prettier as it levels out and curves through a bowl of hills, maintaining its road-like character. Pass an unmarked spur to the left that drops down a set of stairs to a bench. Remain on Pine Meadow Trail through oak and rhododendron cover.

At 1.1 miles, the orange-blazed Hillburn-Torne-Sebago Trail (HTS) appears from the left, and departs again to the right. Continue on the red-blazed Pine Meadow Trail.

As you begin to rise out of this section, Seven Hills Trail appears. You are still on the red trail, which is now joined by the blue-blazed Seven Hills Trail. Just before the bridge, the white-blazed Kakiat Trail enters from the right. At 1.44 miles, at which point you have climbed 500 feet in elevation, cross Pine Meadow Brook on a pretty footbridge. Bear left, following the blue-blazed Seven Hills Trail to a point where, in a couple of hundred feet, Seven Hills Trail heads sharply to the right and uphill. Shortly, a large stone buttress of the ridge appears, which you climb with no great difficulty if it is not snow- and ice-covered.

On top of the first ledge, pitch pine appears. The spot has a remote feeling. There are some dangerous vertical drops in the vicinity. The ledge faces south, with views over North and South hills. As you climb higher and walk north on Seven Hills Trail, white pine, pitch pine, and hemlock appear. Several lookouts follow, some with herd trails to more remote outcroppings. As you gain westerly views, Halfway Mountain is seen to the west.

As you climb higher over a combination of footway surfaces, from soft dirt to bare rock, the orange-blazed HTS Trail joins in at a trail junction. You are now approaching the highest point of Diamond Mountain. You may see the letters "HTS" pointing to the left. Continue straight ahead on Seven Hills Trail and HTS. From the right (east), the red-blazed Pine Meadow Trail comes in. From the summit balds on a clear day, you can see the Manhattan skyline. You are at elevation here; it's as high as you can get. To the east, you look down at Pine Meadow Lake. You've come 2.1 miles and have climbed 975 feet, to 1,240 feet above sea level. From this ridge, you can see the Catskills far away to the west. As you walk north, you will be looking west over Lake Sebago. *Sebago* is an

Rock gardens, flowing water, and streamside hiking characterize the trek to Diamond Mountain.

Algonquian name, meaning "big water." The impoundment was created in 1925 by the Palisades Interstate Park Commission when a dam was installed across Stony Brook, inundating Emmetfield Swamp.

Wintergreen and blueberry appear all along the ridge top. Search carefully as you walk north on the height-of-land for the point at which the orange-blazed HTS departs to the west and downhill toward Stony Brook, as it is not very obvious. (If you reach the yellow-blazed Diamond Mountain Tower Trail, you have gone too far.)

Follow HTS as it drops down off the ridge into the west. Although its departure point is obscure on the ridge, it is well blazed along its descent. Drop down steeply for a while through attractive mature forest and cross a small brook, continuing until you reach the yellow-blazed Stony Brook Trail at 2.75 miles, and turn left. The trail follows the brook for most of the remaining distance of the hike.

The ridges to the right and left of the brook taper down as the river widens and the land flattens out. Patches of hemlock are frequent. As winter loosens its grasp, the river swells noisily; the trail softens as the ice warms and melts. Stands of young beech with their old copper leaves festoon the spring woodlands. Soon, the white-blazed Kakiat Trail comes in from the left.

At 3.9 miles, cross a footbridge over Pine Meadow Brook. A short distance beyond, Kakiat Trail leaves to the right. Ahead, the yellow-blazed Stony Brook Trail crosses the gas pipeline right of way you hiked earlier, though at a lower elevation now. Stony Brook Trail ends at the junction with the red-on-white-blazed Pine Meadow Trail. This heavily shaded trail has the tendency to remain iced-over and slick, especially toward the end of the day, when temperatures drop. You'll be glad to have worn lug-soled boots and even happier if you've got your microspikes. Also, because this trail tends to be seasonally wet, it pays to have waterproof footwear. From here, you will retrace your earlier footsteps, following Pine Meadow Trail back to the parking area.

DID YOU KNOW?

AMC's recently opened Harriman Outdoor Center is located nearby on the shore of Breakneck Pond, offering a number of hiking, paddling, and camping opportunities. Cabins, shelters, and tentsites are available, as well as meals in its dining hall. Reservations are required; visit outdoors.org/harriman or call 603-466-2727.

MORE INFORMATION

Harriman State Park, Seven Lakes Drive
Bear Mountain Circle, Ramapo, NY
845-947-2444
nysparks.com

11

SILVERMINE LAKE AND BLACK MOUNTAIN

This hike is considered by many to be among the best in Harriman State Park. The trailhead is situated along the beautiful Seven Lakes Drive, one of the prettiest roads in the Hudson Valley.

DIRECTIONS

From the Bear Mountain traffic circle, drive west on US 6/ Palisades Interstate Parkway. Pass Exit 19, which goes to the Perkins Memorial Tower.

Get off the Parkway at Exit 18, continuing on US 6. At 2.8 miles, the Long Mountain traffic circle, take Seven Lakes Drive heading toward Sloatsburg. At 4.4 miles, bear left into the Silvermine picnic and parking area. From the south, take NJ 17 north to the New York State Thruway and take Exit 15A into Sloatsburg. Turn left at the bottom of the ramp onto NY 17 north, continuing through the village of Sloatsburg. At the traffic light intersection of NY 17 and NY 17A, turn right onto CR 106 (Seven Lakes Drive) and set your odometer to zero. Take Seven Lakes Drive 10.2 miles to the Silvermine picnic area on the right. *GPS coordinates:* 41° 17.700′ N, 74° 3.600′ W.

TRAIL DESCRIPTION

From the Silvermine parking area, proceed directly onto the run-out area of the ski slope and take the yellow-blazed Menomine Trail, markers for which may be seen on the side of the service building. Don't go directly upslope, where you may see some folks climbing the hill for exercise. Walk across the bottom of the slope, bearing left past two maintenance buildings and toward Silvermine Lake, then bearing right along its shores. The rocky trail follows the scenic western shore of the lake for 0.65 mile then climbs next to Bockey Swamp Brook for 0.4

LOCATION
Harriman State Park, Baileytown, NY

RATING
Moderate

DISTANCE
4.5 miles

ELEVATION GAIN
1,200 feet

ESTIMATED TIME
3 hours

MAPS
USGS Popolopen Lake; NY-NJTC Trail Map 119 16th Edition (2015) Northern Harriman Bear Mountain Trails; National Geographic Harriman, Bear Mountain, Sterling Forest State Parks

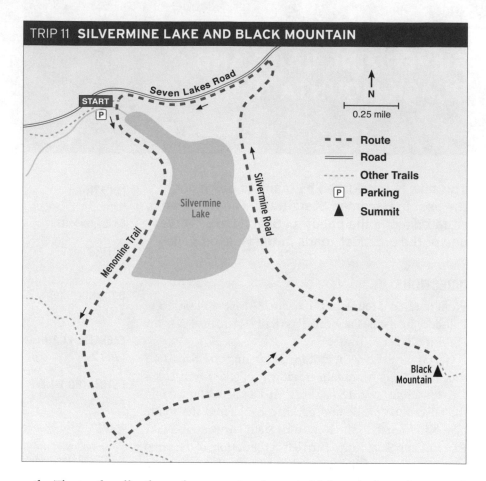

Seven Lakes Road

START

N

0.25 mile

- - - Route
=== Road
······ Other Trails
P Parking
▲ Summit

Silvermine
Lake

Silvermine Road

Menomine Trail

Black ▲
Mountain

mile. The trail walks through a maturing forest, with large oaks and scattered stands of tall tulip trees.

Rocks diminish and the trail becomes more road-like, heavily used and worn down to mineral soil amid boulder-strewn woods. Climb to a junction where the trail levels out and bear left onto a woods road. The trail crosses a small creek and climbs steadily through thick woods where oak mountain laurel is plentiful.

In the next 0.35 mile, you will climb another 246 feet and will come to the stone William Brien Memorial Shelter (elevation 1,077 ft., constructed 1933), previously named Letterrock Shelter. Overnight camping is permitted here. Typically used by AT thru-hikers, this beautifully built fieldstone, lean-to-style shelter has bunks on each side. Its construction was financed by a bequeathal from the naturalist William Brien, the first president of the New York Ramblers hiking club, which was founded in 1923 at the summit of High Mountain in Haledon, New Jersey.

Although the relatively protected area around the shelter lies at a modest elevation with higher ridges nearby, there is evidence of a lightning strike on a middle-aged, slender oak tree out in front of the shelter. Immediately beyond the shelter,

Forests of giant tulip poplars greet hikers on the popular trails around Silvermine Lake.

you will come to the trail junction with the AT and Ramapo-Dunderberg Trail (R-D, white background, red dot in the center). You will leave the yellow-blazed Menomine Trail at this point, bearing left and sharply uphill on the AT/R-D. The trail climbs steeply for only a short distance, leveling out on a ridge of oak-blueberry heath cover at 1,160 feet in elevation and treading northeast easily along a rolling ridge. The trail continues downhill. Avoid a dead-end trail to the left, still following the AT/R-D. At this point, there appears a thick understory of young, thin sweet birch, also called cherry or black birch. These pioneer species usually indicate a past forest fire because they can establish themselves on damaged ecosystems with correspondingly poor soil. Their live twigs have the pleasant taste of wintergreen when chewed. Oil of wintergreen has medicinal properties and was used by American Indians to relieve headaches and fever. The oil contains methyl salicylate, a synthetic version of which is the main ingredient in modern aspirin.

At 2.25 miles from your starting point, you arrive at the unmarked Silvermine Ski Road, a nicely preserved and maintained woods road built in 1934 by the New York State Temporary Emergency Relief Administration, one of Governor Franklin Roosevelt's highly successful, Depression-era unemployment relief programs. Do not be tempted to end the hike here by bearing left back to the lake or you will miss the best part of this outing! The ascent to Black Mountain may look like a big climb from the junction, but the short ascent passes quickly. Cross a tiny seasonal stream and follow the AT/R-D uphill. The trail switches back behind the peak over sections of hand-laid stairs.

You'll soon reach a viewpoint, where you are treated to views over Silvermine Lake and the country you have just traveled. There are some dangerous drops here, so use caution. Pitch pines appear, recognizable by the needles in fascicles of three. These trees typically grow in poor soil at higher-elevation outcroppings and tablelands, and were once widely used for their high quantity of resins. They sometimes hybridize with other pines, such as loblolly, shortleaf, and pond pine.

As you're curving around to the east, you can look far downriver at the mine-ravaged hills of the Palisades. Beginning in the late 1880s, the durable sandstone of the heavily glaciated diabase was mined for various construction uses, including the streets of New York and the buildings known as brownstones. Quarrying became so aggressive and ruinous to the landscape that the Palisades Interstate Park Commission was ultimately formed for their protection.

Continue along the summit ridge, with expanding views to the south and east. At the summit of Black Mountain, which is more like a grassy plateau, you're at 2.5 miles and 1,200 feet in elevation. You see Jackie Jones Mountain and the AT&T microwave towers. You see Haverstraw Bay and Croton Point, Ossining, and views of the Manhattan skyline to the southeast. You see ridges off to the northeast, including Bear Mountain and the Torne. The wetland to the east-southeast is Owl Swamp, with Big Bog Mountain in the background. Ahead, the trail drops downhill to join 1779 Trail. Turn around here; don't descend off the ridge.

As you are hiking back on Black Mountain, you see Letterrock, Stockbridge, and Fingerboard mountains in the northeast. At the height-of-land on Black Mountain, just north of the trail, you may come across the shallow exploration pit of the Spanish Mine, purported site of a fanciful tale about silver coins being hidden by Spanish seamen.

Retrace your route. Descend and bear right onto the Silvermine Road, which you crossed earlier. The road descends gently, and soon you walk next to Silvermine Lake through beautiful woodlands. At the northeast edge of the lake, near its outlet by the dam, is an idyllic stand of tamarack trees where there are many illegal fire rings and evidence of sustained illegal camping. Continue past this point and, nearing the end of the trail, cross a bridge over Queensboro Brook. Bear left onto the road (Seven Lakes Drive). As you crest the hill, observe the white pines on the left. Stands of maturing trees like this are part of what makes Harriman State Park beautiful.

DID YOU KNOW?

In *Forest and Crag*, Laura and Guy Waterman's history of hiking in the northeastern United States, the Ramblers is described as conducting fast-paced hikes. On its web page, the club promotes hikes of 16 to 18 miles for small groups of experienced hikers. The science fiction author H. P. Lovecraft (1890–1937), an avid hiker, mentioned a Rambler outing in a diary entry from the 1920s.

MORE INFORMATION

Harriman State Park, Seven Lakes Drive
Bear Mountain Circle, Ramapo, NY
845-947-2444
nysparks.com

12

WEST MOUNTAIN AND CAT'S ELBOW

This high-ridge hike's many scenic points include a stone shelter and views of the Hudson River, the Highlands, and the New York City skyline.

DIRECTIONS

Take the Palisades Interstate Parkway to Exit 17 (Anthony Wayne Recreation Area). Park in the first parking area to the right. If the lot is full, continue to the far south parking area.

As you drive into the parking area, you will pass the trailhead 200 feet before the ticket kiosk. Park and walk back to the trailhead. Near two stone pillars and a steel gate, look for a sign indicating the hiking and biking trail. You will see the white blazes of Anthony Wayne Trail. Enter the woods here, following the trail on a cinder path. This was once a tarred road. Follow the white blazes, leaving the maintenance buildings to the left. *GPS coordinates:* 41° 17.940′ N, 74° 1.680′ W.

TRAIL DESCRIPTION

At an intersection 0.25 mile in, you'll cross a woods road beneath a power line. Look to the left for a red "F" on a white background. Take this red-blazed Fawn Trail up a pretty rock staircase into a stand of white pines. The trail switches to the left after the stairs. The trail then climbs diagonally across the hill and up over a little hump. Large tulip trees appear. The ones with the large, straight trunks are called yellow poplar but are really magnolias. The well-marked trail climbs easily again through pretty woods. Now you are walking the spine of West Mountain's northerly ridge. At 0.45 mile you will reach the four-way intersection of Fawn Trail and the blue-blazed Timp–Torne Trail (TT), and you will see Bear Mountain in front of you. Turn right onto TT.

LOCATION
Bear Mountain, NY

RATING
Moderate

DISTANCE
5 miles

ELEVATION GAIN
1,467 feet

ESTIMATED TIME
4 hours

MAPS
USGS Popolopen Lake; NY-NJTC Trail Map 119 16th Edition (2015) Northern Harriman Bear Mountain Trails; National Geographic Harriman, Bear Mountain, Sterling Forest State Parks

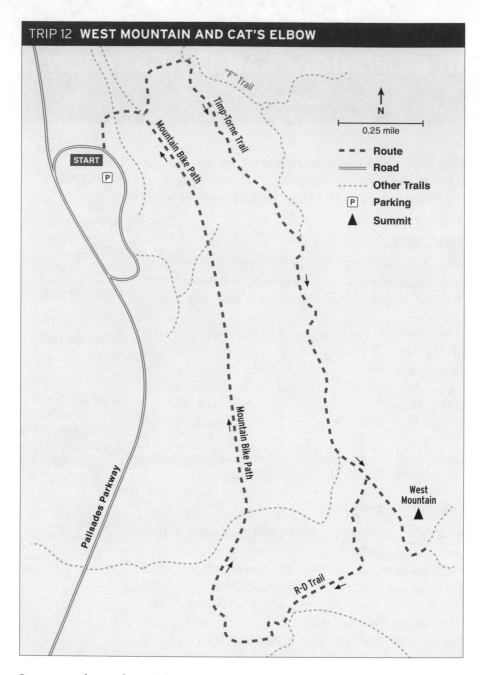

START

N

0.25 mile

- - - Route
═══ Road
······ Other Trails
P Parking
▲ Summit

"F" Trail

Timp-Torne Trail

Mountain Bike Path

Mountain Bike Path

Palisades Parkway

West
Mountain
▲

R-D Trail

Large numbers of small birch trees have established themselves here as the result of recent forest fires.

The trail is very rocky now as it ascends moderately. Pitch pine appears. TT flattens for a while then climbs again, yielding views of Bear Mountain and the Torne. The trail rises through a series of flats with viewpoints here and there. There are some steep sections, with increasingly fine vantage points to the west

West Mountain's ascent offers increasingly fine vantage points for all hikers.

and the east. Perkins Memorial Tower is plainly seen to the northeast.

In a small clearing where there are blue TT blazes and white Appalachian Trail (AT) blazes, you can see the road winding up Bear Mountain. You can also see the Torne with its bright tan summit. Mount Taurus is hidden behind Bear Mountain, but you can see Anthony's Nose to the right of Bear Mountain and a bit of the Hudson River. There's a short spur trail with views to the west, where you look down on the Palisades Parkway and west to Stockbridge Mountain. Continue hiking south, following the blue TT and white AT blazes. The two trails continue together for a while along the ridge top, until the AT leaves West Mountain in a northeasterly direction at 1.1 miles. You are now at 1,100 feet in elevation and have climbed a total of 728 feet. In the forested areas of the ridge, you will see where the bare rock of the ridge has functioned as a firebreak, with thin young birches to the left over damaged soil and mature, unaffected forest growth to the right. A small ground fire beneath an established canopy without significant undergrowth will not necessarily damage mature trees. In some spots where there was no existing natural firebreak, fires have crested the ridge. At a few points facing the southwest, you can see the City of Newark, New Jersey.

At 1.7 miles, you arrive at a west-facing ledge and a signpost stating that the trails here are maintained by the NY–NJTC. At this point, the AT, which you've been following for some time, rejoins TT from the west. From here, you can see Cat's Elbow jutting out in the southwest. (At this trail junction, you can easily shortcut this hike by following the AT down to Beechy Bottom Road and bearing right, back to the Anthony Wayne parking area.) Leaving the AT, you continue south on TT. Continue through beautiful groves of mature red oak with blueberry heath groundcover, a forest type typical of upper elevations in the park. There's evidence of illegal use, with fire rings here and there. Watch carefully ahead for the junction with the yellow-blazed Suffern-Bear Mountain Trail (S-BM), at which point you bear left, following TT and S-BM. In 0.3 mile, you arrive at a junction. Leaving S-BM, bear right onto TT. Within 600 feet or so, you will arrive at West Mountain shelter, built in 1928, where you are treated to views of the southeast-lying Timp and the Hudson River, as well as the New York City skyline. You have now hiked a total of 2.1 hilly miles and gained 1,120 feet in elevation. Retrace your route now, returning to the point where the yellow-blazed S-BM heads downhill to the left (southwest). Follow S-BM as it drops downhill toward Cat's Elbow, descending moderately steeply through ledge-y terrain where you'll see talus that has broken away from the ledges on the uphill side of the trail.

As the trail climbs out of a hollow and flattens on the approach to Cat's Elbow, you discover more fire damage, where many smaller trees have been girdled. S-BM bears right, and at 2.9 miles Ramapo-Dunderberg Trail (R-D; red dot on a white background) comes in. The two trails run jointly for a few hundred feet and arrive at a ledge with views to the south. Many of the birch trees here are infected with chaga, a polypore fungus that is characterized by a black perennial woody growth called a conk. This is a basidiomycete, or a true mushroom that is often harvested in the wild in Europe and Asia for the treatment of cancer, gastritis, and ulcers.

From the ledge, facing south is a magnificent view of New York City. You also see Croton Beach State Park, Haverstraw, Haverstraw Bay, and the Palisades bumping up and curving away into the flatlands. From Cat's Elbow, S-BM departs to the south. Bear right onto R-D and descend to join the blue-on-white-blazed bike trail at Beechy Bottom Road, which was improved in 1934 by the Civilian Conservation Corps. You've come a total of 3.3 miles from the beginning of the hike. Bear right, leaving R-D, and follow this beautiful flat road to the north. At 3.5 miles, you will cross the AT. At a Y, bear right. At 4.7 miles, you'll recognize the point at which you followed Fawn Trail to TT. Bear left here, returning to the parking area.

DID YOU KNOW?

The relationship between the resinous pitch pine (*Pinus rigida*) and the production of iron goes back to pre-Colonial times. Difficult to work, tough and sappy, pitch-pine charcoal proved to be better than coal for the smelting of ore. Iron that was forged in the pine barrens was made into weapons that fed the Revolutionary War. *Wood* magazine calls the pitch pine "The tree that fueled the Army of Independence."

MORE INFORMATION

Harriman State Park, Seven Lakes Drive
Bear Mountain Circle, Ramapo, NY
845-947-2444
nysparks.com

THE SHAWANGUNKS

The enchanting Shawangunk Ridge (a.k.a. Shongums, Gunks, or the Ridge) is the scenic and recreational Mecca of the mid-Hudson Valley. It is among the region's most ecologically important landmasses. An extension of the south-lying Kittatinny Ridge of the Appalachian Mountains, the Gunks stretch from the town of Rosendale in the north to Cragsmoor in the south, rising between the Wallkill and Rondout valleys. Shawangunk Ridge is a place of high, windswept plateaus and cliffs (average elevation 2,000 feet), remarkably clear "sky" lakes, sheer ledges (the highest vertical drops east of the Mississippi), pellucid streams, robust waterfalls, and diverse natural habitats. The Ridge has been identified as one of Earth's "Last Great Places" by The Nature Conservancy, as well as one of the 40 most important natural resources lying within the North American continent and the Pacific Rim Basin.

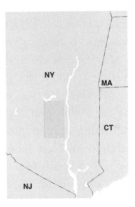

The Shawangunk Mountains look a good deal different from the younger surrounding ranges, such as the Catskills. This is due to the Ridge's prominent, white-quartz conglomerate bedrock and its 450-million-year-old sands and quartz gravels that were deposited at the base of a shallow sea during the Taconic orogeny. Much later, the mountains were eroded, faulted, fractured, and smoothed by a million years of glacial action. The glaciers dragged off the tops of the ridges, breaking them into talus blocks and leaving behind vertical cliffs such as Sky Top, the Trapps, and Millbrook Mountain. The resulting bare rock can be seen from great distances. Folding lifted the sandstone into broad, west-tilting slabs, and retreating ice nearly a mile thick scraped and polished the uplands into bright, open promontories, such as Gertrude's Nose and Castle Point, that are studded with pitch pine and thick with blueberry heaths. This impervious, nutrient-poor rock held water, resulting in the creation of the five sky lakes that are strung across the top of the Ridge. These are among the clearest lakes imaginable (in particular, Lakes Minnewaska and Awosting; see Trips 14 and 16), because aquatic plants cannot grow in their thin, acidic, nutrient-poor soils.

Underlying the conglomerate, the softer, older layer of Martinsburg shale is a few thousand feet thick. Hikers will see the shale layer spilling out here and there around the Ridge, where it was mined for building material, as well as crushed and sprinkled on the extensive carriage roads of the Mohonk and Minnewaska preserves.

As the glaciers retreated, plants took hold in protected crevices and on the bare rocks, beginning a succession that would lead to today's varied vegetation profile. Hikers will often see oak woods with the mountain laurel understory that is so common in the higher woodlands, along with pockets of hemlock and, less frequently, white pine and red spruce. The northern hardwood group (beech, birch, maple, and associated species) appeared about 8,000 years ago, followed by southern trees of the Carolinian forest types, including oak, chestnut, and hickory. Composing a good deal of the often dense understory are flowering dogwood, shadbush, striped maple, viburnum, witch hazel, lowbush blueberry, huckleberry, and raspberry.

The southern area of the ridge (the Badlands, or Pine Plains) is dominated by the widely distributed pitch pine, for which the Shawangunks are famous. Although extensive pitch-pine barrens can be found in places such as Long Island and New Jersey, those forests grow on sand, not rock. The naturalist Erik Kiviat points out that the Shawangunks contain "the only extensive high-altitude pitch-pine barrens, and the only bedrock dwarf-pine plains in the world." Hikers will see these forests in patches all around the Gunks, but they are most profuse in the otherworldly Badlands.

In addition to its alteration by physical forces and soil type, the distribution of the Gunks' vegetation groups was altered significantly by human intervention. Although the ridge area was not fertile enough to attract anything more than seasonal use by indigenous, valley-dwelling peoples, it is possible that they manipulated the land with fire, opening it up for deer browse and nut trees or berry growth. Resource-extractive industries followed when, by the early 1700s, settlers were using the forests for lumber, charcoal production, tanbarking, barrel hoop and furniture making, and for the production of the very desirable Shawangunk millstones. Particularly in the southern Shawangunks, the ridge was perennially burned to enhance growth (by removing competing vegetation) when the commercial berry-picking industry thrived here until the 1930s. Pickers' shacks can still be seen along the trails of the southern ridge. Ongoing efforts to protect the ridge from commercial and residential development have been difficult, but several potentially ruinous projects have been defeated, sustaining a broadening acquisition of buffer lands to protect this precious resource. At this time, four independent, cooperating management partnerships are stewarding the ridge.

THE MOHONK PRESERVE

The largest member-and-visitor-supported nature preserve in New York State, the Mohonk Preserve protects 6,400 acres of the northern Shawangunk Ridge. Established in 1963, its mission to protect and preserve the ridge includes fostering an "understanding of the relationship between people and nature." The preserve is committed to providing open space for "contemplation and recreation in keeping with the peace and natural beauty of the land." The Smiley family (who, in 1869, began building what would become today's Mohonk Mountain House resort hotel) initiated the tradition of land stewardship in the Shawangunks. Their holdings grew to 7,500 acres over the next century. The Smileys created the Mohonk Preserve (previously called the Mohonk Trust) to provide a management presence for the public use of preserve lands lying beyond the Mountain House boundaries.

The preserve's recreational resources include 100 miles of multiuse carriage roads and trails for hiking, jogging, mountain biking, cross-country skiing, snowshoeing, and horseback riding. There are an estimated 1,000 rock-climbing routes on the preserve's lands. All of these resources are heavily used; the greatest challenge the preserve faces, next to the preservation of the ridge itself, is the management of human impact. Those with annual memberships constitute most of the user group.

Take the time to stop at the Mohonk Preserve Visitor Center on your trip to the Gunks; you'll go past it on your way to the Trapps trailheads. Here you will find interpretive displays, a gift shop with books and maps of local interest, a kids corner and butterfly garden, and a self-guiding nature trail. You can purchase day passes and memberships.

Access Fees. The visitor center and its immediate grounds are free to the public, but to access the land, you need to have a current membership or pay a day-use fee (basic membership is $55, $45 for seniors; day use is $12 per person for hikers). Children 12 and under are free and must be accompanied by an adult. Fees may vary annually. The relatively high day-use fees can be substantially reduced through the purchase of a membership. As a member, you enjoy additional privileges and access to the preserve lands from sunrise to sunset, 365 days a year.

Parking. On peak weekends, the preserve parking areas fill up extremely fast—and early. Try to arrive before 10 A.M. to be assured a spot. Parking is limited to 30 minutes at the scenic overlook and hairpin turn above the visitor center on US 44/NY 55, and tickets are issued for violations. Although the preserve's Wawarsing and West Trapps parking lots fill quickly on weekends, weekdays are seldom a problem.

Camping and Pets. You must leash and clean up after your pets. Camping and fires are not permitted. Drive-in and walk-in camping is available at the Samuel F. Pryor III Shawangunk Gateway Campground, located on Route 299 in Gardiner, near the visitor center and within walking distance of the Trapps trailheads. For information call 845-255-0032.

Directions and Information. Mohonk Preserve Visitor Center is on US 44/NY 55, 0.5 mile west of its intersection with NY 299 in Gardiner, New York, 6 miles west of New Paltz. Contact the Mohonk Preserve at P.O. Box 715, New Paltz, NY, 12561; 845-255-0919; mohonkpreserve.org.

MOHONK MOUNTAIN HOUSE

Named a National Historic Landmark in 1986, this private, nineteenth-century, Victorian-style castle and the beautiful lands, trails, and carriageways surrounding Lake Mohonk are a separate entity from the Mohonk Preserve. The resort began in 1869 with the Smiley brothers' purchase of 280 acres of the ridge, on which they built a ten-room boarding house. Subsequent purchases and improvements resulted in today's hotel of 250 rooms, 138 with working fireplaces, and 238 balconies providing world-class lake and mountain views.

Day access is pricey. Although a membership with the Mohonk Preserve will allow you access to the Mountain House property and trails, additional fees and restrictions apply. Parking at the gatehouse is included. Hikers are asked not to enter the hotel, and hotel facilities are reserved for guests only. Hikers purchasing day-use passes at the hotel gatehouse rather than at the Preserve Visitor Center will be charged $26 per person on weekends, $21 on weekdays. A shuttle-bus ride from the gatehouse to the hotel trailheads is included. No pets are allowed on the property, even if left in a vehicle.

Directions and Information. From Exit 18 of the NYS Thruway (I-87), drive west through the village of New Paltz on NY 299. As you cross the bridge over the Wallkill River, take the first right onto Springtown Road and set your trip odometer to zero. At 0.5 mile, turn left onto Mountain Rest Road (CR 6), where you'll see signs for Mohonk. At 1.7 miles, go through the intersection of Butterville-Canaan Road. Continue up Mountain Rest Road, and at 4.0 miles, you'll pass the Mohonk Mountain House main gate on the left. Contact the Mohonk Mountain House at Mountain Rest Road, New Paltz, NY, 12561; 845-255-1000; mohonk.com.

MINNEWASKA STATE PARK PRESERVE

Encompassing nearly 12,000 acres of forested land on the Shawangunk Ridge, Minnewaska is just as beautiful as Mohonk but more remote. Originally owned and developed as a rustic resort area by the Smiley brothers, this day-use park is connected to the Mohonk Preserve by the same extensive trails and carriage roads that were built more than a century ago. It contains three lakes—Minnewaska, Awosting, and the remote Mud Pond—as well as the high ledges, cliff-top promontories, and dwarf pitch-pine barrens that have made the ridge one of the world's most distinctive natural resources.

Recreational use in the park includes cycling, hiking, biking, snowshoeing, cross-country skiing, horseback riding and horse carriages, swimming (ADA accessible), and scuba diving under permit in Lake Minnewaska. Cartop boats are allowed in Lake Minnewaska by permit. Rock climbing is permitted at the Peter's Kill area, 1 mile east of the park's main gate on US 44/NY 55. Leashed pets are allowed. The lands of Minnewaska State Park are every bit as beautiful as those of the Mohonk Preserve and can be enjoyed at a fraction of the preserve and Mountain House trail-use fees.

Note: The terms *carriageway, carriage road,* and *road* are used interchangeably on maps, in publications, and in speech, in both the Mohonk Preserve and Minnewaska State Park.

Directions. From Exit 18 of the NYS Thruway (I-87), head west through the village of New Paltz on NY 299 for 7.5 miles. Turn right onto US 44/NY 55 and drive past the Mohonk Preserve Visitor Center. Continue up the hill and under Trapps Bridge, and go another 3 miles to the Minnewaska State Park entrance on your left (a total of 11.4 miles from I-87).

13

BONTICOU CRAG

A walk along a carriage road precedes a short introduction to rock scrambling on the Shawangunks' white-quartz conglomerate talus fields, followed by a bare summit with vertical cliffs and excellent views.

DIRECTIONS

The most convenient access to Crag Trail is from Upper 27 Knolls Road, just west of the Mohonk Mountain House main entrance on Mountain Rest Road in New Paltz. From Exit 18 of the NYS Thruway (I-87), drive west through the village of New Paltz on NY 299. As you cross the bridge over the Wallkill River, take the first right onto Springtown Road and set your trip odometer to zero. At 0.5 mile, turn left onto Mountain Rest Road (CR 6), where you'll see signs for Mohonk. At 1.7 miles, go through the intersection of Butterville-Canaan Road. Continue up Mountain Rest Road, and at 4 miles, you'll pass the Mohonk Mountain House main gate on the left. (Ask for a map here.) At 5 miles, turn right onto Upper 27 Knolls Road, and in another 0.3 mile, park in the Spring Farm trailhead parking area. *GPS coordinates: 41° 47.729′ N, 74° 7.658′ W.*

TRAIL DESCRIPTION

This short but rigorous hike includes a stretch of the northernmost Shawangunk forests, a stroll on the foot trails and carriage paths of the Virginia Smiley Preserve, and an invigoratingly quick rock scramble through the savage, broken talus of the Gunks' conglomerate cliffs. What you get in exchange for a relatively short half-day hike are sweeping views of the Catskills and the southeastern Hudson Valley lowlands, as well as a hands-on feel for a remarkable cliff-and-talus environment of dark green

LOCATION
New Paltz, NY

RATING
Moderate

DISTANCE
3 miles

ELEVATION GAIN
500 feet

ESTIMATED TIME
2.5 hours

MAPS
USGS Mohonk Lake; Mohonk Preserve Trail Map, Northern Section; NY-NJTC Shawangunk Trails

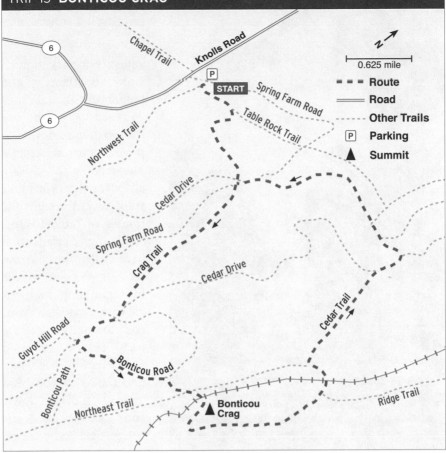

pitch pine and white, tilted slabs. This hike is not recommended for very small children, or dogs.

Locate the red-blazed Crag Trail across the road from the parking lot kiosk and follow it through open fields past cedar hedgerows. You will be treated to immediate views of the Catskills over the Esopus and Rondout valleys, and these views improve dramatically as you ascend the Crag. Cross Cedar Drive and Spring Farm Road, climbing through open hardwoods as you bear east. At the four-way intersection of Cedar Drive and Bonticou Road, go straight ahead on Cedar Drive. This will bring you to circuitous Bonticou Road again, where you will turn nearly 180 degrees to the northeast. Stay alert here so that you leave the red-blazed Bonticou Path to your right (it descends to Northeast Trail, out of your way), remaining on Bonticou Road. This level carriageway soon treats you to open views of Bonticou Crag, looming from the north. Within a few minutes, follow the yellow-blazed Bonticou Ascent Path, which leaves to the right. There's a flat rock to the right of the ascent where you can

The challenging scramble up to Bonticou Crag brings hikers to a long, tilted slab, or "table rock."

adjust your pack, tighten your bootlaces, and prepare for the climb. If you wear a watch, you may wish to remove it to protect it from scrapes. You're going to be using all fours now as you make your way through the tumult of broken, radically angled slabs that have fallen away from the cliff. As a general rule in scrambling high-angle rock faces, keep your body low and close to the rock. Search for good foot-, hand-, fist-, and fingerholds as you head upward, moving slowly and deliberately. The going is generally easy if you're reasonably agile and fit. Follow the yellow blazes. There's one challenging point at the upper end of the climb where you'll ascend through a narrow crack. Some members of your party may need assistance. Be careful and stick together.

Feel that cold air coming from the deep crevices of the talus? These moist fissures, some of them seemingly endless, may well be one of the last known habitats of the endangered eastern woodrat, which, although once common here, has not been on the Mohonk Preserve since 1967. Erik Kiviat, author of *The Northern Shawangunks* and a founding ecologist of the nonprofit environmental research group Hudsonia Limited, observes that the woodrat, which resembles an "oversized Norway rat (house rat) . . . with larger ears and longer whiskers," has been found in the Ice Caves Mountain area of the southern Shawangunks, a locale that may be the most northeastern station in the animal's range. In the fortunate event you see a woodrat, do not be alarmed: They are not aggressive. One thing you will notice is how little soil there is in these crevices and how little vegetation is able to grow among the blocks of talus, which shift over time.

Here and there are trees that are perhaps twenty years old. As you ascend, more appear, along with mountain laurel and, at last, pitch pine, the most dominant and obvious member of this cliff-and-talus plant community.

Very soon after cresting this narrow ridge, bear right (south) following the yellow blazes. The escarpment opens up, and you'll walk across the tilted summit rocks. These open slabs provide you with several choices for relaxing and observing the magnificent views to the west and southeast. You'll also be treated to the antics of curious turkey vultures. Note the two-toned wings, with the flight feathers lighter in color. This scavenger, nearly the size of an eagle and with up to a 6-foot wingspan, gets its name from the bare red heads of the mature birds. They are gregarious, commonly soaring in groups of a dozen or more, in search of carrion. As you watch, beware of the extremely high vertical drops of the cliffs.

Follow the spine of the Crag north and find the yellow blazes again; go past your ascent point and continue north and downhill. Join the obscure blue-blazed Northeast Trail, where the yellow blazes of Ascent Path end. After fifteen minutes, you're down to forest level again. Pass beneath one last ledge and bear right onto Cedar Trail (red blazes), following through reclaimed fields—now ash groves—and join Cedar Drive in a mature oak forest. Follow the carriageway along an even, northerly contour, passing Spring Farm Road, and you're back at a point where you'll recognize Crag Trail. Go right to the Spring Farm parking area and your point of origin.

DID YOU KNOW?

The Mohonk Preserve is New York State's largest member- and visitor-supported nature preserve. It features more than 70 miles of carriageways for hikers, cyclists, and cross-country skiers, with 40 miles of foot trails. On its cliffs are more than 1,000 established rock-climbing routes.

MORE INFORMATION

A self-pay fee collector (a.k.a. iron ranger) is located in the parking lot for winter, spring and fall weekdays, when the booth is not staffed. There's a kiosk with map and trail information adjacent to the attendant booth; mohonk.com; 845-255-1000.

EASTERN WOODRAT

The friendly, curious, and bushy-tailed eastern woodrat was last seen on Storm King Mountain in 1980. Because woodrats proliferate in the kind of rocky slopes found in the Shawangunks, an attempt was made to reintroduce them into the ideal cliff talus habitat of Bonticou Crag in 1991. Introduced from Virginia and equipped with radio transmitters, the rats all perished due to the raccoon nematode, an insidious roundworm parasite that can survive for more than ten years in dens and remain virulent. Biologists were puzzled by this outcome because raccoons and woodrats have been sharing the same habitat for thousands of years.

At this time, the only active population of the eastern woodrat in New York State is in the Palisades, although it has been extirpated from the northern part of this range. Four principal causes for population declines have been suggested: increased predation by great horned owls (*Bubo virginianus*); changes in the landscape, such as forest fragmentation and changing forest composition; reduced availability of acorns and American chestnuts (*Castanea dentata*); and infection and mortality from the nematode parasite, *Baylisascaris procyonis*, carried by raccoons (*Procyon lotor*).

The disappearance of the woodrat here is an indicator more of unknown negative changes in the local environment than of the potential endangerment of the species. Healthy, reproducing populations of the woodrat survive throughout the South.

14

CASTLE POINT, LAKE AWOSTING, AND MARGARET CLIFF

An easy if long hike passes two sky lakes along the old Shawangunk carriage roads, with swimming in Lake Awosting and far-reaching valley views from Castle Point.

DIRECTIONS

From Exit 18 of the NYS Thruway (I-87), head west through the village of New Paltz on NY 299 for 7.5 miles. Turn right onto US 44/NY 55 and drive past the Mohonk Preserve Visitor Center. Continue up the hill and under Trapps Bridge, and go another 3 miles to the Minnewaska State Park entrance on your left (a total of 11.4 miles from I-87). From the gatehouse, drive 0.7 mile to the upper lots. *GPS coordinates:* 41° 43.723′ N, 74° 14.223′ W.

TRAIL DESCRIPTION

Many hikers walk the easy, scenic carriage roads of Minnewaska to Castle and Hamilton points, taking a brief side trip to swim in Lake Awosting's sapphire waters. But few venture beyond Awosting, where this hike turns north to approach Castle Point across the lonely rim rocks of Murray Hill, Spruce Glen, and Margaret Cliff.

Plan for a long outing and bring your bathing suit. Try to reach Minnewaska State Park before 9:30 A.M. on nice weekends or you may have to park in the Lower Awosting lot, adding 1.5 more miles of hiking and 400 feet of elevation gain to this already long hike.

There are two levels to the upper (Wildmere) parking area. The trail begins at the southwest corner of the higher lot, at the north end of Lake Minnewaska. A map and an interpretive kiosk are posted on the picnic-area lawn nearby. Walk toward the lake—the view is terrific—and bear right (south) to find the trailhead. With Lake Minnewaska to

LOCATION
New Paltz, NY

RATING
Moderate

DISTANCE
10 miles

ELEVATION GAIN
500 feet

ESTIMATED TIME
6.5 hours

MAPS
USGS Gardiner, USGS Napanoch; Minnewaska State Park Preserve Hiking Map; NY-NJTC Shawangunk Trails

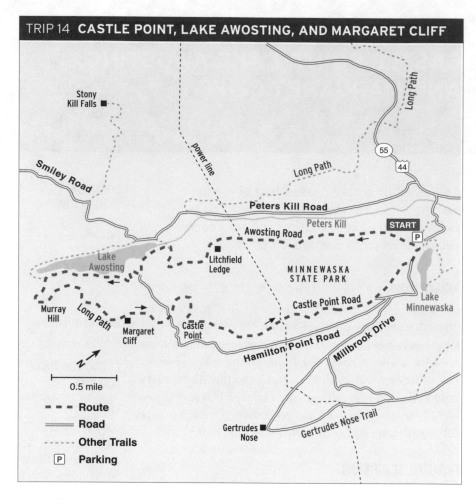

Stony Kill Falls ■

Long Path

power line

Smiley Road

Long Path

55

44

Peters Kill Road

Peters Kill

Awosting Road

START

P

Lake Awosting

■ **Litchfield Ledge**

M I N N E W A S K A
STATE PARK

Lake Minnewaska

Castle Point Road

Murray Hill ■

Long Path

■ **Margaret Cliff**

■ **Castle Point**

Hamilton Point Road

Millbrook Drive

N

0.5 mile

- - - **Route**
——— **Road**
······· **Other Trails**
P **Parking**

Gertrudes Nose ■
Gertrudes Nose Trail

your left, bear left at the first fork (don't take Sunset Trail), and walk down to the Lake Minnewaska swimming area, where you'll find a map and a battalion of chemical toilets. Bear right onto the green-blazed Upper Awosting Road (a.k.a. carriage road). You will be sharing the path with bikers and equestrians. The surface is hard-packed shale with no rocks. Those will come later.

Views of the Catskills appear intermittently to the right (west) as you travel south on the carriage road. Within a half hour, you'll pass a stone streambed to the left. Pass under the power line, where you'll get a look at some white conglomerate bedrock. A few ledges offer views of Peter's Kill Valley to the right as Litchfield Ledge begins to build on your left. Leaving the long ledge behind, climb easily to the intersection where Lake Awosting Road goes right; you'll bear left here, staying on the green-blazed Upper Awosting Road.

Soon the seemingly long walk (more than 3 miles) will begin to pay off as you climb the ramparts of Lake Awosting's north shore. These provide long views of the Catskills to the northwest and south, over the lake. Short spur trails lead to expansive panoramas and vertical pitch-pine ledges as you level out on the carriage road. At the intersection of Hamilton Point Road and Upper Awosting Road, turn right onto the black-blazed Lake Awosting Road. You'll pass through a thick hemlock glen before arriving at Awosting's stone beach, where swimming is allowed only when lifeguards are on duty. There's a restroom here. Continue along the lake's edge, passing two small peninsulas where people frequently sunbathe.

As you approach the south end of the lake, ledges appear across it to your right. Be alert for an unmarked left turn here. As the trail departs to the south, two rocks lie across the trail next to a "No Bikes" sign. Very old blazes are detectable on the trees. Follow this trail and bear left as the aqua-blazed Long Path enters from the right. This will bring you uphill easily to the deeply fractured, southerly summit of Murray Hill, a ledge outcropping facing southwest with sprawling views of the Badlands that take in High Point and Sam's Point Preserve, with the Kittatinnys lying beyond to the south. Peekamoose Mountain, in the Catskills, lies due north. As you cross Murray Hill, stay on Long Path; some spurs lead to dangerous drops that are concealed by low vegetation.

As you work your way north toward Margaret Cliff, views to the northwest and southeast are dramatic, with the Catskills rising beyond the glacially ravaged, pitch-pine tablelands. Battlement Terrace, Castle Point, and Lake Awosting appear ahead. The landscape looks raw and weather-beaten; cairns appear to help you stay on course, and blazes show up more frequently on rocks. Margaret Cliff lies ahead, identifiable by its two deep cracks. Stay with the blue-blazed trail as you pass a few established-looking spurs that head east to create a herd connector along the extensive Margaret Cliff. At a third T, bear right. Blue blazes are not obvious at this junction until you follow the trail for a moment. This is one of the few areas in the park where red spruce occurs in numbers. You can distinguish it from surrounding hemlock and white pine by its pointed, spear-like spires.

Nearly three hours into the hike, the trail joins an old carriage road. The change in tree type to hemlock is dramatic; at this point, watch very carefully for Long Path as it climbs left onto a narrow, slightly eroded laurel path.

As the trail levels, you will pass a small rock balanced on a cannonball-sized stone adjacent to a high and dangerous fissure. Shortly after, the trail heads downhill steeply but then soon levels, crossing a talus field among oaks and a dewy glen with a few very large hemlocks at the site of a grassy, dead-end carriage road. Climb now, tunneling through the rocks before ascending to meet the intersection of Hamilton Point Road and Castle Point Road. Follow the blue-blazed Castle Point Road uphill. Walk under the large, overhanging ledges of Battlement Terrace, then wind around to cross the top of it, climbing into the east and enjoying far-flung views from east to west across the Badlands. Soon you will reach Castle Point, a high, white conglomerate ledge forming the eastern-most cliff of the Terrace. The views are the culmination of most everything

you've seen so far, only better; to the southeast, you'll see the fertile, agricultural lands of the Wallkill River floodplain with the Hudson Highlands beyond.

Castle Point Road treats you to fine views to the north and east as you continue descending north along the ledges. Perhaps nowhere else is the view of Gertrude's Nose so complete and vivid. The little dimples to the north of it is the backside of the otherwise dramatic Millbrook Mountain. You can see the white, obelisk-like Patterson's Pellet balanced on the ledge next to Millbrook Drive, across the Palmaghatt Ravine. In another 45 minutes or so, you will arrive at a T, where Hamilton Point Road goes right. Go left, staying with Castle Point Road. Lake Minnewaska's high northern ledges appear to the right as you descend, and soon you'll arrive back at the swimming area for the short climb back to the parking lot.

DID YOU KNOW?

The Badlands, or Pine Plains, in the area west of Castle Point, are among the largest dwarf pitch-pine barrens on Earth. The nearest large barrens are in the Hamptons area of Long Island.

MORE INFORMATION

Parking requires a per-car entry fee of $10. For more information, visit lakeminnewaska.org.

Facing page: The dazzlingly bright conglomerate sandstone of the Shawangunks rises in the foreground, with the hazy Catskills beyond.

15

MILLBROOK MOUNTAIN AND GERTRUDE'S NOSE

A long and fascinating hike passes through glacial cobble fields and pitch-pine balds next to the sheer cliffs of Millbrook Mountain.

DIRECTIONS

From Exit 18 off the NYS Thruway (I-87), head west through the village of New Paltz on NY 299 for 7.5 miles. Turn right onto US 44/NY 55 and drive 0.8 mile up the hill to the Mohonk Preserve Visitor Center. Just beyond the entrance, turn right into the Wawarsing parking area. *GPS coordinates:* 41° 44.224′ N, 74° 11.074′ W.

TRAIL DESCRIPTION

The hike across Millbrook Mountain to the white conglomerate cliffs of Gertrude's Nose is among the longest outings in the Gunks—and easily the most memorable. These landmarks are frequented less than the popular destinations nearer to the Trapps or Lake Minnewaska. Bring plenty of food and water, a good map, and boots with enough support to protect your feet from the rocky trails.

Park at either the Mohonk Preserve Visitor Center Wawarsing area or the West Trapps parking area and make your way up to Trapps Bridge. (See Trip 17 for details.) Turn west, crossing the bridge onto Trapps Road (carriage road). Watch carefully to the left while still in sight of the bridge and bear left (southwest) onto the blue-blazed Millbrook Ridge Trail. As you climb, you'll see views to the west across Coxing Kill valley, including the ledges of High Peter's Kill, as well as Dickie Barre and Ronde Barre in Minnewaska State Park. Signage and blazes are faint at the trailhead. The trail begins by climbing the low-angle, pitch-pine slabs of the Near Trapps and continues southwest along the cliffs. Interesting views develop back across the Trapps as the

LOCATION
New Paltz, NY

RATING
Strenuous

DISTANCE
9.5 miles

ELEVATION GAIN
850 feet

ESTIMATED TIME
5.5 hours

MAPS
USGS Gardiner, USGS Napanoch; Minnewaska State Park Preserve Map; NY-NJTC Shawangunk Trails

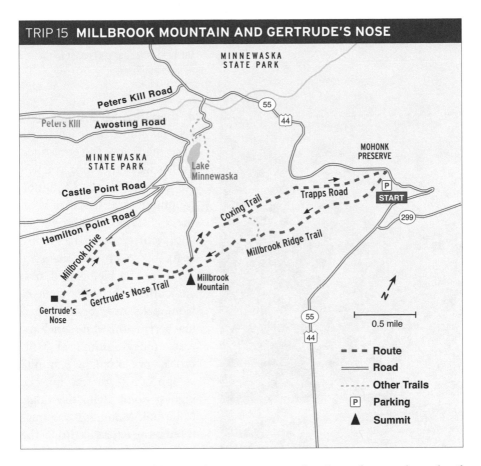

trail winds in and out of the woods over a variety of surfaces, from rocks and soil to pine needles, sometimes coming close to high vertical ledges.

This area of the Shawangunk Ridge is part of the Appalachian hawk migration route. In certain conditions, updrafts and tailwinds allow hawks to soar long distances with little energy expenditure. During fall, the preserve conducts its annual hawk watch along these slabs and cliffs, where you can see hawks, harriers, and vultures moving through the flyway. You will almost always see vultures and hawks here, and sometimes a bald or golden eagle.

You will pass Bayard's Path (red blazes) when you are 25 minutes into the hike. Continue through rolling oak and laurel woods into the southwest. Here and there you'll have a glimpse of Millbrook Mountain ahead of you.

An hour or less into the hike, turn left at the blue blazes as the red-blazed Millbrook Cross Path departs to the right. (It's easy to absentmindedly bear right here.) Continue left on Millbrook Ridge Trail, rising into an open area before descending to a little hemlock glen, where the trail crosses an unnamed, mossy creek that dries in the summer months. From this point, you will ascend consistently along the northern spine of Millbrook's steep ridge. Dramatic views of the Trapps and Sky Top appear as you progress, and the trail walks the lip of

Day-hikers take in the easterly view from Millbrook, which has some of the highest sheer cliffs east of the Mississippi River.

a spine-tingling, 350-foot-high vertical cliff to your left (east). Walking below the west-tilted knife edge of the ridge, you will see the red-blazed Millbrook Mountain Trail appearing on the right (west). This will be your return route to the Trapps, so fix this spot in your memory.

Where the blue-blazed trail ends, the vegetation changes from oaks over bedrock and blueberry to the white conglomerate, piney summit of Millbrook—not exactly a "summit" in appearance or feel, but the highest point along the ridge. Millbrook Mountain was fractured more or less in two by the Wisconsin ice sheet, so what you're standing on is roughly half of its preglacial shape. (The other half of the mountain can be seen lying in chunks below the cliffs.) Here are extensive views of the ridges to the west, the flatlands to the south and east, the Hudson Highlands and Fishkill Ridge beyond them, and the Catskills to the northwest. You can see both Hamilton and Castle points to the west and the lands of the Mohonk Preserve to the north.

Millbrook Mountain marks the boundary between the Mohonk Preserve and Minnewaska State Park. Adjacent and downhill from the summit of Millbrook Mountain, Millbrook Drive (carriage road) ends in a hairpin turn. Here the red-blazed Gertrude's Nose Trail begins, and Millbrook Ridge Trail ends. Follow the red blazes, continuing along the ridge to the southwest. For a while, Gertrude's Nose Trail parallels Millbrook Drive. You will have glimpses of Gertrude's Nose ahead, a diminished version of Millbrook without the rocks. The trail traverses variable terrain, crossing a beautiful, flat-rock, pitch-pine barren before descending steeply past a deep hole near a hemlock ledge to the left; then you'll walk beneath a power line at 1,500 feet. Now you ascend again, following a level contour along the cliffs. The forest type will change several times, from hardwood to hemlock to pitch pine over blueberry heaths. Then, with little warning, you're on Gertrude's Nose, about 3 hours into the hike. The trail curves to the northeast to cross the wind-punished conglomerate flats.

The southwest-facing promontory of the Nose, though lower in elevation, is similar in many respects to Hamilton and Castle points. Each is a high, level plateau of faulted and fractured conglomerate cap rock, the white stone that is the signature geology of the Shawangunks. Long fractures reach from the cliffs' edges back to the woods; some are dangerously deep and can be obscured by a significant snowfall. Signs are posted on the cliffs reminding hikers to move cautiously across the rocks and to avoid trampling the fragile vegetation off-trail. Below the cliffs are large talus blocks and rubble that have fallen away from the cliff face, forming crevices that are old enough and deep enough to support a significant plant and animal habitat. The rock margins are covered in thick mats of blueberries. As you move west, you'll walk in and out of the woods along the upper-northerly edge of wild Palmaghatt Ravine and the Kline Kill (pronounced kline-ah-kill). The trail continues next to the cliffs, past erratics (boulders, pebbles) and isolated patches of pitch pine, hemlock, and hardwoods before it rises through an enchanted hemlock forest and up to a high, rocky ledge.

Soon you will arrive at Millbrook Drive. Turn right and follow the carriage-way back to Millbrook Mountain. You'll recognize the summit area soon. Turn left on the blue-blazed Millbrook Ridge Trail, backtracking on your earlier route a short distance to the red-blazed Millbrook Mountain Trail, where you bear left and descend. After another ten minutes, make sure to turn right on the blue-blazed Coxing Trail, descending from open pitch-pine slabs with northerly views into dense woods. These westerly slopes of Millbrook Mountain—the boisterous Coxing Kill's watershed—are often wet. Puncheons have been placed in the wettest areas to protect the soft soils. You will pass Millbrook Cross Path on your right, remaining on the blue-blazed Coxing Trail until you reach Trapps Road. Bear right onto Trapps Road and walk northeast, back to Trapps Bridge and your point of origin.

DID YOU KNOW?

Millbrook Mountain has one of the highest sheer cliff faces east of the Mississippi River.

MORE INFORMATION

Arrive before 9:30 A.M. on a nice weekend or you won't find a parking spot. If you can't get a spot in the Wawarsing parking area, continue on US 44/NY 55 to the West Trapps parking area ($12 fee for day-hikers; members park free), just beyond Trapps Bridge on the right. For more information, visit mohonkpreserve.org.

16

LAKE MINNEWASKA

This moderate hike passes a crystal-clear lake hemmed by white conglomerate sandstone cliffs, with far-reaching vistas of the Catskills and the Hudson Valley.

DIRECTIONS

To reach the Minnewaska State Park Preserve from Exit 18 off the NYS Thruway (I-87), head west through the village of New Paltz on NY 299 for 7.5 miles. Turn right onto US 44/NY 55 and drive past the Mohonk Preserve Visitor Center. Continue up the hill and under Trapps Bridge, and go another 3 miles to the Minnewaska State Park entrance on your left (a total of 11.4 miles from I-87). *GPS coordinates (upper parking area): 41° 43.723′ N, 74° 14.223′ W.*

TRAIL DESCRIPTION

This fine, short hike is among the great scenic treks available in the Minnewaska State Park Preserve. The highlight is Lake Minnewaska itself, one of the clear sky lakes (upper elevation) of the Shawangunk Ridge. In addition to the lake's striking blue water and bright conglomerate sandstone cliffs, hikers will be treated to far-reaching views of the Catskills in the west and of the Hudson Highlands to the southeast. The hike around Lake Minnewaska is short and easy enough to leave time for other activities, such as sightseeing, a visit to the Mohonk Preserve Visitor Center, a swim in the lake, or perhaps a picnic in the scenic overlook area atop the lakeside cliffs along the Lake Minnewaska carriage road, the former site of the Cliff House.

The trail begins at the southwest corner of the upper parking lot, at the north end of Lake Minnewaska. Walk toward the lake and bear right (south) to find the trailhead. Follow the carriage road downhill, with the lake to your left (avoiding Sunset Trail on your right), to lake level,

LOCATION
New Paltz, NY

RATING
Moderate

DISTANCE
1.5 miles

ELEVATION GAIN
230 feet

ESTIMATED TIME
2.5 hours

MAPS
USGS Gardiner, USGS Napanoch; Minnewaska State Park Preserve Hiking Map; NY-NJTC Shawangunk Trails

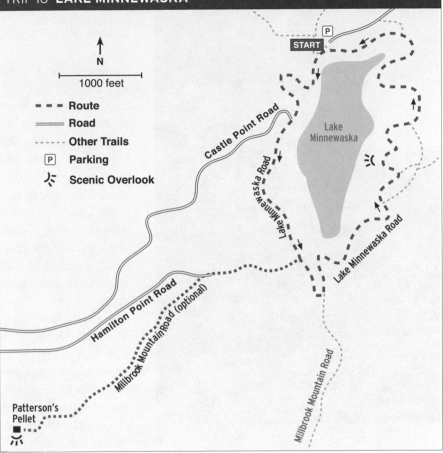

Legend:
- – – – Route
- ═══ Road
- ········ Other Trails
- P Parking
- 人 Scenic Overlook

N
1000 feet

(Map labels: START, Lake Minnewaska, Castle Point Road, Lake Minnewaska Road, Hamilton Point Road, Millbrook Mountain Road (optional), Millbrook Mountain Road, Patterson's Pellet)

where you will see the red trail blazes of Lake Minnewaska Road (carriageway). Bear left at the bathing beach. There are chemical toilets here. The carriage road ascends slightly, heading south. The vegetation is hemlock and oak woods, and in spring, shadbush is in bloom. Continue this easy climb past the junction where Castle Point Road goes off to the right. Avoid it and continue. Soon you will see the yellow-blazed Millbrook Mountain Road on your right. If you have time and want to extend your hike, consider following the Millbrook Mountain Road for a visit to Patterson's Pellet, a white conglomerate glacial erratic that sits on the lip of the wild Palmaghatt Ravine. This easy side jaunt is a nearly flat, 1.4-mile round-trip.

The vantage from Pellet will give you the lay of the land in the west, where the long, high ridges lead to Hamilton and Castle points and into the far reaches of the Shawangunk Badlands (Pine Plains). Patterson's Pellet is marked as such, although the boulder itself can't be mistaken; there are no others like it in the vicinity.

Hikers can savor the indigo views of Lake Minnewaska from the surrounding sandstone cliffs.

Along Lake Minnewaska Road, you will enjoy isolated views to the north toward Mohonk, including Sky Top. These views will improve ahead. Hiking around the south side of the lake, you'll come downhill and walk along the water's edge. You'll pass Millbrook Mountain Road on your right. A few isolated lookouts present themselves ahead, but the best views will be had as you climb to the picnic area. Continue uphill on the east side of the lake now, still following red diamonds and bearing left at a fork. Suddenly, you arrive at a broad, flat, open field with the vertical ledges of Lake Minnewaska on your left. The views are exceptional in every direction. The Catskills appear in the west, a long array of peaks stretching from the northerly Indian Head Wilderness through all of the high peaks in the south. Sky Top is immediately to the east over the Trapps. The Hudson Valley sprawls away to the southeast. In the near northwesterly realms of the state park preserve, you can see beyond Napanoch Point, Pulpit Rock, and Four Mile Camp on Tombstone Trail.

You are standing on the former site of the Lake Minnewaska Cliff House, also known as the Minnewaska Mountain House. Built by Alfred H. Smiley (famed cofounder of Mohonk Preserve) in 1879, the Cliff House could accommodate 225 guests and enjoyed immense popularity during its operation. In 1972, the cost of maintaining Cliff House led to its abandonment, and it burned down in 1978. The barn still stands to the north of the site, which you will see as you descend toward the lake again. Smiley built another hotel, Wildmere, which stood near the lake at the site of the present upper parking lot. It, too, was abandoned, and it burned in 1986. The property's future was in question for years. The Marriott Corporation wanted to build a hotel there, but a succession of lawsuits blocked the plans, and the state purchased the property and established the Minnewaska State Park Preserve in 1993. Today the Palisades Interstate Park Commission manages the preserve.

Perhaps Lake Minnewaska itself, with its remarkably clear and colorful water, will fascinate you as much as the sweeping views of the high ledges. The 34-acre, 78-foot-deep lake is so clear and beautiful because its acidic water and rocky shoreline cannot support aquatic vegetation. It is, in essence, dead. This is not to say that vegetation is absent, but it is limited to the minimal presence of water lilies, pipewort, and milfoil. The last recorded fish caught in the lake was in 1922. Collectively, the upper-elevation Shawangunk lakes are known as sky lakes. The lakes fill the surrounding streams with spring-fed waters; the entire volume of the Coxing Kill depends on Lake Minnewaska. During droughts, conditions can lead to fish kills on the creek. Although the waters of Lake Minnewaska may be nutrient-poor and provide only a marginal vegetation profile, the forests surrounding the lake are diverse, and many significant biological features exist in the area. Peregrine falcons, which live in nesting sites on Millbrook Mountain, hunt over the lake. Unusually old pitch pines grow in the former Cliff House area and are believed to have lived longer than most pitch pines on the ridge due to the presence of open rock, which acts as a natural fire barrier. (Larger pitch pines are also naturally fire-resistant.) Rare plants such as broom crowberry and mountain spleenwort grow near Lake Minnewaska, but some species have been locally extirpated, including yellow lady's slipper and maidenhair fern. There are rhodora, pink lady's slipper, nodding ladies' tresses, slender ladies' tresses, and rattlesnake plantain in the area. Minnewaska State Park Preserve is also the only known area where the noctuid moth (*Zale curema*) exists.

From the high cliffs along the lake's east shoreline, continue north, following the trail as it winds its way downhill above the lake. You may follow either the trail or the carriage road from this point back to the parking lot, passing a private inholding on your left (west) as you descend slightly. Leaving the barn to your right, you will pass beneath a pretty pedestrian bridge that spans the carriage road. Bear left to follow the red blazes back toward the parking area for one last look at the lake from a low ledge.

Even if hikers coming to Lake Minnewaska go no farther than the lake itself, they will become acquainted with some of the northern Shawangunks's significant geologic, physiographic, and biological communities. The varied aquatic, cliff-and-talus slab rock, and pitch-pine habitats encountered on this hike are a microcosm of what hikers can expect on longer, more involved forays across the fascinating Shawangunk Ridge.

DID YOU KNOW?

Alfred Smiley, a former owner of Lake Minnewaska, was a temperate Quaker who was distressed by the presence of a rum tavern near Minnewaska's main entrance. Smiley was able to purchase the property after the previous owner's death, and when he had the tavern cleaned out, he found many tools—spades, picks, and shovels—marked with his name. Smiley surmised that his employees had given the tools to the owner of the tavern in exchange for drinks.

MORE INFORMATION

Arrive at the gate before 9:30 A.M. on weekends or you may have to park in the Lower Awosting lot, which will add 1.5 miles of hiking and 400 feet in elevation to this hike. There are two levels to the upper (Wildmere) parking area. A map and an interpretive kiosk are posted on the picnic-area lawn between the parking lot and the lake. Pets are permitted on a leash of no more than 6 feet. A yurt near the edge of the trail provides a nature and activity center for visiting school groups. Other activities allowed on and near the area include scuba diving, boating (cartop boats only), biking, swimming, horseback riding, cross-country skiing, hunting (in designated areas), and fishing (though there are no fish). There is a day-use fee of $10. For more information, visit lakeminnewaska.org.

17

THE TRAPPS

An easy, enchanting hike along carriage roads passes under high cliffs popular with rock climbers.

DIRECTIONS

From Exit 18 off the NYS Thruway (I-87), head west through the village of New Paltz on NY 299 for 7.5 miles. Turn right onto US 44/NY 55 and drive 0.8 mile up the hill to the Mohonk Preserve Visitor Center. Just beyond the entrance, turn right into the Wawarsing parking area. *GPS coordinates:* 41° 44.224′ N, 74° 11.076′ W.

TRAIL DESCRIPTION

The century-old Undercliff and Overcliff carriageways (gravel roads) form a loop around the famous cliffs known as the Trapps, creating one of the most popular scenic hikes and bike rides in the Shawangunks. The route travels beneath then above the high vertical cliffs of bright conglomerate that are unique to the Gunks. Here, you will become intimately acquainted with the diverse cliff, talus, and slab-rock communities that have made the Trapps the most fascinating scenic attraction of the mid-Hudson Valley, as well as an ecological preserve of global significance.

Both the Undercliff and Overcliff roads are multiuse, so you will encounter many cyclists, hikers, and joggers, as well as the knowledgeable preserve rangers who patrol the cliffs and carriage roads. (You may be asked to show or purchase your day pass at this point.) These carriage roads are also popular cross-country skiing routes, their surfaces carved into dual, diagonal striding tracks by local skiers the moment there is a 4-inch snowfall. By far, though, the Trapps are most renowned for the world-class

LOCATION
New Paltz, NY

RATING
Moderate

DISTANCE
5 miles

ELEVATION GAIN
400 feet

ESTIMATED TIME
2 hours

MAPS
USGS Gardiner, USGS Mohonk Lake; Mohonk Preserve Trail Map; NY-NJTC Shawangunk Trails

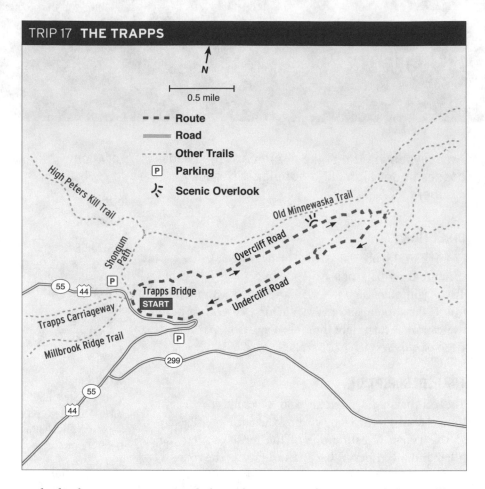

rock-climbing routes pioneered along their eastern face. As you hike, you'll see climbers in action on the vertical walls, some as high as 250 feet.

Begin at the Mohonk Preserve Visitor Center. Take the short but steep East Trapps Connector Trail from the north end of the Wawarsing parking area up to Undercliff Road. Catch your breath after climbing the Connector Trail's 250 stone steps and turn left (southwest) onto Undercliff Road. Signage is good. From here, the hike remains fairly level.

In a few minutes you will arrive at the wooden hut and information kiosk (with a restroom) in the general meeting area known as the Uberfall. The carriage road continues directly under the sheer cliffs, where dozens of climbers can be seen top-roping (a method by which an anchor, or protection, is placed above the climber, who is then held on belay from below by another person, protecting the climber in the event of a fall). It will amaze you to see how some climbers are able to scale a vertical wall that seems to have no handholds or ledges on it; for a non-climber, difficulty is hard to judge. Some very technical climbs are adjacent to very easy ones. You'll find yourself enthralled, maybe even eager to give this thrilling sport a try. Although climbers are a friendly bunch, many of those who are "on belay" are in close vocal contact with their partners and can't risk being distracted. The atmosphere is somewhat solemn and highly focused. The white stains on the rock are from chalk, which is used by climbers to keep their hands dry and maximize friction. Chalk has an erosive effect on sandstone.

Continue, ascending slightly past a southerly view and rising to Trapps Bridge. Don't cross the bridge. Turn right here where the Overcliff Road departs to the west. Shortly, the flat carriage road turns northeast, and views to the west appear, slowly revealing the Coxing valley, the broad lowlands of the Rondout Valley, and the southern Catskills beyond. The viewshed expands as the carriage road cuts through sunny, low-angle pitch pine and oak-covered slab rocks. The entire east-facing silhouette of the Catskills, from Ashokan High Point in the south to Overlook Mountain in the north, forms the western horizon. Continue into the woods as the road descends slightly and curves past ledges on the left, passing an unmarked connector road on the left (avoid it) to Laurel Ledge Road. Within minutes, you'll arrive at Rhododendron Bridge, a shaded, five-way intersection in the densely wooded heart of the Mohonk Preserve. Bear right onto Undercliff Road, winding below the massive cliffs of the Trapps as the road turns south. Soon you will enjoy views of the broad, flat Wallkill Valley and its little hamlets and farms, and the Fishkill Ridge and Hudson Highlands beyond the village

Encircled by a multiuse trail, the cliffs known as the Trapps draw both technical and beginner rock climbers.

of New Paltz. On the talus alongside the carriage road, climbers will be bouldering, or practicing overhang holds, and relaxing between routes. The yellow-blazed spur trails lead through the labyrinths of talus to reach climbing routes. On slower-traffic days, it is not unusual to see copperheads sunning themselves in the middle of the road. Give them space. You'll be pleased to know there have been few, if any, incidents involving hikers and snakes here.

From time to time, the cliffs may be closed to hikers to protect a peregrine falcon or black vulture nest; often you will see observers set up along the carriageway with telescopes trained on the nests. Most are volunteers and enthusiasts who help with census and tracking studies. If you've never seen a raptor up close, this is your chance to study the head of a falcon. Watch as it completely fills the view field of a high-power telescope—a surprising and unforgettable image. Soon you will come to the East Trapps Connector Trail junction you used earlier. Descend to return to your car.

Undercliff Road was built by hand and steam power in 1903. The area became a climbing destination when Fritz Wiessner, a climber scaling the cliffs around Breakneck Ridge, spotted the white cliffs of the Gunks. He pioneered the first routes on Millbrook Mountain (the so-called Old Route) then pioneered routes up Sky Top.

DID YOU KNOW?

In 1941, the renowned climbers Fritz Wiessner and Hans Kraus established the route known as High Exposure in the Trapps. This is considered by many world-class climbers to be the best technical rock-climbing pitch in the world. Today there are an estimated 1,000 climbing routes in the Shawangunks, visited by more than 50,000 climbers annually.

MORE INFORMATION

Arrive before 9:30 A.M. to find a parking spot. If you can't get a spot here, continue on US 44/NY 55 to the West Trapps parking area ($12 fee for day-hikers; members park free), just beyond Trapps Bridge on the right. Walk east up the gravel path to Trapps Bridge. For more information, visit mohonkpreserve.org.

BLACK VULTURE

The black vulture (*Coragyps atratus*) is an exciting recent addition to the Shawangunks' bird population, along with the clay-colored sparrow and the peregrine falcon. The vulture, a large southern scavenger, has been expanding its habitat into more rugged areas farther north due to warming trends. The first documented nest in the state appeared near Bonticou Crag in 1997. By 2004, there were three confirmed nesting sites in Mohonk Preserve, now the bird's northernmost known breeding area in the United States. Eggs, two to a clutch, take 38 to 41 days to incubate. The birds fledge at around 70 days.

The black vulture likely will do well in the Shawangunks and in similar areas of moderate-to-intensive human use because it is not overly sensitive to human presence during its breeding season. From time to time, the Trapps cliffs have been closed to protect falcon and vulture nesting sites from disturbance by rock climbers. The increasing populations of turkey vultures and now, smaller black vultures, often confuse observers. Black vultures have a short, square tail, with whitish patches toward the wingtips. They have a black head (as opposed to the adult turkey vultures' easily identified bald, red head) and a smaller wingspan. They tend to flap vigorously and glide in short intervals.

18

SKY TOP

A boulder scramble from Mohonk Mountain House through a deep and exciting crevice leads to a 360-degree view from Sky Top Tower, with an easy walk back.

DIRECTIONS

From Exit 18 off the NYS Thruway (I-87), drive west through the village of New Paltz on NY 299. As you cross the bridge over the Wallkill River, take the first right onto Springtown Road and set your trip odometer to zero. At 0.5 mile, turn left onto Mountain Rest Road (CR 6), where you'll see signs for Mohonk. At 1.7 miles, go through the intersection of Butterville-Canaan Road. Continue up Mountain Rest Road, and at 4 miles you'll enter the Mohonk Mountain House main gate on the left. *GPS coordinates:* 41° 46.727' N, 74° 8.150' W.

TRAIL DESCRIPTION

This historical, scenic hike to Sky Top is perhaps the Shawangunks' most popular outing. The hike winds to the crowning glory of the Mohonk Mountain House property that adjoins the 6,400-acre Mohonk Preserve. The walk, as described here, begins at the gatehouse parking lot. (You can save distance by taking the shuttle directly to the trailhead.) Follow Huguenot Trail at the southwest corner of the parking lot to Whitney Road (carriage roads). Follow scenic North Lookout Road until you see signs for Picnic Lodge, where food, restrooms, and phones are available. From Picnic Lodge, walk across Garden Road, past the greenhouses, and up through the gardens to the Mountain House. The estimated time from the gatehouse is 40 minutes.

For casual visitors and Mountain House guests, the main attraction of Sky Top is the views it affords of six

LOCATION
New Paltz, NY

RATING
Moderate

DISTANCE
6 miles

ELEVATION GAIN
650 feet

ESTIMATED TIME
4 hours

MAPS
USGS Mohonk Lake;
Mohonk Preserve
Trail Map; NY-NJTC
Shawangunk Trails

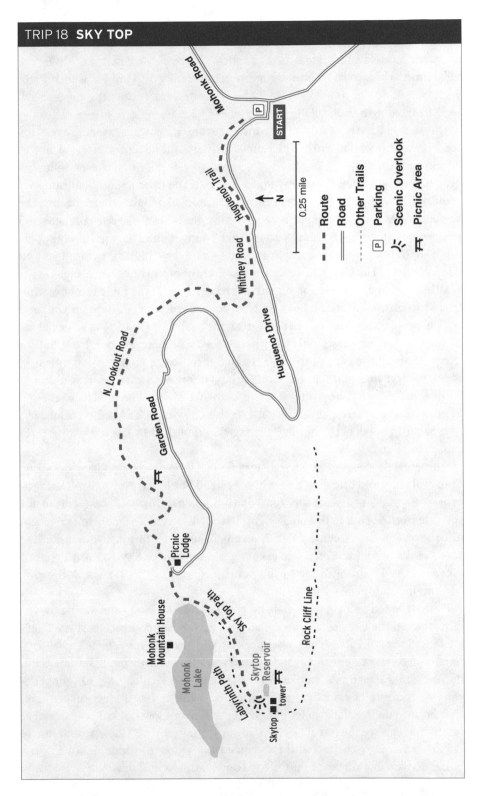

Mohonk Road

P

START

Huguenot Trail

N

0.25 mile

- - - Route
— Road
.... Other Trails
P Parking
Scenic Overlook
Picnic Area

Whitney Road

Huguenot Drive

N. Lookout Road

Garden Road

Picnic Lodge

Mohonk Mountain House

Sky Top Path

Labyrinth Path

Mohonk Lake

Skytop Reservoir

Rock Cliff Line

Skytop tower

states; some say seven. Hikers have the bonus of tunneling their way through the white conglomerate talus fields below the cliffs, then scaling the cliff face on rustic ladders and bridges as they follow the cool, dark path known as the Labyrinth. The two most popular approaches to Sky Top are Labyrinth Path, your ascent route, and Sky Top Path, your descent route. The designated, well-traveled Labyrinth Path is a serious rock scramble requiring all-fours agility, a good share of gumption, and, in some instances, raw courage. This trail is recommended only to the physically fit and adventurous, and not to anyone who is unsteady or afraid of heights. Sky Top Path, however, follows a graded, easily-managed footway and takes half the time to climb, although it requires the same 350-foot ascent from Mohonk Lake to the tower's base as the Labyrinth. Many parties split up at the Mountain House's East Porchere and rendezvous at the tower. Make certain that younger children are closely supervised. Both hikes approach and in some cases traverse high vertical ledges and deep crevices. The Labyrinth requires boulder hopping and tunneling.

While your party is getting organized, have a look at the huge rainbow trout that swirl around Mohonk Lake under the East Porchere, waiting for the food pellets you can buy from dispensers near the archway. (Fishing is reserved for Mountain House guests only.) With the East Porchere at your back, follow the path along the edge of the lake (Lake Shore Road), go under a footbridge, through a crevice, and join Sky Top Path. (Follow Sky Top Path if you do not want to take Labyrinth Path.) Cross a boardwalk and go a short distance to Sentinel Rock, where Labyrinth Path to the Crevice (a.k.a. Lemon Squeezer) and Sky Top appears to your left. Signage is good. Follow the red paint blazes into the Labyrinth.

Immediately you will make your way through holes and crevices, stooping, crab-walking, and crawling under house-sized boulders. You'll climb ladders, cross catwalks, and scale the tops of tilted slabs. You will pass connector trails to both Spring Path and Sky Top Path, where you will continue straight ahead toward the Crevice. Within a half hour of beginning your hike, the trail breaks onto the sunny, treeless scree slopes west of Sky Top, with rugged views of the Hudson Valley to the south, as well as the Trapps, Millbrook Mountain, and Eagle Cliff.

Follow the red paint blazes carefully now as you rock-hop your way below the cliffs toward the Crevice. (Stay alert so that you do not continue past the Crevice onto Staircliff Path.) The Crevice appears in the cliff on your left as a high, narrow fissure. A series of wooden stairways ascends through several dark, damp pitches. The final climb out of the Crevice is a challenging, 10-foot vertical wall (be sure of your foot- and handholds, and assist younger hikers here) that brings you to a flat slab with high, vertical drops, overlooking the preserve lands. You can see the top of Sky Top Tower from here if you look up and north.

Walk back over the top of the Crevice on a wooden bridge, following the blazes for a short distance up to Sky Top Road. Go left, pass the Armstrong

Seat, turn right onto the paved walkway (note that Sky Top Path meets Sky Top Road here; this is your descent route), and walk a short distance to Sky Top Tower. The tower is open, and you can climb to the observation deck, where you'll enjoy 360-degree views, from Vermont's Green Mountains to New York's Taconics, Catskills, and Hudson Highlands, and to New Jersey's Kittatinnys. Below are the Mountain House and Mohonk Lake. The tower, which stands over Sky Top Reservoir, was originally constructed for fire control. There is a picnic table next to the map kiosk on Sky Top. Return via Sky Top Path for the fastest descent (25 minutes) to the Mountain House.

There are several other choices for return routes to the Mountain House. Many hikers opt for the longer, gentler Sky Top Road, or the Reservoir, Pinkster, or Bruin paths. Sky Top hikers who have parked at the gatehouse often return by way of Sky Top Road and Fox Path, crossing Garden Road onto Glen Anna Path, North Lookout Road, Whitney Road, and Huguenot Path.

DID YOU KNOW?

Built in 1921, the internationally famous monument of Sky Top Tower commemorates Albert K. Smiley (1828–1912), who founded the Mohonk Mountain House with his twin brother, Alfred.

MORE INFORMATION

The Labyrinth is not recommended as a descent route. Carry as small a pack as possible and bring a first-aid kit. For more information, visit mohonk-preserve.org.

From the Alfred K. Smiley memorial tower on Sky Top, visitors can see several states.

PEREGRINE FALCON

Probably the most successful wildlife reintroduction effort in the United States has been that of the peregrine falcon (*Falco peregrinus*), or duck hawk. Before the 1950s, the birds bred from the southern states as far north as the high arctic islands. Peregrines were nearly wiped out by the use of the pesticide dichloro-diphenyl-trichloroethane (DDT) and were extirpated from the area east of the Mississippi River by 1964. When DDT was banned in North America in the early 1970s, a captive-breeding program administered by Cornell University reintroduced the birds to places where it was believed they would thrive—especially bridges and skyscrapers. Because of this, and to the surprise of many people, their reappearance occurred around large population centers.

Peregrines are common migrants and can be observed in increasing numbers along the Appalachian Highlands and into the upper Hudson Valley. One of the most popular places to watch them is from the Trapps area of the Shawangunks, where the Mohonk Preserve conducts an annual hawk watch. Often you will meet volunteer observers tracking nesting pairs of falcons along the Undercliff Carriageway. The birds are sensitive to disturbance, and parts of the Trapps have been closed to rock climbing from time to time to protect their breeding sites.

19

EAGLE CLIFF AND MOHONK LAKE

A carriage road from Mohonk Mountain House heads to the gazebos and cliffs overlooking the Shawangunks and the Catskills, with a walk around Mohonk Lake.

DIRECTIONS

From Exit 18 off the NYS Thruway (I-87), drive west through the village of New Paltz on NY 299. As you cross the bridge over the Wallkill River, take the first right onto Springtown Road and set your trip odometer to zero. At 0.5 mile, turn left onto Mountain Rest Road (CR 6), where you'll see signs for Mohonk. At 1.7 miles, go through the intersection with Butterville-Canaan Road. Continue up Mountain Rest Road, and at 4 miles you'll enter the Mohonk Mountain House main gate on the left. *GPS coordinates:* 41° 46.727′ N, 74° 8.150′ W.

TRAIL DESCRIPTION

Rivaled only by Sky Top for dramatic views, this short, easy hike reveals the kind of bewitching and far-reaching landscapes for which Mohonk is famous. It ranks as a Mountain House favorite, and perhaps because of its gentle, easy grades and scenic payoffs, it may be the most popular hike on the hotel property. The jaunt to Eagle Cliff—with views of Sky Top, the southlands, and the Victorian "castle" of Mountain House along the shores of Mohonk Lake—will be among the stateliest and most alluring easy hikes you'll ever take. Eagle Cliff is an east- and south-facing escarpment of vertical white conglomerate. Its rugged beauty results partly from the jumbled tonnage of talus that has broken away from the cliff and lies glistening among moss- and tree-clad pockets below. The serpentine route of the carriage road will introduce you to an awe-inspiring series of panoramic surprises,

LOCATION
New Paltz, NY

RATING
Easy

DISTANCE
6 miles (2 miles if you begin at the Mountain House)

ELEVATION GAIN
625 feet

ESTIMATED TIME
3.5 hours

MAPS
USGS Mohonk Lake; Mohonk Preserve Trail Map; NY-NJTC Shawangunk Trails

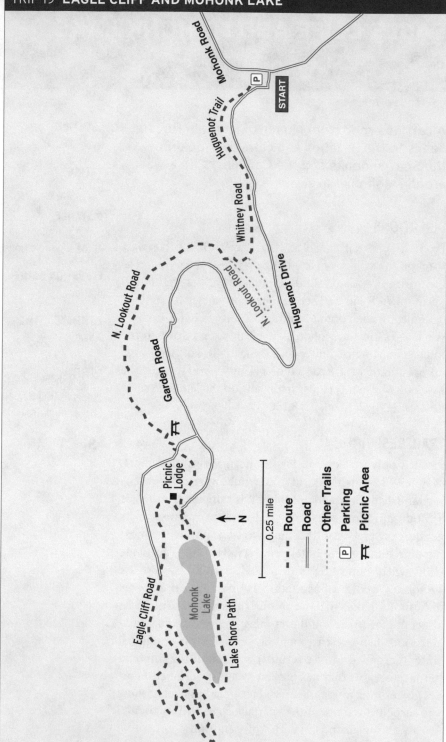

TRIP 19 **EAGLE CLIFF AND MOHONK LAKE**

Mohonk Road

Huguenot Trail

START

P

Whitney Road

Huguenot Drive

N. Lookout Road

N. Lookout Road

Garden Road

N. Lookout Road

Picnic Lodge

N

0.25 mile

Eagle Cliff Road

Mohonk Lake

Lake Shore Path

- - - Route
——— Road
········· Other Trails
P Parking
Picnic Area

The easy yet rewarding hike to Eagle Cliff includes views of Mohonk Lake, with the famous mountain house at its far end.

from the Catskills in the west through the southerly rolling hills of western New Jersey, Minnewaska State Park, and the Hudson Valley Highlands. In the foreground, the jagged rocks of the Mohonk Preserve form a fitting picture frame for some of the east's most startling vistas and one of the world's most enchanting carriage roads, created by the Smiley brothers to delight their guests.

The walk, as described here, begins at the gatehouse parking lot. (You can save distance by taking the shuttle directly to the trailhead.) Follow Huguenot Trail at the southwest corner of the parking lot to Whitney Road (carriage roads). Follow scenic North Lookout Road to a point at which you will see signs for Picnic Lodge, where you can find food, restrooms, and phones. From Picnic Lodge, walk across Garden Road, past the greenhouses, and up through the gardens to the Mountain House. The estimated time from the gatehouse is 40 minutes.

Begin at the front entrance of the hotel and turn left onto the main service road (Garden Road). Follow the road a few hundred feet to the apex of the hairpin turn. Here you will find Eagle Cliff Road. Follow this cinder carriage road, leaving the tennis courts to your right. Entering the forest, you're surrounded by moss-frocked boulders sticking out of the ground like fuzzy emeralds. Ascend easily amid the hemlock and laurels, passing a small bench on a slab of stone to your right with limited views to the west. Keep climbing and soon you will come to a pair of small gazebos with views of the Trapps and Millbrook Mountain. The trail turns through the south now, passing another west-facing gazebo with extensive views of the Catskills from Overlook to Peekamoose.

Soon you will reach an H intersection. Bear right now, and, although you can't sense it just yet, you're climbing the tilted northwest slopes of Eagle Cliff and Huntington Ledge. Red and white oak appears, along with hemlock, white pine, and pitch pine. Suddenly, you arrive at Huntington Lookout, a stunning tableau across the preserve lands and beyond. Beneath you are the pristine lands of the Trapps and Millbrook Mountain, and rising to the west are the retreating folds of hills that reach up across Rondout Valley to Ashokan High Point. The south is enveloped in the scrubby pitch pines of the Badlands. At your feet is the thin valley of Rhododendron Brook, which you can locate by pouring an imaginary torrent of water between you and the Trapps and following its course eastward, downhill.

Humpty Dumpty Road is just below you, amid the dizzying, bright chunks of talus rock. Continuing the hike, the next gazebo is the magical Artist's Rock, and more follow as you turn toward the south. On your right, you'll pass the Eagle Cliff descent, a rough path that shortcuts down to Short Woodland Drive and Humpty Dumpty Road. Eagle Cliff Road now heads north, and suddenly the vertical cone of Sky Top comes into view. The carriage road threads in and out of the woods, walking the cliff's edge past a collection of the world's finest handmade cedar gazebos, constructed by the Mountain House's rustic builders. Take in the sweeping valley views and close-ups of the Mountain House and its terra cotta roof, with Sky Top on your right, perched on its monolith of bright conglomerate. Mohonk Lake, shimmering in deep shades of viridian, lies beneath you. Views to the northeast are striking, with the hotel imposed before the northern lowlands of the Hudson Valley.

Vistas don't get much better than those you'll enjoy from the Arthur's Seat gazebo, and surely you will think this stretch of carriageway ranks as one of the finest short walks in the world. The carriage road curls into the forest again, passing the Cuyler Castle gazebo. Pass the H intersection you saw earlier, bearing right toward the Mountain House. Just after crossing a wooden bridge turn right and descend Lambdin's Path, then turn left under the bridge and descend a three-pitched flight of stairs to join Undercliff Path. Bear right, walk around the southwest shore of Mohonk Lake, and follow the lake's edge on Shore Path, joining Lake Shore Road (east) back along the water's edge to the Mountain House.

Return to the gatehouse by the route you came.

DID YOU KNOW?

Lambdin's Glen (reached by Lambdin's Path) was named for the nineteenth-century American landscape artist James Reid Lambdin, who painted many scenes of the Shawangunk Mountains and the area around the Mohonk Mountain House. He was a registered guest at the Mountain House in the years 1873, 1881, and 1883. The Glen is a tribute to Lambdin's contribution to American art.

MORE INFORMATION

Maps are available at the gatehouse parking lot. For more information, visit mohonkpreserve.org.

THE EASTERN MID-HUDSON REGION

The Hudson Valley developed slowly in comparison with the English settlements of New England and Virginia. The Dutch East India Company lost interest after Henry Hudson determined that what would later be called the Hudson River was not the sea route to the Orient. (When Hudson returned to the Netherlands, the British seized his ship, the *Half Moon*; Hudson's last expedition to the Northwest Passage, in 1610, was under the British flag in the ship *Discovery*.) Hudson did, however, interest a powerful group of private investors in the region's lucrative fur trade, and this group formed the Dutch West India Company, which was chartered in 1621 with a 21-year trading monopoly.

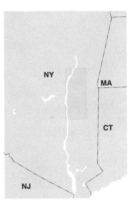

The company established trade connections with the colonies, built forts in Albany and New York City, and introduced patroonships as an inexpensive means of encouraging colonization. A patroonship was, in essence, a land grant given to a patroon (a lord or feudal master), who could establish a colony of 50 settlers within a four-year period. Because patroonships were so large (8 miles square), and because those who farmed the land could not own it, the system prevented permanent settlement on both sides of the river. Ultimately the patroonships failed. Most farmers found that life was better in the Netherlands, where land could be privately owned. The best-known patroon was Peter Minuit, who is remembered for the purchase of Manhattan Island from the Canarsie tribe. Only one patroonship, Rensselaerwyck, survived the transition to British rule intact.

After the patroonships, much of the open land remained unsettled until the German Palatines, religious refugees from the Electoral Palatinate of Germany's Rhine Valley, arrived in 1710. Fleeing persecution in their homeland, 3,000 refugees relocated to America after seeking asylum in Britain. Robert Hunter, appointed as first governor of the New York province, oversaw the Palatines' settlement. They were encamped in the vicinity of Germantown on both sides of the river, in an East Camp and a West Camp, and employed by the crown for the manufacture of naval stores, such as tar. The lands on the east bank were purchased from Robert Livingston; the west banks were the queen's lands. Despite a concentrated effort, the production of naval stores was unsuccessful, and the Palatines disbanded. Later marble, slate, and iron mining contributed to the region's prosperity. Eventually the area took part in the lucrative world trade, a development made possible by proximity to the Hudson River.

The eastern mid-Hudson Valley is bounded in the east by the Taconic Range, in the south by the Fishkill Ridge, and in the west by the Hudson River. Substantial open space exists along the river's edge, where most of the hikes in this guide are located.

20

OLD CROTON AQUEDUCT

This easy, flat walk through deep woods is ideal for children.

DIRECTIONS

To reach the park, take NY 129 (Maple Street) east from US 9. Go 2.4 miles to the park entrance on the right. Follow the park road past the dam into the parking area. *GPS coordinates: 41° 13.493′ N, 73° 51.499′ W.*

By train, take the Metro-North Hudson line to Croton-Harmon station. The hike ends near Ossining station.

TRAIL DESCRIPTION

Many hikers feel that the most attractive section of Old Croton Aqueduct Trail (OCA) is the one described here, which connects Ossining to Croton Gorge Park. Each end of the trail has attractions, and in between are 5 miles of quiet woodlands, with one or two diversions through the surrounding communities. It is best to leave a shuttle car at both ends of the hike described here, but you can also hike from the north end to the south and back (a total of 10 miles), or hike from one end to any point where you want to turn around. It would be a mistake, however, to miss either the Heritage Community Visitor Center in Ossining, which features an exhibit on the aqueduct's construction, as well as original cells and an electric chair from neighboring Sing Sing prison, or the remarkable Croton Dam.

Begin the hike from the north end, at Croton Gorge Park. Take a few minutes to walk across the dam from the trailhead picnic area. To do so, walk to the east edge of the playing fields, turn left on OCA, and climb to Croton Dam Road (not open to private vehicles). The dam is on the left at this point. This will allow you the option of seeing New Croton Reservoir.

LOCATION
Croton-on-Hudson, NY

RATING
Moderate

DISTANCE
4.75 miles

ELEVATION GAIN
420 feet

ESTIMATED TIME
3 hours

MAPS
USGS Haverstraw; Old Croton Aqueduct State Historic Map and Guide; Westchester County (road map)

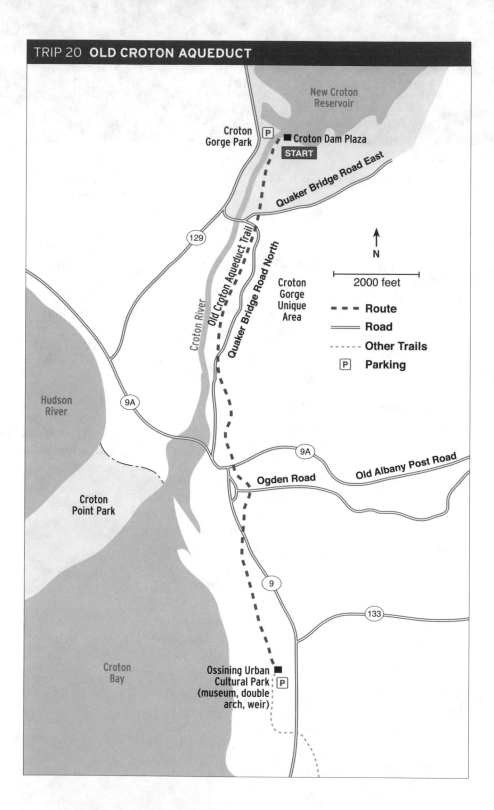

New Croton
Reservoir

Croton
Gorge Park

P

■ Croton Dam Plaza
START

Quaker Bridge Road East

129

Croton River

Old Croton Aqueduct Trail

Quaker Bridge Road North

Croton
Gorge
Unique
Area

N

2000 feet

- - - **Route**
——— **Road**
········· **Other Trails**
P **Parking**

Hudson
River

9A

9A

Ogden Road

Old Albany Post Road

Croton
Point Park

9

133

Croton
Bay

Ossining Urban ■
Cultural Park
(museum, double
arch, weir)

P

The dam is just as impressive from ground level, where you can see the spillway up close. From the Croton Gorge Park picnic area, go to the south side of the parking lot and follow the trail south (right) as it walks between rows of tall, thin white pines. Soon you will be presented with the chance to walk along River Trail, which lies between the Croton River and OCA. This option, however, is ultimately confusing because the blazes (blue paint and assorted disks) are poor and this side trail is not well managed. There are no maps posted at the site. Continue straight ahead on OCA. Pass beneath a large power line. Soon large oaks and poplars appear, and you will see some trail signs. The trail is flat, hard-packed sandy loam, about 18 feet wide. After walking for twenty minutes, you will reach Quaker Bridge Road, which you cross. You're moving away from the

The New Croton Dam is a part of the New York City water supply system and can be seen from Croton Gorge Park.

river now and have risen above it. Barriers across the trail prevent its use by motorized vehicles. Cross the road once again. Pass the 19-acre Croton Gorge Unique Area (Department of Environmental Conservation [DEC] managed), which lies between the trail and the river. Some herd trails, which lead downhill to the river's edge, are evident.

Continue along OCA. Soon a 10-mile-long vista opens up to the southwest, showing Hook Mountain (the Palisades) and Haverstraw Bay across the Hudson River. Where there are no trees, OCA blazes are posted on green stanchions. Soon you'll circumvent the perimeter of the beautifully landscaped General Electric Management Development Institute, walking next to a chain-link fence. You'll escape this residential area as you cross Albany Post Road and follow blue blazes under CR 9A. The trail turns left onto Ogden Road and goes uphill about 500 feet, where you bear right onto OCA again. The low, cylindrical stone towers you see along the route are ventilators that equalize the pressure in the aqueduct and aerate the water.

At the Ossining welcome sign, cross US 9 on the pedestrian crosswalk, where signposts identify the trail. You'll pass through the property of the Avalon Ossining apartment complex on the sprawling grounds where the historical Kane mansion (1843) stands (it is now the Avalon community's club house). The white post on the lawn once identified the center of the aqueduct.

Now you will cross several streets in the village of Ossining. Descending a flight of stone stairs at the south end of a green strip, you will arrive at the Double Arch bridge. On the north side, before you cross, you'll come to the stone weir chamber, which controlled the flow of water through the aqueduct. When the tunnel needed to be emptied for repair, the weir chamber would release water into the Sing Sing Kill.

Cross the bridge, leave OCA, and follow an informal trail to the observation platform to look at the Double Arch bridge. You're nearly in the center of Ossining. Go back and cross OCA again to reach the Heritage Area Visitors Center (part of the Joseph G. Caputo Community Center), where there are outstanding displays recounting the aqueduct's history.

From the lower parking lot of the Caputo Community Center, you can take an interesting scenic walk on Sing Sing Kill Greenway, a concrete walkway that will allow you to see the Sing Sing Kill Gorge up close. The elevated walkway has steel railings for its full length (0.33 mile), where it currently ends on Central Avenue. Ultimately it will connect with Henry Gourdine Park on the Ossining waterfront. A walk on the Greenway combined with a weir visit makes for an interesting outing in itself.

The Sing Sing Kill Greenway, completed in 2015, is an elevated walkway above the riverbed at the base of a steep gorge. A maintenance trail had to be put in to make the sanitary sewer line more secure by encasing it in cement because the pipe was above ground due to the bedrock. Pilings were built, and the walkway was built above it.

Paid for by the village of Ossining, it will eventually connect to the riverfront. It now goes to Central Avenue, and interpretive displays line the path connecting it to the Henry Gourdine Park. You can park on Central Avenue.

Ossining's original name of Sing Sing came from the Sint Sinck ("stone upon stone") tribe, which sold the land in 1685. The name survives in both the Sing Sing Kill and the infamous Sing Sing state prison, which stands just to the west on the Hudson's banks. The historical exhibit at the visitor center contains original prison cells, dating from 1826. There are also photos, personal effects, and dioramas of prison life. Sing Sing was considered a model prison because it earned a profit for the state of New York, as no prison had done before. While the Old Croton Aqueduct display in the Ossining Museum will remain in place at the Caputo Community Center, the Sing Sing prison exhibition, which shares the same space at the museum, is currently being updated in anticipation of a move to the power-house building just outside the walls of the prison.

When you've finished, return to your car in the parking lot, or continue the hike back to Croton Gorge Park.

DID YOU KNOW?

The expression *sent up the river,* meaning "to be in prison," references Sing Sing state prison in the village of Ossining, 30 miles upriver from New York City. The phrase dates from 1891.

MORE INFORMATION

The entry fee for Croton Gorge Park varies from year to year. To begin this hike from the south, take the Tarrytown exit (Exit 9 from the NYS Thruway) and go north on South Broadway 7.2 miles. Take the first left after Main Street into the Caputo Community Center. You can also use local street parking.

Old Croton Aqueduct State Park is administered by the New York State Office of Parks, Recreation and Historic Preservation. An interactive map of the trail may be seen online, and paper maps requested from Friends of the Old Croton Aqueduct, which conducts guided tours of the OCA Trail and the weir; aqueduct.org. Park management may be contacted at 914-693-5259. For more information about the Caputo Community Center and Ossining Heritage Visitor Center, call 914-941-3189.

OLD CROTON AQUEDUCT

The Old Croton Aqueduct was built to supply New York City with water, and it did so from 1842 to 1955. Around the beginning of the twentieth century, when Manhattan started to expand north of Wall Street as its population exploded, the city began the construction of reservoirs in the Catskill Mountains (see Trip 35). But the Old Croton Aqueduct, an impressive feat of engineering referred to simply as "the aqueduct," was the one by which all others were measured. Thirty-five million gallons of water flowed into the city daily through the aqueduct from Croton to two reservoirs, one in today's Central Park, the other in the present location of the Main Branch of the New York Public Library.

Neither reservoir exists today, but the 26-mile-long aqueduct does, along with many of its disused aerators and weir chambers. The aqueduct still provides the village of Ossining with drinking water. Its combined length and width have been designated as one of the Hudson Valley's longest linear parks, with a surface that has been improved along its entire length, from Croton Gorge Park in Cortlandt to the Bronx. Here and there the trail is interrupted by development, but it is still a continuous, marked trail with a flat dirt surface.

21

STISSING MOUNTAIN

A steep ascent to a fire tower overlooking agricultural lands leads to views of the Southern Taconic Plateau and the Catskills.

DIRECTIONS

From the Taconic State Parkway, take Exit 44 to NY 82 north. Turn left at the firehouse onto Lake Road; from here you will see Stissing Mountain and its fire tower ahead. (From the center of Pine Plains, go south on NY 82 for 0.4 mile and turn right onto Lake Road.) At 1.6 miles, pass the Thompson Pond Preserve trailheads. (There is one on each side of the Stissing Pond outlet.) At 2.2 miles, park at the Friends of Stissing Landmarks (FOSL) trailhead, on the right. The trail begins across the street. You can also park here to reach the Thompson Pond trailhead, just down the street. *GPS coordinates:* 41° 58.192′ N, 73° 40.933′ W.

TRAIL DESCRIPTION

Choose a clear, sunny day for this short hike to Stissing's summit (1,403 feet) and fire tower, leaving time to hike the loop trail around Thompson Pond. Together they make an unforgettable outing to a diverse, 507-acre preserve located midway between the Hudson River and the Southern Taconic Mountains.

The area's natural value was recognized by a group of local citizens whose dedication led to the involvement of The Nature Conservancy (TNC) in 1957 and, finally, to the preserve's designation as a registered National Natural Landmark in 1973. FOSL continues to act as liaison to the conservancy.

Though short, the trail to Stissing summit is steep and rocky. It is also unmarked at this time, but it is self-guiding and easy to follow. Especially during spring and fall, come prepared for high winds and a chill factor if you plan

LOCATION
Pine Plains, NY

RATING
Moderate

DISTANCE
3 miles

ELEVATION GAIN
1,000 feet

ESTIMATED TIME
2 hours

MAPS
USGS Pine Plains; Thompson Pond and Stissing Mountain Trail Map; co.dutchess.ny.us/CountyGov/Departments/DPW-Parks/tmsthompson pondstissingmnt.pdf

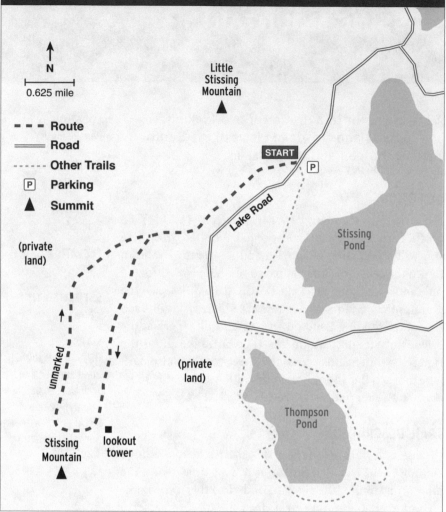

N

0.625 mile

- - - **Route**
—— **Road**
- - - - **Other Trails**
P **Parking**
▲ **Summit**

Little
Stissing
Mountain
▲

(private
land)

START P

Lake Road

Stissing
Pond

unmarked

(private
land)

Thompson
Pond

Stissing
Mountain
▲

lookout
tower

to climb the fire tower, which is not on the true summit of Stissing but on its
northerly slope.

From FOSL trailhead, cross the street to the Stissing trailhead, identified by
preserve sign markers. Climb immediately up the rocky, steep trail as it bears
left onto an old fire access road. A seasonal brook sometimes shares this road-
way, which served the fire tower, but soon you will climb above it. At a Y—where,
as of this writing, there are no trail markers—bear left for the most direct and
steepest route to the summit.

The incline relaxes only slightly as the trail cuts east across the northerly side
of the mountain, then it climbs stiffly as it turns south toward the summit. You
will begin to see open farmland to the east, through a second-growth hardwood forest that was originally clear-cut for charcoal production. Just as you're

From the fire tower on Stissing Mountain, hikers could glimpse raptors soaring over Thompson Pond in search of food.

wondering where the tower could be, it appears. As you top out on the summit, you'll see the foundation of an old observer's cabin. The tower, open and maintained by FOSL, is now 200 feet to your left. It is so tall that the squeamish may be content with limited views from partway up. The tower has a cab (a waist-high steel enclosure) and a roof but no windows, so you're going to feel the full force of the wind here. It's in need of maintenance, undertaken by means of private donations. Without significant improvement, this tower may not be considered safe in the near future. Exercise caution and watch your step.

Stissing Mountain is isolated within a relatively flat, peripheral plain of softer sandstones. Its Precambrian gneiss is erosion-resistant, representing some of Earth's oldest surface rock. The views from Stissing's heights are expansive, taking in a 360-degree panorama of the north and east farmlands of Columbia and Dutchess counties, and of the Southern Taconic Ridge stretching from North Egremont and Mount Washington State Forest in Massachusetts to Bash Bish Mountain, Alander Mountain, and Brace Mountain as the ridge tapers down to the flatlands around Millerton, New York. At your feet, north to south, are Twin Island Lake, Stissing Pond, and Thompson Pond. To the southwest, you see long Shawangunk Ridge sweeping across Minnewaska State Park, from

Sam's Point all the way to Sky Top Tower in the Mohonk Preserve. With binoculars, you can see High Point tower in northwestern New Jersey and the jagged Kittatinnys.

In the west, you can take in the entire Catskills, from Peekamoose and Table mountains through the Burroughs Range (the High Peaks area of Slide, Wittenberg, and Cornell mountains) and into the vast northerly wilderness areas to the "big three" of Thomas Cole, Black Dome, and Blackhead mountains. Beyond these are the Helderbergs, and to the north and east on a good day you may see the southern Adirondacks and the Green Mountains of Vermont. Your compass will not function in the steel tower, so map orientation and peak identification present a challenge.

At one time, it was easier to follow the old truck trail down from the summit (it leaves from the base of the tower to the west), but there are no markers at this time, and the trail is interwoven with other unmarked trails. For the return trip, retrace your steps back to Thompson Pond Preserve trailhead (see Trip 22).

DID YOU KNOW?

At the Town of Pine Plains town meeting of 1794, it was voted that 80 pounds (currency of the time) be raised for the use of the poor the following year. Also voted was that all hogs would have a right to run on the common if ringed and yoked. The following year, it was voted that 6 pounds' bounty be paid by tax on the inhabitants of the town for every wolf killed in the year 1795.

MORE INFORMATION

For more information, contact The Nature Conservancy's Eastern New York Chapter by visiting nature.org or calling 518-690-7878.

GOLDEN EAGLE

Visitors to Stissing Mountain and Thompson Pond are likely to get a glimpse of the majestic golden eagle (*Aquila chrysaetos*) wheeling overhead in search of food. This large bird is capable of hunting animals as big as house cats, foxes, turkeys, geese, and similar game. Considered a threat to livestock in the western states, the golden eagle had a bounty issued on it at one time.

Although similar in appearance to bald eagles from a distance, adult golden eagles are distinguished by a darker, obscurely banded tail. Immature golden eagles have white tails, not unlike those of the bald eagle. The golden eagle's hindneck appears copperish or golden, but don't expect to get close enough to see it. While golden eagles have lived in this area for many years, their range in New York is shrinking. Once common breeders in the Adirondacks, the eagle has moved south, to an area threatened by habitat degradation and reduction. Golden eagles need as much as 35 square miles of uninterrupted hunting and breeding ground, and even under ideal circumstances, juvenile mortality can be as high as 75 percent. At one time considered a pest, these endangered birds are now protected under the Migratory Bird Treaty Act.

22

THOMPSON POND PRESERVE

The pond and surrounding wetlands of this excellent family hike are a National Natural Landmark where golden eagles and king rails nest.

DIRECTIONS

To reach Pine Plains from the Taconic State Parkway, take Exit 44 to NY 82 north. Watch carefully for the firehouse on the left; turn left here onto Lake Road, where you will see Stissing Mountain and its fire tower ahead. (From the center of Pine Plains, go south on NY 82 for 0.4 mile and turn right onto Lake Road.) At 1.6 miles, you'll see the Thompson Pond Preserve trailheads. (There is one on each side of the Stissing Pond outlet.) If these lots are full, continue 2.2 miles and park at the Friends of Stissing Landmarks (FOSL) Stissing Mountain trailhead, on the right. Walk back along the road to the Thompson Pond trailhead. *GPS coordinates: 41° 58.192′ N, 73° 40.933′ W.*

TRAIL DESCRIPTION

Thompson Pond lies east and directly beneath Stissing Mountain in the town of Pine Plains. You can hike both destinations for a scenic day outing. The pond was named for Amos Thompson, who in 1746 was among the earliest white settlers in Dutchess County. During King George's War (1744–1748, one of the French and Indian wars), a Moravian mission also existed nearby, ministering to the Mahican group that was soon disbanded by settlement and by the king's dissolution of the mission.

Reach the trailhead from the same parking lot as the Stissing Mountain trailhead (see Trip 21). Ideally you should wear waterproof boots for the hike around Thompson Pond, which forms the soggy headwaters of Wappingers Creek. If the water table is high, you might

LOCATION
Pine Plains, NY

RATING
Easy

DISTANCE
3 miles

ELEVATION GAIN
50 feet

ESTIMATED TIME
2 hours

MAPS
USGS Pine Plains; The Nature Conservancy, Thompson Pond Nature Preserve; Thompson Pond and Stissing Mountain Trail Map; co.dutchess.ny.us/ CountyGov/ Departments/ DPW-Parks/ tmsthompsonpond stissingmnt.pdf

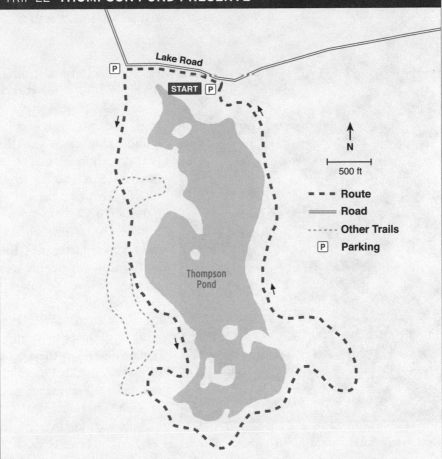

find yourself ankle-deep or more in standing water at the pond's south end, where a series of boardwalks is sometimes submerged. These conditions occur mostly in early spring, usually the best time to observe the birdlife for which this area is known. Many naturalists consider Thompson Pond the best location for viewing water birds in the entire central Hudson Valley area. Nesting golden eagles are found here, something not mentioned in most of the literature on the preserve. You'll have a very good chance of seeing them if you arrive early in the season before hikers have appeared in numbers.

If you're parked at the Stissing Mountain trailhead (FOSL trailhead) and want to leave your car there, walk 0.2 mile south along the road to the well-identified Thompson Pond trailhead, where there's also a small pull-off. Equip yourself with a bird guide and binoculars (you might also want trekking poles to safely ford the high water and slippery boardwalks) and set out along the preserve's yellow-blazed trail. This is a roadwide dirt path. Up to your right are the steep eastern slopes of Stissing. To the left is Thompson Pond. The

The boardwalks encircling Thompson Pond may be submerged in spring, so wear your boots.

forest is full of sweet birch here (a.k.a. black or cherry birch), identifiable by the thin, horizontal lines on its trunk. This aromatic tree is the traditional source of birch beer, fermented from its sap, and was the original source of wintergreen oil, which is now chemically manufactured. The buds and seeds of this tree provide browse for rabbits, deer, and ruffed grouse.

Soon you will arrive at a kiosk, with maps and information describing the details of this calcareous limestone wetland. What makes the preserve so unusual is its high biological diversity in a relatively small space of 507 acres: 387 species of plants, 162 of birds, and 20 of mammals. The exquisite, small, orchidlike milkwort called fringed polygala (a.k.a. gaywings) is also found here in the damp woods, blooming in late spring. You may also find pipewort, round-leaved sundew, Saint-John's-wort, and jack-in-the-pulpit. The forest cover includes hemlock, ash, hickory, maples, and some very large specimens of red oak.

Follow the yellow-blazed trail. Another trail (blue blazes) approaches the pond at this point and forms a loop around the main trail. Remain on the yellow-blazed trail, continuing south through pockets of hemlocks past a pair of stone commemorative benches. Follow along the pond's western fringes, passing a cornfield and descending to a swampy section of trail with a long boardwalk at the south end.

Turning north to cross the Wappingers' headwaters, you'll walk adjacent to a farm along several sections of boardwalk. Tread carefully on the slick surfaces of pressure-treated boards. This area is muddy and low. At a culvert where the ponds drain, you may see schools of good-sized smallmouth bass. A boardwalk crosses the outlet.

Views to the west reveal Stissing's fire tower. The trail rises above the pond now and remains dry. In the dense cattails, look for large, rust-colored king rails, a critically imperiled water-bird species in its northernmost habitat limits, which are now substantially farther north than the range mapped by naturalist and ornithologist Roger Tory Peterson in 1980.

Bear left at a Y and continue walking close to the pond. As you reach the trail's northern terminus, a stand of Norway spruce grows beside an open cornfield at the edge of a new housing development. As the desirability of scenic home sites increases, we should appreciate the efforts of FOSL and The Nature Conservancy that have led to the preservation of this remarkable place. Hunting, trapping, fishing, camping, bicycling, motorized vehicles, and fires are prohibited in the preserve, which is why it is still pristine. Cross-country skiing and canoeing are allowed.

Bear left as you reach the road and cross the outlet of Stissing Pond. The trail entrance appears to the left as you complete the loop.

DID YOU KNOW?

With 162 bird species, Thompson Pond is considered to be the best location for viewing water birds in the Hudson Valley region.

MORE INFORMATION

For more information, contact The Nature Conservancy's Eastern New York Chapter by visiting nature.org or calling 518-690-7878.

23

NORRIE POINT

This shoreline hike along the Hudson River is a great family outing, with a fine example of a Hudson River mansion and estate.

DIRECTIONS

Take Exit 19 from the NYS Thruway (I-87) at Kingston. Bear right out of the toll pavilion and set your trip odometer to zero. Cross over the thruway and bear right onto NY 209, heading north toward the Kingston–Rhinecliff Bridge. At 5.5 miles, cross the bridge (toll), and as you enter Dutchess County, NY 209 becomes NY 199. At 7.9 miles, turn right (south) at River Road (CR 103). Bear right at the fork you reach after 8.6 miles. At 11.2 miles, turn left onto Rhinecliff Road. At 12.4 miles, you're in the center of Rhinebeck. Re-set your trip odometer to zero here. Turn right onto NY 9G (south), and at 4.3 miles, turn right onto Staatsburg Road. At 5.3 miles, turn right into the Staatsburgh State Historic Site. Drive through the grounds. The mansion appears on your left. Take the first right into a shady parking area adjacent to the beautiful, old brick carriage houses that serve as the grounds' maintenance buildings. This is the designated parking area for hikers and sledders. (Sledding is popular on the long, sloping hillside in front of the house.) Take Gardener's House Lane from the southwest corner of the lot and head for the river between rows of elegant sugar maples. *GPS coordinates:* 41° 51.502' N, 73° 55.760' W.

TRAIL DESCRIPTION

What distinguishes this hike from others in the Hudson Valley is its proximity to the river. For more than 2.5 miles, you walk next to the water, enjoying far-reaching views. When you've finished the hike, you can look at the Mills Mansion ($8 admission fee) or sit on the open sweep of

LOCATION
Staatsburg, NY

RATING
Moderate

DISTANCE
5 miles

ELEVATION GAIN
200 feet

ESTIMATED TIME
3 hours

MAPS
USGS Hyde Park; Staatsburgh State Historic Site (Mills-Norrie State Park) Trail Map

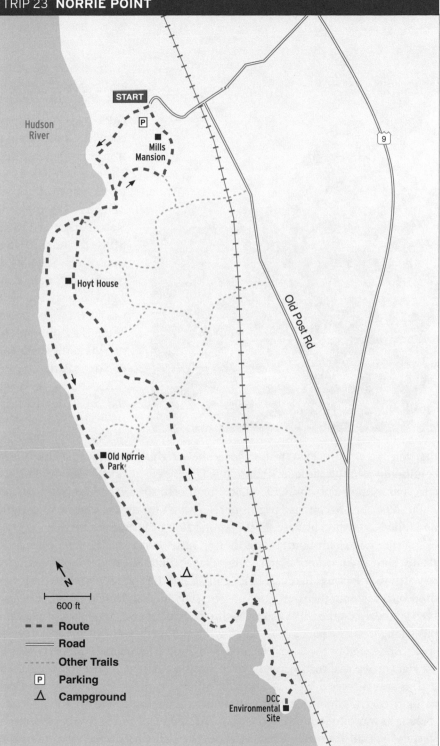

Hudson
River

START

Mills
Mansion

Hoyt House

Old Post Rd

9

Old Norrie
Park

N

600 ft

△

DCC
Environmental
Site

- - - Route

——— Road

- - - - - Other Trails

P **Parking**

△ **Campground**

An avian visitor alights on a nameless Greek goddess at the Mills Mansion.

lawn above the river and ponder the opulent lives of one of the Gilded Age's wealthiest couples, Ruth Livingston and Ogden Mills. The area consists of two parks joined together, Margaret Lewis Norrie State Park and Ogden Mills & Ruth Livingston Mills State Park, comprising more than 1,000 acres. You will walk through both. There is a campsite and marina at the south end of Norrie Park.

As you walk down the road toward the river, you'll pass a stone boathouse on the right that you can explore. Pass the boathouse, bear right, and follow the blue blazes, continuing past the gardener's house (the large, elegant brick homestead on the left), and soon you're at water level, looking north toward the Esopus Meadows Lighthouse. Just as the road begins to rise, watch for the trail kiosk, bear right, and follow the white blazes into the woods along the river's edge.

You will rise to Dinsmore Point as the trail turns south over the craggy hemlock-shaded path and provides several open vantage points. The trail is rooty and rocky, so watch your footing. Take care in icy conditions; there are spots where the ledges drop vertically into the river. Continue, passing an abandoned pump house, and keep your eyes on the white blazes, as they become sparse. You'll notice a few fire pits dating from the park's origins in the 1920s. Shortly you will arrive at a grassy spot with several picnic tables enclosed by old stone foundation ramparts. Stay to the right on a paved road along the river, passing a large gazebo with a fireplace in it. This area is accessible by car, and in season many people drive down for a look at the river. The white-blazed trail continues on the south side of this cul-de-sac, making its way into secluded woods again. At a point where the riverbank becomes steeper, the trail veers uphill and east, goes through a hardwood forest of mature oaks, and climbs gently above the river to the cabin camping area. Keep the cabins to your left and continue with the river on the right. Markers are scarce here for a short stretch.

At the rear of the last cabin, the white-blazed trail turns right, dropping downhill toward the park road. Cross a small wooden bridge and turn right at the road, leaving the Indian Kill to your left. Continue along the road (yellow blazes appear), very shortly passing the marina, and head to the Norrie Point environmental research station that you will see straight ahead. Consisting of an aquarium, a museum, and a field station belonging to Dutchess County Community College, the research station is open to the public (hours are posted). From the dock on the south side of the building, treat yourself to a rest and enjoy the far-reaching southerly views across the river—maybe even spotting harbor seals, which have been known to sun themselves off the northern tip of Esopus Island.

Return to the stone bridge and go north on the road beyond the white-blazed trail until you reach an intersection. Go left at the blue- and yellow-blazed trail junction, and in 50 feet, go right to follow the red blazes of the multiuse trail (also marked as a horse trail). Ascend gently through young sugar-maple woods and cross the park road, continuing on the red-blazed trail through secluded woods. At the next road, which leads to the river gazebo you passed earlier, turn left and very soon after go right (north) on the blue-blazed carriage path. The blue-blazed trail will take you past the Hoyt House and its reclaimed gardens, barn, and carriage house. This parcel of land on Dinsmore Point was given to the Mills's daughter, Geraldine, and her husband, Lydig Hoyt. The large cedars and runaway ornamental Norway spruce trees hint at what the place must have been like in the mid-1800s. To get a better idea, continue to the park road (Gardener's House Road) where you began, turn right, and, leaving the gardener's house to your right, follow the trail along the south side of the mansion grounds to the garden complex. To the north, a footpath crosses the lawn to the mansion, a gift shop, and offices, then leads back to your starting point.

DID YOU KNOW?

Darius Ogden Mills, Ogden Mills's father, found wealth in the California gold rush and became one of the richest men in the gold business. He bequeathed his fortune to his son Ogden, who married into the Livingston family. At one time, the Livingstons owned more than a million acres in the Hudson Valley.

MORE INFORMATION

Guided tours of the Staatsburgh State Historic Site are available April 1 to October 31, Thursday through Sunday (fee), and on weekends during the winter. There are extended hours during the holiday season; nysparks.com/historic-sites/25/details.aspx; 845-889-8851.

24

POETS' WALK ROMANTIC LANDSCAPE PARK

A fun family river walk among open fields and stone walls with rustic gazebos provides unforgettable views of the Catskills.

DIRECTIONS

Take Exit 19 off the NYS Thruway (I-87) at Kingston; bear right out of the toll pavilion and set your trip odometer to zero. Cross over the thruway and bear right onto NY 209, heading north toward the Kingston–Rhinecliff Bridge. At 5.5 miles, cross the bridge (toll), and as you enter Dutchess County, NY 209 becomes NY 199. From the center span of the bridge, you will see the Rondout Lighthouse a few miles to the south, on a small island off the western shore. To the north, along the east shore, are the marshes of Tivoli Bays. Closer to the bridge and just beneath you as you approach the east shore are the fields of the old Astor and Delano estates, the location of Poets' Walk. Take the first left off the bridge onto River Road, also known as CR 103. You're 7.8 miles from the thruway now; at 8.5 miles, turn left into the Poets' Walk parking area. *GPS coordinates:* 41° 58.902′ N, 73° 55.102′ W.

TRAIL DESCRIPTION

This scenic park, located within a few minutes' drive of Tivoli, Red Hook, and Rhinebeck villages, offers one of the prettiest, easiest walks in the valley. It is regarded by many as the crown jewel of the nonprofit Scenic Hudson's open-space preservation efforts. At just over 2 miles round-trip, the walk can be done in an easy hour by most. Plan to stay longer, if you can, to ponder what Scenic Hudson rightly calls the "breathtaking, unparalleled vistas" of the Hudson Valley and the Catskill Mountains. The park has proven very popular with locals who

LOCATION
Red Hook, NY

RATING
Easy

DISTANCE
2 miles

ELEVATION GAIN
200 feet

ESTIMATED TIME
1.5 hours

MAPS
USGS Kingston East; Scenic Hudson, Poets' Walk Romantic Landscape Park Map (available onsite and online)

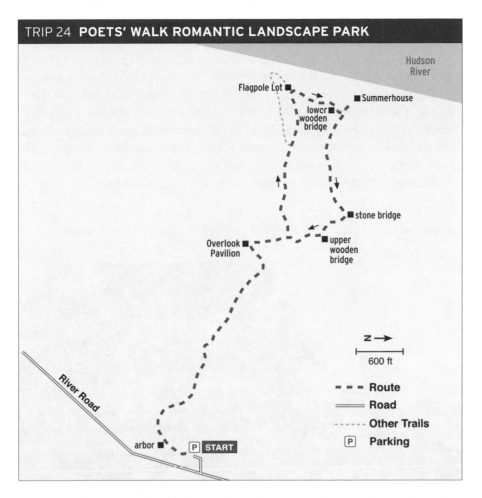

Hudson
River

Flagpole Lot ■

■ Summerhouse

lower
wooden
bridge

■ stone bridge

Overlook ■
Pavilion

■ upper
wooden
bridge

N →

600 ft

- - - **Route**

— **Road**

...... **Other Trails**

P **Parking**

arbor ■

P START

River Road

visit the grounds and its rustic pavilions to cavort, picnic, walk, write, paint, or simply relax and do nothing.

Orient yourself at the trailhead information kiosk, where you can help yourself to a trail map and a copy of "Scenic Hudson's Adventure Guide to Parks, Preserves, and Trails." Don't worry if the trail maps are gone; the trail is self-guiding and well posted. (You can also print out a map from Scenic Hudson's website ahead of time.) Take the path west, into open fields cloistered by mature hardwood forests.

The sunny fields of the park offer a warm western exposure. There are benches along the path as it winds in and out of the hardwoods over gentle terrain. The theme of the park—the Romantic "sublime," a notion that captured the imagination of the valley's early poets and writers—commemorates Washington Irving (1783–1859) and his friend/mentee, the Knickerbocker writer Fitz-Greene Halleck (1790–1867). The period takes its name from Irving's fictitious character Diedrich Knickerbocker, the sobriquet under which Irving penned *A History of New York* and "Rip Van Winkle." A satirist and a lesser-known poet, Halleck served as John Jacob Astor's personal secretary, a position that brought him to these grounds. It is unlikely Irving frequented this area.

At approximately 0.65 mile, you'll arrive at the Overlook pavilion, an elegant rustic gazebo and the focal point of the park. Here you can sit back and enjoy views of the Catskills' eastern escarpment. The long wall of ridges and peaks forming the northeast headlands reaches from Overlook Mountain (325 degrees) at the edge of the Indian Head Wilderness north past Kaaterskill High Peak and Round Top to North Mountain. You can see the Catskill High Peaks as well, from Peekamoose and Table mountains in the south all the way through the Burroughs Range, including Slide (284 degrees), Wittenberg, and Cornell

The cedar gazebos along the trails of Poets' Walk reflect a high degree of rustic craftmanship.

mountains. Countless other peaks and low hills invite your curiosity and stir your romantic imagination.

Continue along, you'll arrive at a signed trail junction. Go left (west, toward the river) and descend gently to the flagpole lot, where three rustic benches overlook the river. After a brief respite, proceed to the right and downhill, descending a flight of steps into the woods. Cross a tiny creek and ascend easily through a wooded glen, arriving at a T. Turn left to see the Summerhouse, a large cedar gazebo facing west. We can imagine artist Frederic Church having mixed feelings after learning that the cedar used in the structures at Poets' Walk came from Olana, his picturesque estate nearby. The trees in this wooded glen are junipers, or eastern red cedars. The Summerhouse is the most secluded spot along the trail. Retrace your steps to the T and ascend easily to the east, along the northern edge of the grounds, crossing a pretty stone bridge and another wooden one before arriving back at the trail junction below the Overlook Pavilion. From here, the trail retraces its steps to the parking area.

DID YOU KNOW?

In 1849, the Astors and Delanos commissioned a German-born landscape architect named Hans Jacob Ehlers to beautify their lands. Among his creations, Ehlers developed a small path he called Poet's Walk, in commemoration of Washington Irving and others who once walked in the area. It is rumored that Irving came up with the idea for the short story "Rip Van Winkle" (published 1819) as he gazed toward the Catskill Mountains. "When I wrote the story," Irving later admitted, "I had never been on the Catskills."

MORE INFORMATION

Dogs are allowed in the park, but you must leash and clean up after them. Closing time varies by season; scenichudson.org; 845-473-4440.

SCENIC HUDSON

Scenic Hudson is the grandparent of all Hudson River environmental watch-dog groups. The mission of this member-supported organization is to "protect and restore the Hudson River, its riverfront, and the majestic vistas and working landscapes beyond as an irreplaceable national treasure for America and a vital resource for residents and visitors." Scenic Hudson was formed in 1963 to oppose the electric company Consolidated Edison's Storm King pumped-storage project, which would have been the world's largest hydroelectric plant. The organization was successful and has since added to the inventory of publicly protected open space in the valley through an aggressive acquisition policy. Scenic Hudson's precedent-setting battle against Con Edison continues to serve as a model and cornerstone for federal environmental law.

Through a separately incorporated land trust and a sizable endowment, Scenic Hudson acquires and protects lands, in many cases creating easements and marked trails that provide public access to scenic properties adjacent to the Hudson River. Scenic Hudson also partnered with other organizations and townships to pioneer the creation of the Hudson River Valley Greenway. Many of the parks and preserves described or referenced in this book were created by, funded by, or formed in partnership with Scenic Hudson. Additionally, the organization spearheaded the campaign that led to the Hudson Valley being designated a National Heritage Area by the National Park Service (1996) and the Hudson River being named a National Heritage River (1998). These designations provide the Hudson Valley with a wider range of protection and more funding on a national level.

In addition to ongoing local advocacy, as well as community development and improvement programs, Scenic Hudson promotes its smart-growth principles in the river towns of Yonkers, Haverstraw, Hyde Park, and Beacon. Scenic Hudson is also active at the state level, promoting energy plans and environmentally friendly technologies for power plants.

25

TEATOWN LAKE RESERVATION

Ideal for families with young children as well as seasoned hikers looking for easy-to-moderate terrain, the Teatown Lake Reservation is a 1,000-acre preserve that includes the 41-acre Teatown Lake, the 7-acre Shadow Lake, and the 9-acre Vernay Lake, with streams, waterfalls, hardwood swamps, mixed forests, and meadows.

DIRECTIONS

To Lakeside and Twin Lakes Trails

Follow the Taconic Parkway north and exit at Route 134/Ossining. Turn left onto Route 134. Drive for approximately 0.25 mile and turn right onto Spring Valley Road. Drive for about 1 mile and bear left at the fork/Teatown sign. The nature center will be on your right over the crest of the hill. The main parking lot is on your right immediately after the nature center. This parking lot is for access to the Lakeside Trail and the Twin Lakes Trail. *GPS coordinates:* 41°12.660′ N, 73°49.620′ W.

To Cliffdale Farm/Catamount Hill Trail

From the nature center, bear right out of the main parking lot onto Spring Valley Road and go 0.5 mile to Teatown Road. Bear right onto Teatown Road and go another 0.9 mile to the trailhead parking area on the right side of the road. Here a trail kiosk displays a map of your route. *GPS coordinates:* 41°12.360′ N, 73°51.060′ W.

TRAIL DESCRIPTION

Lakeside Trail

From the bottom right side of the main parking area, immediately adjacent to the nature center (facing Teatown Lake), follow the blue-blazed trail, leaving the rustic sugarhouse to the right. Descend slightly to the lake's

LOCATION
Ossining, NY

LAKESIDE TRAIL:
RATING
Easy
DISTANCE
1.5 miles
ELEVATION GAIN
187 feet
ESTIMATED TIME
45 minutes

TWIN LAKES TRAIL:
RATING
Moderate
DISTANCE
2.3 miles
ELEVATION GAIN
450 feet
ESTIMATED TIME
1 hour 30 minutes

CLIFFDALE FARM/
CATAMOUNT HILL TRAIL:
RATING
Moderate
DISTANCE
2.25 miles
ELEVATION GAIN
480 feet
ESTIMATED TIME
1 hour 30 minutes

MAPS
NY-NJTC Trail Map Teatown-Kitchawan Trail; Teatown map available at trailhead

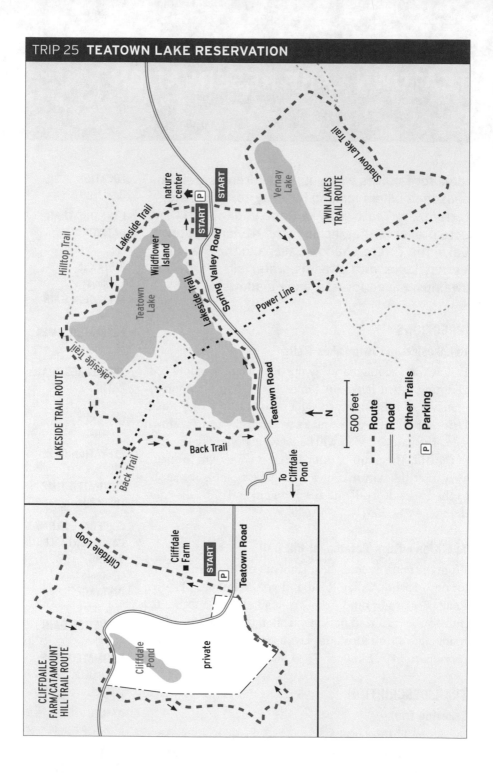

eastern shore. At the junction, go straight, following blue blazes. Interpretive signs and maps detailing tree species, watersheds, and other subjects appear along the trail. Several trails leave from Lakeside Trail, but your route for this loop hike follows close to the lake itself.

Continue along the blue-blazed trail with the lake immediately to your left and pass the boathouse, which can be used for picnics and events or for just taking a break. Beyond the boathouse, the trail splits briefly. You can go either way, but bearing left at this point will take you along the shore, which is the more scenic choice. Continue to the north end of the lake and bear left, crossing the outflow of Teatown Lake, which forms the headwaters of Bailey Brook and feeds the New Croton Reservoir, part of the New York City public water supply. The 33-acre lake was created in 1924 when the area of the Swope farmstead known as "Big Meadow" was flooded. The lands were originally acquired by then General Electric president Gerard Swope Sr., who expanded the property into a country estate, where he lived until his death in 1957. His heirs donated the bulk of the estate in 1963, including the farm complex at Cliffdale, to create the Teatown Lake Reservation.

Continue on Lakeside Trail, passing a hand-laid stone wall in a sugar-maple woods. The hardware cloth, or wire mesh, around the base of the trees protects them from damage by beavers. Avoid Lakeside Shortcut Trail to the right and hike along the shore of the lake. Pass beneath the power lines, which, though unsightly, are important for maintaining extensive shrub habitat, an understory that thrives following the removal of trees. This woody plant and bush cover contributes to species diversification by providing habitat for wildlife that is not common to the bulk of Teatown's woodlands. The artificially created ecosystem acts to balance the effects of deer, the high numbers of which are contributing to the shortage of flowering plants for birds, butterflies, and insects—all important pollinators for sustained plant regeneration.

You'll come to a stand of large conifers; these are Norway spruce. A native of Europe, this variety is the largest, most widespread, fastest-growing, and most disease-resistant spruce in the northern hemisphere. This tree does not thrive in warm environments and grows best in areas where there are at least 25 inches of annual rainfall. Norway spruce reach more than 100 feet in height and live in excess of 100 years.

As you hike uphill away from the water's edge, you'll pass Northwest Trail and Briarcliff-Peekskill Trailway on the right. Continue ahead and, just before reaching Teatown Road, you'll bear left onto the beautiful Bergmann Boardwalk and follow it across the western arm of the lake. From here you'll walk through the woods again, continuing along Lakeside Trail. Soon you will arrive at Wildflower Island, which you can explore in season. Twenty-five years in the making, the island is a unique conservation garden and home to more than 230 species of wildflowers. A 90-foot-long wooden bridge connects the island to the mainland. The island is accessible only by guided tours from April through September, and reservations are required. A bloom list is available online. At 1.5 miles, you are back at the nature center. If you're in the mood for more mileage, walk across Spring Valley road to Twin Lake Trail and follow the next trail description.

Twin Lakes Trail

Vernay Lake is named after Arthur Stannard Vernay (1877–1960), a well-to-do dealer of English antiquities and the original owner of Teatown. Vernay built the elegant Tudor-style manor house (the Croft), which you'll see adjacent to the trail on the left. Not long after completing the Croft, Vernay sold it to Daniel R. Hanna, a Cleveland newspaper and iron magnate who built the stable that houses Teatown's administrative offices and nature center. Teatown bought the property in 2010 along with its 67 acres of woodland. Today, the reservation is 1,000 acres, with 15 miles of trails.

From the parking area across the street from the nature center, walk 100 feet or so to the trailhead kiosk. There's a small pond on your right, and maps are available here. Follow the orange-blazed Twin Lakes Trail 0.1 mile to the shore of Vernay Lake and turn left (northeast). Follow the trail next to the lake for a while. At 0.3 mile, at the north end of the lake, the trail winds into the southeast, climbing easily through a maturing hardwood forest. The trail switches back gently and rises into an area where beech and oak trees grow quite large.

You'll also see maturing tulip trees, with their huge trunks and high canopies. Considered the largest of the northeastern trees, these deciduous giants can grow to 165 feet. Although they go by the common name of yellow poplar, they are actually *Magnoliaceae*, members of the magnolia family. They belong to the genus *Liriodendron*, whose Latin translation means "lily tree." Their very distinct flowers resemble tulips. Also called canoewood, the lumber is used for furniture and resembles poplar with its green and yellow hues.

The trail continues to rise, never strenuously, and tops out on a fairly flat ridge passing a vernal pond and, beyond it, Shadow Lake at 0.6 mile. The trail winds away from the lake and heads south. Descending slightly, it crosses a power line and drops downhill. Follow the trail easily downhill for some time, turn northeast, and walk next to Vernay Lake again before bearing left. Markers are consistent and the trail is self-guiding. At 2.3 miles, you'll arrive back at the trailhead and nature center.

Cliffdale Farm/Catamount Hill Trail

The trailside structure visible from the Cliffdale trailhead is no longer used as a barn but is instead Teatown Reservation's education center. The center provides environmental education to more than 12,000 schoolchildren annually, with programming designed to instill a "love for the environment, positive attitudes towards conservation, and a sense of personal and civic responsibility."

Walk to the right of the red education center and you'll see orange blazes. Take Cliffdale Loop Trail—not Cliffdale Teatown Trail Loop. This is an old settlement area, with second-growth hardwoods along the road. In an old pasture, make a 90-degree turn left. The signage is good. At the end of the pasture, the trail goes through a rock wall and back into the woods, where there are some very large oak and hickory trees. The trail drops downhill to the left and heads south. Go through a gate and at 0.75 mile, turn right on the road. Cliffdale Pond is to your left. Pick up the trail on the other side of the road. This is an old woods road, which you reach through a gate. Throughout the reservation in winter, you will likely see evidence that you've been sharing the trail with deer, as well as coyotes, which have a den in this area. (See trailhead posting for more information.)

The trail is easy underfoot. Drop downhill and cross a small footbridge. The trail is well marked, but in some areas is not entirely self-guiding. Watch for blazes, as there are several side trails and old roads. The trail crosses a brook and rises somewhat steeply. Switch back uphill and cross an open field. You'll come up to a T at 1.5 miles; go right on blue-blazed Catamount Hill Trail, avoiding the shortcut trail. Catamount Hill Trail is wide and flat, with some climbing involved as you ascend Catamount Hill heading northeast. Pass the shortcut

A blue heron fishes in the thick lily pads of Teatown Lake.

trail again on your left and come down to the road for a total distance of 2.25 miles. Cross the road to the trailhead.

DID YOU KNOW?

The name Teatown dates to 1776, when tea was scarce due to British taxation. A man by the name of John Arthur moved to the northern Westchester area and brought with him a hoarded chest full of tea, with thoughts of selling it at huge profit. A group of women called the Daughters of Eve found out about the tea and demanded Arthur sell it at a reasonable fee. After he refused, the women laid siege to the farmhouse. Arthur finally agreed to sell the tea at a fair price in exchange for the women's peaceful withdrawal. Hence, the area became known as "Teatown." The original owner of Teatown, Arthur Stannard Vernay, sold his wares and services to members of the Vanderbilt, Altman, and Guggenheim families, as well as to Tiffany Studios. A big-game hunter, he both financed and participated in the collections expedition for what became the Museum of Natural History's Vernay-Faunthorpe Hall of South Asiatic Mammals (established 1930). He later moved to Nassau, Bahamas, where he cofounded the Bahamas National Trust, joining an expatriate community that included the Duke and Duchess of Windsor. The rodent genus *Vernaya* was named after Vernay.

MORE INFORMATION

Teatown Lake Reservation: 1600 Spring Valley Road, Ossining, NY, 10562; 914-762-2912.

Nature Center hours: Daily 9 A.M. to 5 P.M. Trails: Open dawn to dusk, 365 days; info@teatown.org; teatown.org.

26

ROOSEVELT WOODS

A shore-and-forest walk on easy carriage roads begins at the museum, library, and home of Franklin D. Roosevelt and leads to points along the Hudson River.

DIRECTIONS

The Home of Franklin D. Roosevelt National Historic Site is located on the west side of US 9 in Hyde Park. Drive into the main entrance on FDR Drive, heading straight back to the visitor parking area, past the National Park Service (NPS) headquarters. *GPS coordinates:* 41° 46.223′ N, 73° 56.077′ W.

By bus, take Coach USA from Port Authority to the FDR Home (call 201-263-1254).

TRAIL DESCRIPTION

The beautiful trails of Roosevelt Woods, lying within the heavily wooded estate of the Franklin D. Roosevelt home, library, and museum complex, are patrolled and maintained by the NPS. On this hike, you are introduced to each loop in the woods (Cove, Forest, and Meadow trails), with a short side trip to Crum Elbow Point on the Hudson River's banks.

These trails are unlike many of the foot trails you may be familiar with in the valley; they are wide, well marked, and immaculately maintained "carriageways." Today they are footpaths only; bicycles are not allowed. Because the elevation change is minimal and the trails are generally flat and wide, this is a walker's paradise, leading you through parklike woods in a peaceful, wild setting with views of the Hudson River. These paths are ideal for children and seniors. The Roosevelt Woods trail system is a part of Hyde Park Trail (HP), a cooperative effort of several organizations, including NPS, the town of Hyde Park, Scenic Hudson, the Winnakee Land Trust, and multiple private

LOCATION
Hyde Park, NY

RATING
Moderate

DISTANCE
5 miles

ELEVATION GAIN
200 feet

ESTIMATED TIME
2.5 hours

MAPS
USGS Hyde Park; National Park Service, Hyde Park Trail

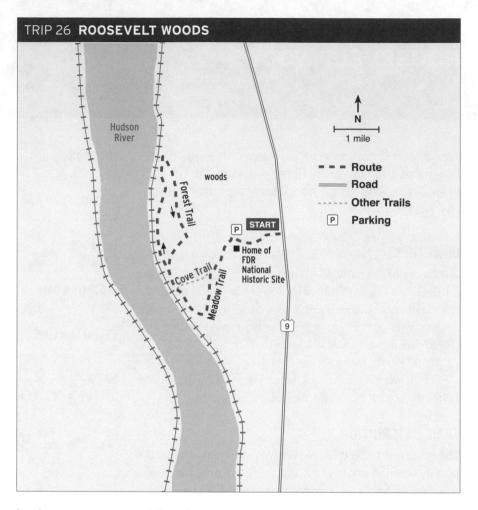

landowners. It is a model trail system under continued development with the help of the Hudson River Greenway.

Before heading into the woods, request an HP trail map at the visitor center. Curiously, the map provided by NPS is far from ideal for trail navigation, but it does provide a helpful overview of the area. Trails are accurately designated and well marked, however, so there's little chance of getting lost or even disoriented. HP is a long, linear trail that is still being developed. You will be walking only a short section of it here.

Begin your hike on the paved walkway to the south of the visitor center that runs next to the museum—a long, fortresslike, hand-laid stone building. A small sign near a cluster of Norway spruce indicates HP to your right. From here you are guided a short distance to the trailhead, where there's a signboard and a map with information. Follow the paved path downhill. Where it turns to dirt you'll follow Meadow Trail south; HP, Cove, and Forest trails go straight ahead.

Immediately you will note the fine, mature forests of red oak, hemlock, poplar, hickory, and sycamore, most of them planted and managed by Roosevelt and his father, who imported many varieties from Europe, making the grounds a matter of national interest when he later formed the Civilian Conservation Corps (CCC). Many of the regional plantations we enjoy today, as well as the trails that run through them (such as those of the Catskills), were CCC projects. You'll pass a pond and a seasonal waterfall to your right as you descend through a shady glen.

Bear right at the first trail junction, where Cove Trail goes left (south). Now you're on Forest Trail. HP goes north, beyond the NPS boundary, to the Vanderbilt Mansion (signed at 2.4 miles from this junction), but that is a trip for another day. Unfortunately, HP follows paved roads for some distance once it leaves these woods, which you may not find appealing. Continue nevertheless, passing the return loop of Forest Trail on your right. (You'll emerge from that trail later.) Within fifteen minutes or so, you will arrive at a junction where Forest Trail departs to the right. Bear left here, remaining on HP. This is the NPS boundary. Within a few hundred yards, bear left again. This will take you across the Metro-North train tracks via a trestle bridge, directly to the river's edge at Crum Elbow Point. There's a large, bright navigation day marker here to help ships make their

Franklin D. Roosevelt's birthplace, lifelong home, and now a National Historic Site, Springwood (below), sits on the same grounds as his Presidential Library and Museum.

way up the channel. You'll have close-up views of tankers and tug barges, most of them carrying oil to the Port of Albany. This is a fine spot to sit on the grassy point and while away the day. Aside from the estate grounds, it's also the best place to have a picnic.

Retrace your steps to the junction of HP and Forest Trail. Follow left onto the latter as you curve north and east, along the park boundary. Following a knoll of red pines on the north side of the trail, bear right once again onto Forest Trail, walking amid stately hemlocks and very tall white pines, then join HP and bear left. Walk back to the Cove Trail junction and follow Cove (and Meadow) Trail to the right (south). Meadow Trail continues south, and Cove Trail goes west (right). This 0.2-mile spur trail takes you along the fringes of a pretty, tidal cattail marsh and dead-ends at the railroad tracks. The large building you see on a hill to the south is the Culinary Institute of America. More interesting yet are the bright yellow blooms of marsh marigold you see everywhere in early spring, their flowers submerged by the incoming tide.

Now retrace your steps to Meadow Trail, bear right, cross the stream via a wooden bridge, and enter a hemlock wood. The trail turns east then north along the edge of a broad meadow where Springwood, the Roosevelt family estate, comes into view. You are soon back at the first junction, where you turn right toward the trailhead and estate grounds. Take a few moments to appreciate Springwood and the magnificent, soft hues of the Hudson's hills, and walk through the rose garden and the Roosevelt gravesite. Treat yourself to a look at the sculpture of two figures, cut from the thick concrete of the Berlin Wall and fashioned into art by Winston Churchill's great-granddaughter, Edwina Sandys. Follow your way back through the grounds to the parking area to complete the walk.

DID YOU KNOW?

One of the most popular programs of the New Deal was the Civilian Conservation Corps (CCC), Roosevelt's personal favorite. The program employed more than 250,000 young men nationwide; see page 152.

MORE INFORMATION

You can enter the grounds and visitor center year-round, free of charge; there's a fee, however, for the museum, library, and house tours. Dogs must be leashed at all times. For more information, visit hydeparkny.us/Recreation/Trails/TrailsRooseveltWoods.html or nps.gov/hofr.

THE TACONICS

The Nature Conservancy has named the South Taconic Range of New York, Connecticut, and Massachusetts one of Earth's "Last Great Places" because it is among the largest and healthiest contiguous forests in the Lower New England Ecoregion (Maine to Virginia). It is also considered one of the most diverse forests in southern New England, supporting rare natural communities such as the scrub oak and pitch-pine woods found on cliff and talus slopes, as well as the rare species that inhabit them, such as Gerhard's underwing moth and the purple clematis. Both the North and South Taconic ranges are heavily forested with northern hardwood species and dense hemlock woods in wet ravines.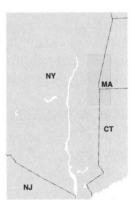

The Taconics get their name from the ancient continental collision known as the Taconic orogeny, or mountain-building process. Formed near the location of today's Costa Rica, the Taconic Island chain moved northward to collide with Proto North America about 470 million years ago. This event marked the beginning of a mountain-building episode that lasted for 35 million years and stretched from the Canadian Maritime provinces to North Carolina. (The Taconic orogeny was distinct from the east- and north-advancing Acadian orogeny that created the Northern Appalachian Mountains.) At the time, the Iapetus Ocean covered most of North America. Achieving an elevation of about 4 miles, the Taconics were eroded during the Mesozoic and Cenozoic eras, and in the Quaternary Period, the mile-high glaciers of the Great Ice Age finished the billion-year process by sculpting the Taconic landscape we see today. These two distinct ranges define the Taconic Mountains from Williamstown, Massachusetts, to the borders of New York and Connecticut.

Protection of the Taconics began around 1920 with the acquisition of lands that eventually became Taconic State Park on the New York side of the range, the Mount Washington State Forest and Bash Bish Falls State Park in Massachusetts, and the Mount Riga State Park in Connecticut.

The Southern Taconics is a 36,000-acre mountain range that is bounded in the north by Hillsdale, New York, and South Egremont, Massachusetts, and in the south by Millerton, New York, and Lakeville, Connecticut. The plateau's highest peak is Mount Everett (2,602 feet), and the average elevation of the ridge is 2,000 feet above the surrounding valley, or 2,700 feet above sea level. Two major trails cross the Southern Taconic Plateau. The Appalachian Trail enters the ridge in the south, at Salisbury, Connecticut, and follows the ridge's eastern edge along the Housatonic watershed, crossing Bear Mountain, Mount Race, and Mount Everett before leaving the range in Egremont. On the west side of the range is South Taconic Trail (ST), a 15-mile scenic ridge trail with its southern trailhead in the town of Northeast, New York. ST traverses South Brace Mountain, Brace Mountain (passing west of Mount Frissell and the highest point in Connecticut), Alander Mountain, and Bash Bish Falls before descending to Taconic State Park and continuing north to Mount Fray and the town of Hillsdale. Several trails join the ridge from the east and west sides, providing a number of access options.

MORE INFORMATION

For more information about the Southern Taconics, contact the following organizations:

- Taconic Hiking Club, taconichikingclub.org
- Berkshire Natural Resources Council (South Taconic Range and Greylock maps), 20 Bank Row, Pittsfield, MA, 01201; 413-499-0596; bnrc.net.
- New York State Office of Parks, Recreation and Historic Preservation/Taconic Region, P.O. Box 308, Staatsburg, NY, 12580; 845-889-4100; nysparks.state .ny.us.

For inquiries about Northwest Camp, contact the Appalachian Mountain Club, Connecticut Chapter, ct-amc.org.

27

BRACE MOUNTAIN

A short, very steep climb followed by a ridge walk across the scenic Southern Taconic Plateau yields valley and mountain views.

DIRECTIONS

From Millerton, New York, follow NY 22 for 5.4 miles to Whitehouse Crossing Road and turn right. At 6.1 miles, turn left onto CR 63. At just under 0.2 mile, turn right onto Deer Run Road, then left onto Quarry Hill Road. Go an additional 0.5 mile and look for the small (obscure) trail-head parking area on the left. A sign identifies the Taconic State Park Brace Mountain Area. *GPS coordinates: 42° 1.940′ N, 73° 30.286′ W.*

TRAIL DESCRIPTION

Brace Mountain (2,311 feet) and its sister peak, South Brace (2,304 feet), are the southernmost trailed peaks in Taconic State Park. This is the tristate highlands area of New York, Massachusetts, and Connecticut (nearby Mount Frissell, at 2,453 feet, is Connecticut's highest point), the watershed divide of the Hudson and Housatonic rivers. Climb Brace on a very clear day, when the exceptional views include points from Mount Greylock and northwest through the Helderbergs and the Catskills, south along the Shawangunks, and as far away as the Hudson Highlands.

Like most of the western approaches to the Taconic Plateau, South Taconic Trail (ST) is steep, and because of its rocks and ledges, this trail is not recommended under icy conditions. Though steep, the climb is short, and you'll reach ridge elevation of 1,800 feet from the trailhead elevation of 1,000 feet in about one hour.

Begin hiking along an open field, following the white-blazed trail. These blazes (and ridge cairns) may be the only trail identification you'll see. Signage, typically sparse in the Southern Taconics, is scarce here. The climb

LOCATION
Ancram, NY

RATING
Moderate

DISTANCE
3.8 miles

ELEVATION GAIN
1,300 feet

ESTIMATED TIME
4 hours

MAPS
USGS Copake; Mount Washington State Forest Trail Map, mass.gov/eea/docs/dcr/parks/trails/mwashington.pdf; NY-NJTC South Taconic Trails

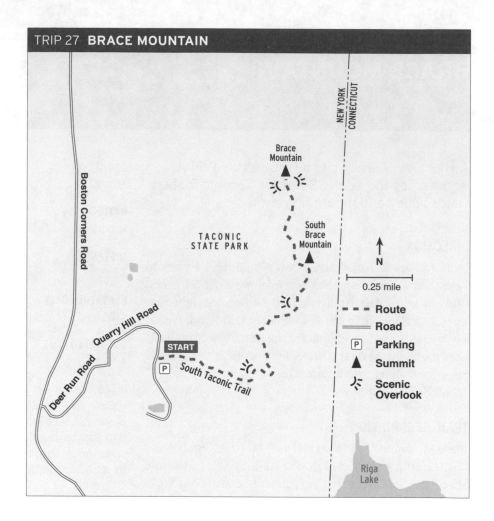

NEW YORK
CONNECTICUT

Brace
Mountain

South
Brace
Mountain

TACONIC
STATE PARK

N

0.25 mile

- - - Route
—— Road
P Parking
▲ Summit
⅄ Scenic
   Overlook

Boston Corners Road

Quarry Hill Road

Deer Run Road

START

South Taconic Trail

Riga
Lake

The southeast lowlands present a panoramic view of Brace Mountain's long, flat summit.

is gentle until, at 1,200 feet in elevation, a shallow gorge appears to the right. Now the trail climbs steeply through magnificent red-oak woods, following the scoured and exposed boulders of this once much larger stream course. As the trail steepens, you'll encounter a high-angled cascade of about 60 feet. Now the trail veers north, away from the falls, and requires an all-fours approach for the next ten minutes as you vault your way upward through ledges with increasing views west and southwest. The trail relaxes at 1,700 feet, and arrives at a flat spot on the ridge, where you turn left. This was the junction with the red-blazed trail to the high ledges of New Point, which you can see just to the south, but the blazes have disappeared and the trail has vanished. You can still follow the vague footpath to the right a little way to take a look at a fairy glen, where tiny falls create a clear pool beneath a small, thick hemlock stand. Hunters have left fire rings and evidence of makeshift bivouacs here.

ST heads north now and is well-marked with white blazes. You face some additional climbing, but it is spread out as the trail continues level for a while along the western ridge, then climbs through oak woods and scattered laurels. Soon you will cross a small, grassy slab with sweeping views south over Riga Lake and South Pond. Climb a bit farther and you'll arrive on South Brace, its summit identified by a cairn. Here, your views to the west develop into a wider panorama of the Hudson Valley, and you begin to see more in the east as well, including Mount Frissell, Round Mountain, Gridley Mountain, and Bear Mountain. On the other side of that ridge, the Appalachian Trail corridor runs up over Lions Head and Bear Mountain, and through Sages Ravine to cross Mount Everett. From here, you can see the burnished open balds of Brace. As the trail makes its way north again around the scenic, windy western side of South Brace, it dips down into a sheltered saddle, then climbs gradually up the south slopes of Brace. The summit is identified by a more impressive rock pile than on South Brace. This broad, open, grassy summit looks directly at Mount Frissell and nearby Alander Mountain to the north, in Massachusetts. Hidden behind Mount Frissell is Mount Everett, but lying in the northeast like an inverted molar is the unmistakable Mount Greylock (Massachusetts' highest peak at 3,491 feet), pale

gray in the haze, with Mount Prospect forming the left part of the tooth. The viewshed is spectacular and complex, and to fully identify surrounding mountain ranges and river valleys, you will need USGS metric topographical maps in the 1:100,000 scale. The westerly Catskills skyline is the most comprehensive, including most of the prominent peaks from the Blackhead range to the southern Sundown Wild Forest area. A dizzying complex of mountains and unnamed peaks dissolves across Berkshire County in the direction of Great Barrington and Lee and away to the north-northeast. The north-northwest flatlands rise imperceptibly to the low Helderbergs, and to the east across Litchfield County, you can see Housatonic State Forest and the bumpy hills of Canaan. No matter which point of the compass you face, you will enjoy extensive open space.

At one time, this hike could have been fashioned into a loop using the blue-blazed trail to Riga Lake and an informal trail back to ST; however, private lands to the west prevent this. Several of the maps still in use for this area are no longer accurate, so be careful. For example, note that the blue-blazed trail from South Beacon to Riga Lake has been erased, covered with tree paint and posted by the Mount Riga Corporation. Return the way you came.

DID YOU KNOW?

Charcoal makers who supplied the iron furnaces and manufacturing needs of the Revolutionary War effort denuded the countryside around Mount Riga. The Riga blast furnace, the last such furnace in Connecticut, stands at the southeast corner of South Pond, north of Mount Riga. It supplied raw product for the ironworks in nearby Lakeville, Connecticut, which were partly owned by the Revolutionary War leader Ethan Allen. When large steelmakers began to use bituminous coal for smelting ore, the charcoal industry disappeared, and the Southern Taconics began their slow process of reforestation.

MORE INFORMATION

To get a good feel for the spectacular Southern Taconic Range, take a drive north along Mount Riga Road from Salisbury, Connecticut, to Mount Washington Road and the Mount Washington State Forest area, where you can camp for free, although you have to hike in. (The headquarters has relocated, but the area is maintained by the state. You can get maps here at the kiosk north of the maintenance building.) The Connecticut Chapter of the Appalachian Mountain Club maintains a rustic camp (Northwest Camp) on its property just west of the Appalachian Trail on the Massachusetts–Connecticut line, making for an ideal alternate staging point for climbing Brace from the east. For more information on Taconic State Park, call 518-329-3993 or visit nysparks.state.ny.us/parks/83/details.aspx.

APPALACHIAN TRAIL

Conceived in 1921 and completed in 1937, the Appalachian Trail (AT) is a 2,190-mile, National Park Service-protected trail corridor stretching from Springer Mountain in Georgia to Maine's Katahdin, passing through fourteen states.

The first section of the AT was built in Bear Mountain State Park in an effort led by Major William A. Welch, the general manager of the Palisades Interstate Park from 1912 to 1940. (Hikers to Bear Mountain follow Major Welch Trail.) He was the first chairman of the Appalachian Trail Conference and designed the AT logo. Although present-day hikers will see few if any of the original logos marking the trail, the AT is marked with its standard rectangular white paint blazes.

Day hikers bound for Bear Mountain and Anthony's Nose will use sections of the AT and stand a good chance of meeting a thru-hiker, who will have walked nearly 1,400 miles to reach Bear Mountain. The trail is most often hiked from south to north, beginning in April and taking about six months to complete. Using the south-to-north approach, a hiker who begins in Georgia amid freezing temperatures and snow will be walking toward spring. The Appalachian Trail Conservancy (ATC) oversees and promotes the trail with the help of its corporate and nonprofit partner groups. To date the ATC has 31 affiliated trail maintenance clubs, including the Appalachian Mountain Club. Visit the ATC website at appalachiantrail.org.

28

ALANDER MOUNTAIN

A gradual climb to the central Taconic Ridge combines views east over the Hudson Valley and the Catskills with free camping.

DIRECTIONS

From the hamlet of Copake Falls, east off NY 22 (13 miles north of Millerton and 20.5 miles south of Exit B3 off I-90), set your trip odometer to zero. Take NY 344 east 0.3 mile to Taconic State Park and continue uphill past Bash Bish Falls, into Massachusetts. At 3.2 miles, bear right onto West Street. Turn right onto Cross Road at 4.3 miles and follow to its end on East Street at 5.3 miles. Bear right and go 0.2 mile to Mount Washington State Forest headquarters. Turn right into the entrance and park next to the maintenance building at the trailhead. *GPS coordinates: 42° 05.181′ N, 73° 27.726′ W.*

TRAIL DESCRIPTION

Alander Mountain forms the watershed divide between the Hudson and Housatonic rivers, along the high scenic borderlands of Massachusetts and New York. Although it may not seem a formidable peak at 2,250 feet, its position in the Taconic Range allows for generous views westward, giving it the look and feel of a much bigger mountain. Be aware that the open balds and rocky, unprotected ridge trails are subject to rapid changes in the weather. This increased exposure should be considered as carefully here as in any upper-elevation setting. Be prepared with water, food, warm clothes, and rain gear.

The Taconic Ridge is very popular with backpackers, among them hiking groups from the Appalachian Mountain Club (AMC), many of whom begin at the Mount Washington State Forest trailhead. There are several reasons for approaching Alander Mountain (or any point on the ridge) from the east, in Massachusetts.

LOCATION
Mount Washington, MA

RATING
Moderate

DISTANCE
8 miles

ELEVATION GAIN
600 feet

ESTIMATED TIME
6 hours

MAPS
USGS Copake; Mount Washington State Forest Trail Map, mass.gov/eea/docs/dcr/parks/trails/mwashington.pdf; NY-NJTC South Taconic Trails

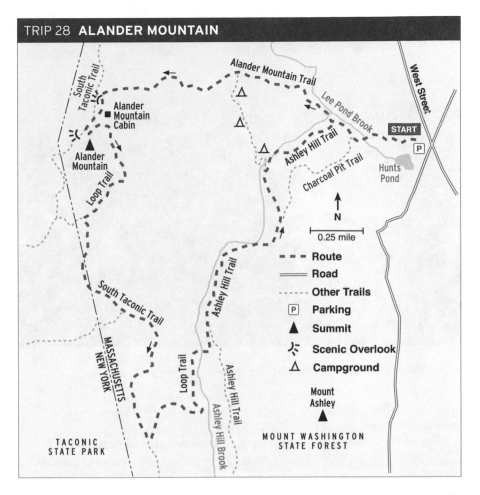

First, you get to choose from several trailheads, all of them beginning at considerably higher elevations than the single western trailhead in New York State, off Mountain Road (750 feet). In contrast, the Alander Mountain trailhead, in Massachusetts' Mount Washington State Forest, begins from the middle of the Taconic Ridge at 1,700 feet, so right away you've saved considerable climbing. The time you would have spent ascending is time you can spend on the ridge. Consider the other advantages: Camping (hike-in) is permitted free of charge in Mount Washington State Forest. You can plan a side trip after your overnight to the Sage's Ravine primitive camp on the Appalachian Trail or take a quick walk up to Guilder Pond in the Mount Everett State Reservation. And you can drive the fascinating, lonely back roads of the Mount Riga area—as wild as it gets in the tristate area of New York, Massachusetts, and Connecticut. But the best part is that with some planning and preparation you can stage from the rustic Northwest Camp of AMC's Connecticut Chapter off East Street, 2.3 miles south of the trailhead. Seldom will you see a cabin as appealing as this one. (There is also a cabin near Alander's summit that is open all year and is

Alander Mountain delivers sweeping views of the northeast Catskills.

available to hikers on a first-come, first-served basis. It has sleeping platforms that comfortably hold six hikers, plus a woodstove.)

Begin at the state forest headquarters. The trail departs just north of the maintenance buildings. There's a kiosk with handout maps, but they are not reliable for way-finding or navigation. Head west into open bluet fields, threading your way in and out of the woods on the blue-blazed Alander Mountain Trail. The trail is well defined and frequently traveled. Marking is good. Pass Charcoal Pit Trail and then Ashley Hill Trail on your left as you walk in proximity to enchanting Ashley Hill Brook. Cross the brook at an idyllic spot on a hand-hewn stringer bridge, and climb easily into a patch of hemlock trees where a sign indicates the primitive camping area at 0.5 mile. The trail assumes the character of a garden path as it passes a blue-blazed connector trail leading to the primitive camping area. Continue straight ahead, remaining on Alander Mountain Trail. Spring-blooming wildflowers appear in profusion: common blue violets, downy yellow violets, and, notably, the critically imperiled, Audubon Blue-Listed (the early warning list for population- or range-reduced North American species) milkwort known as fringed polygala, or gaywings. Its little orchidlike purple bloom looks like a tiny airplane, complete with propeller.

Climbing to a point next to a small brook, you may notice a tin strip on a tree, perforated with the statement, "Last Water In Dry Period." The trail turns hard right (watch for the blue blazes) and climbs more steadily now. At the appearance of the cabin, remaining from the days when Alander had a fire tower, you arrive in a shallow saddle cleaving Alander's ridge.

Continue to follow the blue blazes to the four-way intersection with the white-blazed South Taconic Trail (ST), which goes west. Don't take it, but instead bear left onto the blue-blazed Alander Loop Trail and cross the true summit and the subsequent open ridge rock of Alander. Views to the west are far-reaching, including the Catskills from north to south, Stissing Mountain, the Hudson Valley lowlands, and points southwest. Variations of this view continue as you make your way south in a setting not unlike the Scottish Highlands.

Dropping down off the ridge into a col, the trail makes a sharp right turn, descending briefly west before turning south again below the ridge to join the white-blazed ST. Bear left onto ST at a place identified by a weathered, unofficial sign for Gentz's Corner and climb easily and steadily thereafter on an old grassy tote road that leads to a bygone farmstead. The atmosphere is airy and remote; the forest floor is covered in ferns. The trail takes you around the west side of a hill and gradually up to ridge elevation again (avoid the unmarked trail to the left), where fine views appear from a solitary rock. As you descend this ridge, watch carefully to your left; take the blue-blazed trail that departs northeast over a small rise and then descends. As you hike through the upper elevations of the Ashley Hill Brook headwaters, join Ashley Hill Trail as the terrain levels out. After twenty minutes or so, leave Charcoal Pit Trail to your right—without the trail sign you'd miss it—and continue on Ashley Hill Trail, where you turn right (east). You may be surprised to see a latrine here. It serves the primitive campsites below, along the creek. If you look down the hill across from the outhouse, you'll see a fire ring on the creek's edge. Follow the level Ashley Hill Trail along the lip of a magnificent, steep hemlock ravine. This will bring you to the junction of Alander Mountain Trail, which you'll recognize. Bear right and follow the trail back to the parking area.

DID YOU KNOW?

Today's oak-hickory forest includes the range of the former oak-chestnut forest biome, found in the northeast part of the current oak-hickory range. Following the chestnut blight in the early twentieth century, these forests shifted to the oak-hickory-dominated ecosystem.

MORE INFORMATION

The Mount Washington State Forest is open year-round, sunrise to sunset; access is free; mass.gov/eea/agencies/dcr/massparks/region-west/mt-washington-state-forest-generic.html; 413-528-0330.

29

BASH BISH MOUNTAIN

This trail is rugged, rocky, and steep, with a stream crossing and a spur trail to historical Bash Bish Falls.

DIRECTIONS

From the hamlet of Copake Falls, east off NY 22 (13 miles north of Millerton and 20.5 miles south of Exit B3 off I-90), set your trip odometer to zero. Take NY 344 east 0.3 mile to Taconic State Park and continue a short distance past the park entrance to the Bash Bish Area parking lot on the right. Cross the creek on the cabin access road. *GPS coordinates:* 42° 07.026′ N, 73° 30.461′ W.

TRAIL DESCRIPTION

One of the most beloved wilderness destinations of the nineteenth century, Bash Bish Falls, its gorge, and the sky-clear Bash Bish Brook remain very popular today. Although only a small percentage of the falls' visitors hike the loop using South Taconic Trail (ST) and Blue Trail, this hike is the best way to get a complete feel for this unusually rugged and special place.

This hike is a loop that begins and ends at the Bash Bish Area parking lot on Bash Bish Mountain Road (NY 344). Before heading out, read the historical information at the kiosk in the parking area, where there is a comprehensive map. Adjacent to the parking area and just out of sight on the other side of Bash Bish Brook, the Taconic State Park Commission maintains a number of rustic cabins. From the parking area, follow the cabin access road, cross the bridge, and walk along the south side of Bash Bish Brook among several large Norway spruces until you see the first cabin. Watch carefully to the right, where the white-blazed ST appears next to the cabin; follow this trail. Signs indicate Bash Bish Mountain at 2 miles. Immediately, the trail

LOCATION
Mount Washington, MA

RATING
Moderate

DISTANCE
3 miles

ELEVATION GAIN
1,200 feet

ESTIMATED TIME
3 hours

MAPS
USGS Copake; Mount Washington State Forest Trail Map, mass.gov/eea/docs/dcr/parks/trails/mwashington.pdf; NY-NJTC South Taconic Trails

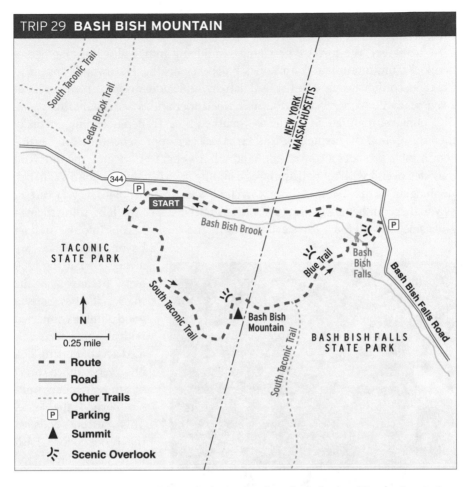

ascends, following a small brook through a hemlock forest. The trail switches back a few times as it climbs the steep northwest shoulder of the mountain through northern hardwood forests.

Just under a mile into the hike, at 1,500 feet in elevation, look for a faint, blue-blazed spur to the left (northwest) of ST. This is easy to miss, and you'll be given few clues. (At the head of the spur, the trail flattens out only slightly before turning east and climbing again.) You've ascended nearly 900 feet at this point and will welcome a break. Follow the spur downhill slightly to a small rocky lookout, where you look straight down into a bowl of pastoral land between Washburn Mountain (1,642 feet) and the ridge you're standing on. You see nearly the entire Catskills Range, from Windham High Peak in the northwest, along the Escarpment north to south, and beyond Overlook Mountain into the Burroughs Range (Slide, Wittenberg, and Cornell mountains and farther south). If you continue a little farther on the blue-blazed spur, you'll discover a pitch-pine outcropping where a limited exposure to the north allows a taunting peek at the north wall of Bash Bish Gorge. This spur provides the hike's best views. Don't miss it. You're right at the New York–Massachusetts border. Backtrack to ST and continue into Massachusetts.

At 1,600 feet, the forest type changes suddenly into a pleasing montage of hemlocks, mountain laurel, and thick blueberry heaths. Hardwoods appear to the right, conifers to the left. The trail flattens, and suddenly you're once again at a vague junction where ST leaves south to Alander and Brace mountains.

Continue straight ahead on the well-marked Blue Trail, descending gradually then steeply into the ravine. The trail turns east as it approaches the safety perimeter. A cable provides a convenient handrail. An engraved rock on the trail (you may step over it without noticing) was carefully inscribed by one John Williams, '46. Judging by the style and script, this stone was carved in 1846. Be very careful as you descend; hemlocks cling tenaciously to the slope. You'll be using them—and sometimes all fours—to steady yourself. The vertical drops into the cataract

beyond the fence are a nerve-wracking 200 feet. Because of the many fatalities here (a good number connected with alcohol and associated acts of derring-do), observers, under threat of a fine, are not permitted beyond the fence. This descent ends at the brook above Bash Bish Falls. From the small gravel apron at the edge of the brook, the trail continues on the other side, bearing right along the bank. The falls are not in view. Walk upstream to find a good crossing point. (This is where trekking poles come in handy.) Once you arrive safely on the brook's northeast banks, look around for the blue blazes and follow the trail up to the

Hikers relax in the cooling mists of Bash Bish Falls.

parking area of Bash Bish State Park in the Mount Washington State Forest of Massachusetts. The cluster of rock to the left is not worth exploring and offers only obstructed views. Your route continues downhill on Blue Trail, well identified on the west side of the parking area. Descend past the trailhead kiosk and walk on a storybook section of trail through a hemlock ravine. As you hear the sounds of falling water, the trail jogs hard left and joins the dirt service road that comes up from the parking area where you began. Bear left to look at the falls and then descend the stone steps to their base. Here a rock protrudes from the lower falls, split by centuries of falling water, the cascade ending in a viridian pool of remarkable clarity. Bash Bish is the highest falls in Massachusetts, falling in multiple tiers to a final drop of 80 feet. Many casual visitors content themselves with painting, writing, photographing, and meditating here; however, few have really seen the whole picture, as you have.

Return to your starting point, 0.75 mile back along Blue Trail (service road) heading west, keeping the brook to your left until you reach the parking area again. Bash Bish Brook continues without you, to join the Roeliff Jansen Kill and go on to dissolution at the Hudson River.

DID YOU KNOW?

John Frederick Kensett (1816–1872), a leading figure among the second generation of Hudson River School painters, made field sketches for a series of five paintings of the falls, most notably his first, *Bash Bish Falls* (1851). Other versions followed, leading to his 1855 masterwork by the same name.

MORE INFORMATION

Bash Bish Falls State Park is open sunrise to sunset, and access is free; mass.gov/eea/agencies/dcr/massparks/region-west/bash-bish-falls-state-park.html; 413-528-0330.

30

HARVEY MOUNTAIN

This little-known trail features views of the Southern Taconics from a blueberry knoll and free camping.

DIRECTIONS

From NY 22 in Austerlitz, New York, 5.5 miles south of Exit B3 off I-90, turn left (east) onto East Hill Road, where you'll see a post office. Go 2.5 miles to the Harvey Mountain trailhead parking area on the left. *GPS coordinates: 42° 19.569′ N, 73° 26.392′ W.*

TRAIL DESCRIPTION

Few scenic vantage points in the Southern Taconics' tapering northern hills offer such unusual views of the Taconic Plateau as Harvey Mountain (2,225 feet). From the east and west as it is viewed from the valley, the range looks like a long, low ridge with minimal relief, but from the north the plateau is seen longitudinally, and the fact that the Taconics are a "real" mountain range—the result of tectonic collision and uplift, not just a dissected plateau from which the shallow seas of the postglacial period receded—becomes strikingly apparent.

Harvey Mountain State Forest (HMSF) is a fairly recent addition to the state forest system, added in the 1990s. Along with Harvey Mountain Trail and its connector trails to the Beebe Mountain fire tower and Barrett Pond, HMSF offers primitive, no-fee, drive-up campsites. Because of low public use, camping site identification and upkeep has been discontinued, but it remains legal to camp. Camping permits are required for more than three consecutive nights or for groups of ten or more. Come prepared: There are no water sources, fire pits, or pit privies, and on-site management is limited to occasional ranger patrols, mostly on weekends. Hunting is permitted here, as it is in most state forests; dress accordingly.

LOCATION
Austerlitz, NY

RATING
Moderate

DISTANCE
3 miles

ELEVATION GAIN
480 feet

ESTIMATED TIME
2.5 hours

MAPS
USGS State Line; New York State Department of Environmental Conservation, Beebe Hill/Harvey Mountain State Forests, dec.ny.gov/lands/66468.html

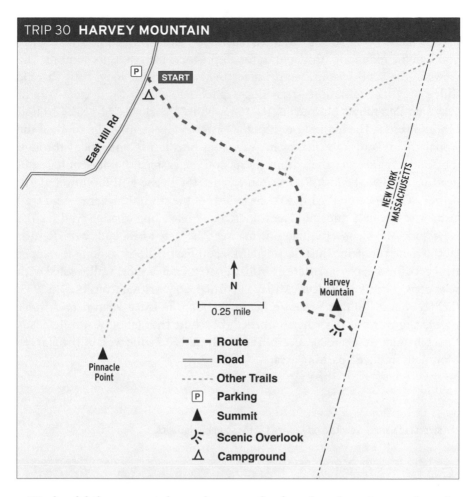

START

East Hill Rd

NEW YORK
MASSACHUSETTS

N

0.25 mile

Harvey
Mountain

Pinnacle
Point

- - - **Route**
——— **Road**
········ **Other Trails**
P **Parking**
▲ **Summit**
☀ **Scenic Overlook**
△ **Campground**

Die-hard hikers may take umbrage at the fact that there is a road to the summit of Harvey Mountain; however, both the summit road (a closed four-wheel-drive route) and the HMSF's dead-end campsite access road get very little use from the sightseeing public. Parking is provided in the well-identified lot on East Hill Road. The Harvey Mountain trailhead is located diagonally across East Hill Road from the parking area, on the northeast side of the Harvey Mountain camping area access road opposite a campsite. Follow the blue blazes.

The trail begins with a sharp ascent then levels out through hardwoods over a smooth, wide dirt surface. Within 0.3 mile, the trail register appears at the junction of the red-blazed trail to Barrett Pond and the trail to the fire tower in Beebe Hill State Forest. Bear right, following the blue blazes into a vigorous young sugar-maple forest on this flat and pretty section of trail. Within fifteen minutes of the trailhead, the trail departs left at a Y (a rough road continues straight ahead), soon becomes a narrow path, descends slightly adjacent to a steep ravine where Harvey Mountain can be spotted ahead, and crosses Big Moon Brook. Now the trail rises consistently but never very steeply, as it ascends the western slopes of the mountain. Soon after climbing through a white-pine stand, the trail rises to an open blueberry heath. Though not the highest point on the mountain, this spot is, for all practical purposes, its summit. The views to the south are the most interesting, showing the long, thin Taconic Ridge with its dramatic eastern slopes pitching steeply down from Mount Fray into Egremont, Massachusetts, followed by the cluster of peaks around Mount Everett. The highest point of the eastern ridge defines the route of the Appalachian Trail as it makes its way from northern Connecticut through the Southern Taconics then drops sharply off the eastern shoulder of Jug End, heading for the Greylock Range. You can see the Beebe Hill fire tower at 310 degrees. Continue up the hill to the east side of the summit, where a herd trail leads across a field and into the woods. Look left along a stone wall for the New York–Massachusetts state-line marker. The state forest ends here. Return by the route you came. Just outside HMSF, on East Hill Road along the upper fringes of the Steepletop Estate, is Millay Poetry Trail, a short walk posted with selections of Edna St. Vincent Millay's nature poetry written from 1917 to 1935. (Millay won a Pulitzer Prize for her collection *The Harp-Weaver and Other Poems* and was noted for her sonnets.) This short trail (about 0.4 mile) leads through quiet woods to her grave. The trailhead is 0.2 mile west of the Harvey Mountain trailhead parking area.

The summit of Harvey Mountain offers views of the southern Taconics.

The nearby Millay Colony for the Arts, established by the poet's sister Norma, is an active artist-in-residence colony and writers' retreat.

DID YOU KNOW?

The town of Austerlitz's historian, Sally Light, has identified several homestead foundations in the state forest dating from 1755, when an iron industry flourished here.

MORE INFORMATION

Pinnacle Point Trail lies to the west of the campsite area and offers lean-to camping in a remote location. Significant trail work has been done in the Harvey Mountain and neighboring Beebe Hill state forests, and these trails merit investigation. For general information on state lands in the area, visit dec.ny.gov/outdoor/7801.html or call 518-357-2234. For information on the Beebe Hill fire tower, visit dec.ny.gov/lands/66468.html.

CIVILIAN CONSERVATION CORPS (CCC)

The Emergency Conservation Work Act (1933) brought together great numbers of unemployed, unmarried men, ages 18 to 23, and the environment. Organized by the departments of Agriculture and Interior, and managed by regular and reserve officers in the Coast Guard, Navy, and Marines, this peacetime "army" of 500,000 men set about improving federal and state lands and parks. Enlistees were housed in tent camps and paid $25 a month. In 1933, the Civilian Conservation Corps (CCC, affectionately known as Roosevelt's "tree army") was formed, and education and training elements were added. Eventually, every state had a CCC camp, as did the then territories of Hawaii, Alaska, Puerto Rico, and the Virgin Islands.

In addition to the CCC's primary duties of planting trees and fighting fires, it built 3,470 fire towers and 97,000 miles of truck and fire roads. The corps also acted as an emergency service organization, assisting with flood and disaster control in the Ohio and Mississippi valleys, and with cropland drainage and irrigation in the Midwest. Nearly 300 CCC veterans were reported missing or dead during the Labor Day hurricane of 1935 in the Florida Keys, and a train derailed on its way to rescue them. Although a close congressional vote in 1942 ended the CCC, its spirit lives on in the state trails and plantation forests you'll enjoy on many of these hikes.

THE CATSKILLS

The Catskills occupy 1,102 square miles (705,500 acres, 287,514 of them publicly owned) and, along with the Adirondacks (6 million acres), are the highest and most rugged peaks in New York State. Despite their appearance and character, the Catskills are not mountains in strict geological terms because they are not the result of tectonic collision. They are a dissected plateau, formed by the erosive action of rivers and streams when vast sheets of thick glacial ice melted and retreated along a north–south axis.

What is perhaps most interesting about the geology of the Catskills is the soil—and hence, the vegetation that flourishes there. The region represents the southernmost occurrence in North America of boreal coniferous forests on glaciated uplands. In contrast with this summit forest of spruce-fir and paper birch is the valley forest type, known as the Carolinian Zone Forest, which consists of oaks, hickories, occasional black birch, tulip trees, and, until recently, chestnut.

After the Contact Period in the 1600s and its destructive consequences for the indigenous peoples of the valley, these same people sold for pittances large blocks of lands that were then "granted" to small groups of patentees. The largest of these land grants was the Hardenburgh Patent, a grant by Queen Anne of England of more than 2 million acres to Johannes Hardenburgh in 1708. For the next hundred years or so, the Catskills remained agricultural.

With the 1781 capitulation of the British, and with the remainder of General Washington's troops still in New Windsor, the Catskills began to grow commercially. Farm products were shipped to New York City on sloops. Dairy products and fruit followed wheat. In 1825, the Erie Canal opened, creating a widening market and turning a good deal of commerce away from Canada. Gristmills graduated to steam power by the middle of the eighteenth century, and by 1840, more than 100 steamships plied the Hudson River. Still, by the mid-eighteenth century, permanent settlement of the original Hardenburgh Patent was limited.

Alongside the tanbark industry (the stripping of hemlock bark for the tanning process) and, later, commercial bluestone quarrying, the great era of hotel tourism began on the high Catskill ledges. Hotel owners were uneasy about the destruction that extractive industries wrought upon their saleable assets— namely the scenic beauty and the dwindling peace and serenity of the wilderness. The Catskill Mountain House set the standard for leisure tourism as early as 1823 when it opened on the ledges east of North Lake in Haines Falls.

The biggest dividend the Hardenburgh Patent yielded was not wealth for its patentees but the unintended preservation of open space, which led directly to the creation of the Catskill Forest Preserve. In an 1885 act of Congress, the forest preserve was created in the Adirondacks and the Catskills, leading to the famous "forever wild" clause in the state's constitution: "All lands now owned or which may hereafter be acquired by the State of New York . . . shall be forever kept as wild forest lands."

By 1887 there was a wooden observatory on Balsam Lake Mountain. In 1892, the state financed the first trail up Slide Mountain. The Catskill Park was created in 1904, and the first fire tower appeared in 1905, replacing the original log structure on Balsam Lake Mountain. Between 1926 and 1931, four public campsites were created. President Franklin D. Roosevelt formed the Civilian Conservation Corps (CCC) in 1933, which led to an era of vast reforestation and trail building. In the ensuing years, the park grew.

Today, in the four forest-preserve counties of Delaware, Greene, Sullivan, and Ulster, there are 143,000 acres of wilderness, 130,000 acres of wild forest, and 5,200 acres of intensive-use lands. There are seven campgrounds, 303 miles of hiking trails, 76 miles of snowmobile trails, 30 miles of horse trails, 33 lean-tos, and 187 primitive campsites. Based on recent trail register sign-ins, a half-million people use the forest preserve annually.

Three long-distance trunk trails are contained within the forest preserve itself: Escarpment, Devil's Path, and Delaware Ridge trails, each roughly 25 miles long. Two longer regional trunk trails, Long Path and Finger Lakes Trail, pass through it. (See "Long Path" on page 283.)

Finger Lakes Trail connects the Allegheny Mountains with the Catskills using a route through the most remote sections of New York State's Southern Tier. The 580-mile trail provides hikers with the opportunity to traverse nearly the entire length of New York State.

JOHN BURROUGHS

Naturalist, poet, and essayist John Burroughs (1837–1921) is considered the guardian spirit of the Catskills, the John Muir of the East. From his boyhood on a farm in Roxbury, New York, to his later years at Riverby estate in West Park on the Hudson, he rose to international prominence as a spokesman for America's wilderness. Most of his writing was done at his handmade cabin, Slabsides, in West Park, New York, built in 1895 and now a National Historic Landmark. Among his visitors were Theodore Roosevelt, John Muir, Thomas Edison, and Henry Ford.

During his lifetime, Burroughs became the most popular author in the field of nature writing. He bridged the gap between his day and the early Romantic artists and writers, alerting his readers to the more concrete, physical wonders of nature. He wrote *Wake-Robin* (1873) while a bank examiner and clerk in the Treasury Department, and followed with another 24 books, among them the first biographical volume on Walt Whitman (*Notes on Walt Whitman as Poet and Person,* 1867). There are 2 miles of hiking trails in the Burroughs Sanctuary, which is open year-round free of charge. Slabsides is open for tours on the third Saturday in May and the first Saturday in October. The sanctuary is located 10 miles south of Kingston, 0.5 mile off US 9W on Floyd Ackert Road in West Park, New York.

31

SLIDE MOUNTAIN

A scenic, daylong hike climbs the Catskills' highest peak, in the Slide Mountain Wilderness area.

DIRECTIONS

From Exit 19 of the NYS Thruway (I-87) in Kingston, take NY 28 west 31 miles to CR 47 (Slide Mountain Road) in Big Indian. Set your trip odometer to zero. Turn left (south) onto CR 47, passing the Giant Ledge trailhead at 7.3 miles and Winnisook Lake at 8.4 miles. At 9 miles, park at the trailhead lot on the left side of the road. *GPS coordinates: 42° 0.529′ N, 74° 25.653′ W.*

TRAIL DESCRIPTION

Slide Mountain (4,180 feet) defied naturalist John Burroughs's climbing efforts in the early 1880s. In Burroughs's time, Slide was, as he suggested, "probably the most inaccessible; certainly the hardest to get a view of, it is hedged about so completely by other peaks, the greatest mountain of them all and apparently the least willing to be seen; only at a distance of 30 or 40 miles is it seen to stand up above all other peaks." Yet within a few years of Burroughs's first ascent in 1885, Jim Dutcher, a bark peeler living at the foot of the mountain, introduced the peak to hikers. Some of Dutcher's trail (constructed in 1886, with many stone steps) remains, but it leads onto private lands.

There are several popular approaches to Slide, but the easiest and fastest route is from the northwesterly Slide Mountain trailhead parking area, using a combination of Phoenicia–East Branch Trail (PE, yellow blazes), Wittenberg–Cornell–Slide Trail (WS, red blazes), and Curtis–Ormsbee Trail (CO, blue blazes). For the final ascent, you again join WS.

LOCATION
Shandaken, NY

RATING
Strenuous

DISTANCE
7 miles

ELEVATION GAIN
1,700 feet

ESTIMATED TIME
5.5 hours

MAPS
USGS Phoenicia, USGS Shandaken; AMC Catskill Mountains; NY-NJTC Catskill Trails, Southern Catskills

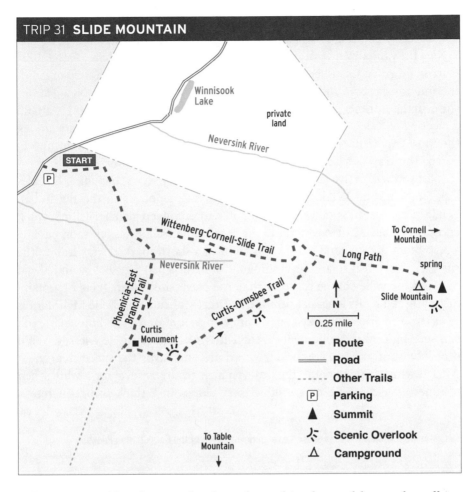

Winnisook
Lake

private
land

Neversink River

START

P

Wittenberg-Cornell-Slide Trail

Neversink River

To Cornell →
Mountain

Long Path

spring

Phoenicia-East
Branch Trail

Curtis-Ormsbee Trail

Slide Mountain

N

0.25 mile

Curtis
Monument

- - - Route

===== Road

------- Other Trails

P   Parking

▲   Summit

Scenic Overlook

△   Campground

To Table
Mountain
↓

Orient yourself at the map kiosk in the parking lot, and locate the yellow-blazed PE. Once under way, you immediately cross the upper reaches of the Neversink River's west branch (it is often dry here but can present a problem at very high water), which flows into the Delaware River. Originating on Slide's northwest watershed is the Esopus Creek, running down through Big Indian Hollow through the village of Phoenicia and into the Ashokan Reservoir water supply, its "wastewater" continuing to the Hudson.

Ascend through a stand of maples over rocks and roots, go up a flight of stone steps, and within fifteen minutes bear right at the T, following a level Jeep trail (a.k.a. the truck trail, the bridle path, or the firetower trail). After five minutes on this section, pass a spring on the left side. Soon you'll arrive at a junction with the red-blazed WS, which goes off to the left. (WS follows the old truck trail up Slide Mountain. It is the shortest way up, but it is rocky and without views. Instead, use this road for your descent.) Continue straight ahead on the yellow-blazed PE. Cross a wooden bridge over an unnamed tributary of the Neversink's west branch. From here, the trail climbs slightly. In another fifteen minutes, you'll reach CO (a.k.a. Long Path). Bear left, following blue blazes.

Note the vandalized stone monument near the junction. William "Father Bill" Curtis and Allen Ormsbee, for whom the trail was named, both died of hypothermia caused by a sudden snowstorm on Mount Washington, New Hampshire, in the summer of 1900. They were on their way up the mountain to attend a meeting of the Appalachian Mountain Club (AMC). These men were among the most experienced hikers of their time, and still they were caught unprepared. This trail was laid out to commemorate them. The trail ascends.

Soon you will arrive at a small ledge with westerly views, including Doubletop, Graham, and Wildcat mountains, and various peaks in the Big Indian Wilderness area. In another fifteen minutes, after a steep but short climb, you'll encounter a beautiful viewpoint to the north. The trail levels off, soon passing a 3,500-foot marker, and within five minutes a short, marked spur trail to the right leads 200 feet to an outstanding overlook at 3,550 feet. Below and ahead of you is the valley of the east branch of the Neversink River. Table Mountain, distinguished by its long, flat summit, is directly ahead, and Lone Mountain is to its left. You also see Rocky and Balsam Cap mountains. With binoculars, you can see High Point Monument on the Kittatinny Ridge in New Jersey. You'll probably want to rest here for a few minutes and savor the spectacular view. After leaving the viewpoint, the trail remains relatively level for a while, then resumes its ascent of Slide's southwestern slopes in a thick spruce-fir forest.

Slide Mountain Wilderness area preserves a stunning swath of the Catskill High Peaks.

Within 40 minutes of the previous lookout, following a fairly steep climb, you'll arrive at the junction of WS.

Bear right (east). This section of trail is relatively flat, and you have only another 200 feet or so of elevation gain and an additional twenty minutes of hiking before you reach Slide's summit. Extensive views appear from a northeast-facing outcropping on the left of the trail. Continue ahead to the summit, passing the site of the former fire tower to arrive at a flat rock with good views to the east. (In Burroughs's time, the encroaching spruce-fir forest had been cut down.) Ahead of you and just to the left are Cornell and Wittenberg mountains, and the Ashokan Reservoir is visible beyond. Directly below the ledge, affixed to the rock face, is a plaque commemorating John Burroughs that reads, in part, "Here the works of man dwindle in the heart of the southern Catskills."

Slide's views include nearly 70 named Catskill peaks, as well as a wide view of the Hudson Valley, Green Mountains, Berkshires, Taconics, Hudson Highlands, and Shawangunks. This is the same view that Forest Commissioner Townsend Cox, climbing Slide in 1886 to recognize the Catskills as part of the New York State Forest Preserve, pronounced "every bit as fine as anything to be seen in the Adirondacks."

Highly recommended is a short descent (off route) to a year-round spring; it's ahead on WS, 200 feet lower in elevation and about a twenty-minute hike beyond Slide's summit along the trail (as if you were continuing to Cornell Mountain). The trail switches back across Slide's eastern face before descending two flights of log stairs, after which the spring appears at the end of an unmarked spur on the left.

To return to your car, retrace your steps on the red-blazed WS, leaving CO to your left and continuing to follow the red blazes. The presence of white quartz here gives the trail the appearance of what has been historically referenced as the "garden path."

Descend for 40 minutes or so over the rocky footpath. Soon after passing a designated campsite on the left, you arrive at the junction with the yellow-blazed PE, which you'll recognize. Turn right and follow the yellow blazes to the next T (the trail continues to Winnisook lands and is usually barricaded with sticks), where you bear left and descend to the parking lot.

DID YOU KNOW?

Slide was not recognized as the Catskills' highest peak until Arnold Guyot, a Princeton professor of geology, published his map in 1879. Previously, Kaaterskill High Peak and Hunter Mountain competed for the title.

MORE INFORMATION

For more information on the Catskill Forest Preserve, visit dec.ny.gov/lands/5265.html. For the DEC Region 3 office in New Paltz, call 845-256-3000.

BICKNELL'S THRUSH

A regular visitor to Slide Mountain in the later years of the nineteenth century, naturalist John Burroughs noted, "Slide Mountain enjoys a distinction which no other mountain in the state, so far as is known, does—it has a thrush peculiar to itself." Burroughs later learned of the work of the amateur ornithologist Eugene Bicknell, who collected a species of thrush on Slide in 1881. Bicknell shot and collected what he thought was a gray-cheeked thrush but on further examination, and to the ornithological community's surprise, it seems Bicknell had discovered a new species. The taxonomic status of the thrush remained in question for a long time, however, until recent DNA examinations confirmed the Bicknell's and gray-cheeked thrushes share no common ancestor in the last million years. Not until 1995 did the American Ornithological Union's Committee on Classification and Nomenclature grant full species status to Bicknell's thrush.

The thrush is a very shy and reclusive species. Bicknell's thrush, said to be the shyest of them all, is found only in high boreal "fog forests" like that of Slide Mountain. It is seldom seen in the open and is small—the size of a sparrow. The bird is olive-brown, with gray and white underneath and yellow at the base of the lower bill. It can be distinguished by its song, a higher, throatier sound than that of the gray-cheeked thrush; both Bicknell and Burroughs noted the Bicknell's song as peculiar to the species. Burroughs reserved his fanciest prose to describe it: "It is . . . a musical whisper of great sweetness and power. It seemed as if the bird was blowing in a delicate, slender golden tube, so fine and yet so flutelike and resonant the song appeared . . . a strain as fine as if blown on a fairy flute . . . it was of the purest harmony. It was but the soft hum of the balsams, interpreted and embodied in a bird's voice."

32

WITTENBERG AND CORNELL MOUNTAINS

A steep climb from the rustic Woodland Valley leads to a favorite scenic area of many Catskill hikers.

DIRECTIONS

From the junction of NY 28 and NY 214 in Phoenicia, drive 0.6 mile west on NY 28 to Woodland Valley Road. Follow Woodland Valley Road to its terminus at the Woodland Valley Campsite (4.8 miles). The trailhead parking area is located opposite the campsite, 0.1 mile east of the campground entrance. *GPS coordinates: 42° 2.178′ N, 74° 21.487′ W.*

TRAIL DESCRIPTION

Wittenberg Mountain (a.k.a. the Wittenberg, 3,780 feet) is a favorite of many hikers who regard its scenery as among the Catskills' finest. A key figure in the skyline peaks of the Burroughs Range (Slide, Wittenberg, and Cornell), Wittenberg's popularity, based on hiker registrations, lags only slightly behind that of Slide, the Catskills' highest peak, and nearby Giant Ledge, the shortest scenic hike in the Slide Mountain Wilderness area. An interesting side trip with open views to the northeast and an area for camping is reached from Terrace Mountain Trail (TM), a short hike from its junction with Wittenberg-Cornell-Slide Trail (WS).

Park in the hikers' parking area on the north side of Woodland Valley Road. Note that WS does not leave directly from this parking lot but from the south side of Woodland Valley Road, within the campsite itself. From the parking area and map kiosk, walk across the road and bear left, keeping the campsite to your right. Within 300 feet, you'll find the red-blazed WS on the right. Follow the

LOCATION
Ulster, NY

RATING
Strenuous

DISTANCE
9.4 miles

ELEVATION GAIN
2,480 feet

ESTIMATED TIME
7 hours

MAPS
USGS Phoenicia, USGS Shandaken; AMC Catskill Mountains; NY-NJTC Catskill Trails, Southern Catskills

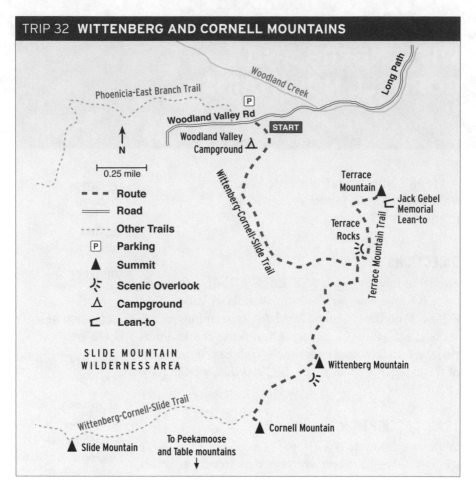

red blazes into the campsite area, bearing left along the edge of Site 46, and cross Woodland Creek on the wooden bridge. The trail ascends at once, soon passing the trail register and climbing thereafter through a dense, boulder-strewn hardwood forest. The trail is well marked here, but due to the many boulders, it is not always self-guiding. Watch for the red foot-trail blazes.

After twenty minutes of hiking, you'll note the dramatic change in forest type to a nearly pure hemlock stand on a flat ledge at 1,950 feet, with spare, seasonal views to the east. Late-arriving backpackers will find many suitable places to camp in the hardwood flats to the right (west) of the trail as they continue past the hemlock stand. After this welcome break, the ascent resumes and the trail crosses a seasonal brook before switching back hard to the left at an obscure arrow (south-southeast). The ascent continues, not as steeply now, through attractive hemlock ledges and soon relaxes, becoming nearly level as the trail turns east-southeast along Wittenberg's northern flanks at 2,700 feet. Nameless seasonal brooks, often lively, increase in volume as you travel east. Beyond the last of these, you'll enter the transition zone from mixed northern hardwoods to stunted paper birch and spruce-fir, and suddenly the trail junction appears in the low saddle between Wittenberg and Terrace mountains. At this point, you are 1.5 hours or more into the hike. Wittenberg is 1.3 miles to the right (south, 1,100 feet higher), and the Jack Gebel Memorial Lean-to is 0.9 mile to the left (north, 200 feet lower) on the yellow-blazed Terrace Mountain Trail (TM).

The ascent to Wittenberg from the WS/TM trail junction is characterized by attractive (albeit steep), terraced ascents, sedimentary rock ledges, and penetrating vertical crevices. The forest cover will have changed notably into spruce and fir at 3,000 feet. Within 45 minutes to one hour of fairly strenuous hiking from the junction, you will arrive at the summit, an east-facing, exposed ledge. Although not panoramic, Wittenberg's view encompasses a 180-degree hemisphere of mountain and valley extending north over the Devil's Path mountains and the Escarpment, east over the Hudson and Taconics, and south over an expanse of hills and valleys, where the Gunks taper off into endless flatlands. To the southwest, hikers are enticed by intimate observations of the nearby Peekamoose and Table peaks, along with the trailless Lone, Rocky, Balsam Cap, and Friday mountains, each of the latter being popular bushwhacking summits above 3,500 feet. In the eastern lowlands, you will see the Ashokan Reservoir, part of New York City's water supply, the impoundment created by the damming of the Esopus Creek. Wittenberg's summit impressed John Burroughs, who reached it after a "long and desperate" attempt at Slide: "The view from The Wittenberg is

The view from Cornell includes Wittenberg Mountain to the east and Slide to the west.

in many respects more striking, as you are perched immediately above a broader and more distant sweep of country . . . and the earth falls away at your feet and curves through an immense stretch of forest until it joins the plain of Shokan, and thence sweeps away to the Hudson and beyond."

After experiencing Wittenberg, you may feel up to the short hike to Cornell (add 30 minutes each way) via Bruin's Causeway, an interesting, boreal section of WS. As you gain Cornell's uppermost elevations, requiring the ascent of one low but nearly vertical ledge that can be hazardous in icy conditions, a short, unmarked spur trail to the left will take you to the summit. This is Cloud Cliff, the site of an illegal, heavily used campsite with limited views. Only Cornell's nearby westerly shoulder provides a good view to the west, including the landslide on Slide's north side that occurred around 1820. To see this memorable view, proceed west 0.1 mile on the trail as if you were hiking to Slide.

Burroughs traveled the range in 1880, relating anecdotes of the porcupines in Volume 6 of his complete nature writings, *Riverby*. If you've dropped your pack off on Cornell's summit to find the westerly view of Slide, don't be surprised, as I was, to discover the omnivorous quill pig sorting through its contents.

Return by the route you came.

DID YOU KNOW?

Many bears have been sighted along a narrow section of trail between Cornell and Slide mountains, giving rise to the name Bruin's Causeway. In the unlikely event that you do sight a bear in close quarters, back away slowly.

MORE INFORMATION

For more information on the Catskill Forest Preserve, visit dec.ny.gov/lands/ 5265.html. For the DEC Region 3 office in New Paltz, call 845-256-3000.

33

GIANT LEDGE

This short and rewarding hike leads to the scenic cliffs of a glacial cirque in the epicenter of an ancient meteorite impact zone.

DIRECTIONS

At the intersection of NY 28 and CR 47 (Slide Mountain Road) in Big Indian, set your trip odometer to zero, turn left, and drive south on CR 47 to the Giant Ledge trailhead at 7.3 miles. *GPS coordinates:* 42° 1.598′ N, 74° 24.238′ W.

TRAIL DESCRIPTION

This fairly short, rewarding hike will take you to the vertical lip of a glacial cirque in the heart of the Catskill High Peaks area. Giant Ledge–Panther–Fox Hollow Trail (GP) to Giant Ledge has become extremely popular with day-hikers and backpackers, so expect company, especially on weekends. Giant Ledge (3,200 feet), so named for its high vertical cliffs, forms the lower, southerly ridge of Panther Mountain (3,720 feet). On the east, it is flanked by the extensive wilds of Woodland Valley and the Slide Mountain Wilderness area, and to the west by the Big Indian Wilderness area. Here, the Esopus Creek (an important source of New York City's drinking water) gains momentum, nurtured within Panther's long ridge and the west-lying Big Indian Valley, with its Bavarian-style homesteads and rustic mountain hotels.

The trail to Giant Ledge begins across the road from the parking lot, where it is well identified. Enter the woods and follow the yellow blazes of Phoenicia–East Branch Trail. Within 300 feet of the road, you'll see the trail register and information kiosk. The initial section of trail climbs steeply at times, goes over a rough and rocky footway, crosses a seasonal streambed on a wooden bridge, and

LOCATION
Shandaken, NY

RATING
Moderate

DISTANCE
3 miles

ELEVATION GAIN
1,000 feet

ESTIMATED TIME
2.5 hours

MAPS
USGS Phoenicia; AMC Catskill Mountains; NY-NJTC Catskill Trails, Southern Catskills

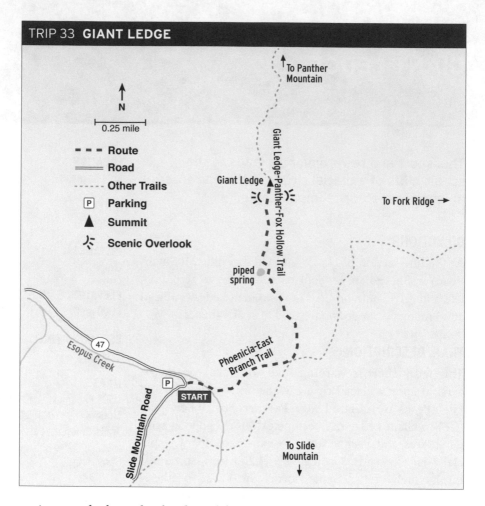

N

0.25 mile

- - - Route
═══ Road
····· Other Trails
P Parking
▲ Summit
ᐞᐟ Scenic Overlook

To Panther Mountain

Giant Ledge-Panther-Fox Hollow Trail

Giant Ledge ▲

To Fork Ridge →

piped spring

Phoenicia-East Branch Trail

Esopus Creek

47

Slide Mountain Road

P

START

To Slide Mountain

again ascends through a hardwood forest. The rest of the hike is easier, except for the last short pitch to the ledges.

After twenty minutes or so of rigorous ascent, the trail flattens out at 2,700 feet in the col between Slide and Panther mountains. Avoid the faint, unmarked trail to your right, which heads southwest across the lands of the Winnisook Club. (This is a legal and significant shortcut to the Slide Mountain trailhead for hikers doing the "loop" from Woodland Valley across the Burroughs Range.) Bear left here, and within a stone's throw, you will be at the trail junction where PE heads for Woodland Valley, passing the blue-blazed GP to Giant Ledge. Bear left again (north) on GP, following blue blazes now. The trail is flat for a while and hops across a series of stones where the footway is often muddy. These conditions vanish as the trail rises again, ascending a long set of stone steps to arrive at a Y. At this point, a spur trail marked "Spring" goes left (west) 600 feet to a piped spring. (Pass the first small pool of water appearing next to a boulder and continue to the pipe. This is the only reliable water source on GP between

Giant Ledge forms the lip of a glacial cirque near the center of a meteorite impact zone.

here and Fox Hollow.) Bear right over level ground for a while and then ascend steeply as the trail rises to ridge elevation, where the first of several herd trails leads to a ledge on your right (east). Explore more lookouts to the north along the trail, each very exposed and dangerous, most poised on fractured sandstone ledges above high, vertical drops. The views are spectacular.

From these easterly points, you look toward Fork Ridge and into Woodland Valley, with Terrace, Cornell, and Wittenberg mountains to your right (southwest). To the northeast, you can identify the lower peaks of Garfield and Sheridan, with Romer to the east and Tremper beyond it, including various peaks of the Devil's Path mountains from northeast to east. With binoculars, you can see three of the Catskills' five fire towers from here: Overlook (easy to spot), Hunter (near the middle of the long ridge top to your left, or northeast), and Mount Tremper (the cab can be seen sticking up between you and the col of Twin Mountain).

From a point roughly in the middle of Giant Ledge, a trail marked with yellow blazes leads to the west into the designated camping area. Continue through the campsites—there are two crude fire rings—where you will discover a west-facing rock with a view revealing, from left to right, Hemlock, Spruce, Fir, Big Indian, Eagle, Haynes, Balsam, and Belleayre mountains in the Big Indian Wilderness area. The appeal of Giant Ledge is that it's a short, fairly easy, and ruggedly scenic hike. You're likely to find many friendly people wandering around or camping here on a nice weekend. To have the place to yourself, plan to come on an off-season weekday.

Giant Ledge is predominantly forested with maple, beech, cherry, and birch, but at its north end is a virgin spruce grove extending to the ledge's base. A few remaining drought-killed red spruce are visible below the eastern cliffs. More recently, forest tent caterpillars and gypsy moths have defoliated much of the mid-elevation forest here, the long-term results of which remain to be seen.

Many hikers elect to continue to Panther's summit for a longer outing. Panther is another 1.75 miles beyond Giant Ledge and an additional 750 feet in elevation. If you'd like to extend your hike from Giant Ledge to Panther's summit, you have another 40 minutes of hiking each way, dropping slightly downhill at first and then climbing vigorously through large boulders and thick hardwood forest. On the ascent, you will have several views of Slide, Wittenberg, and Cornell as you cross open rock terraces, most of them similar if inferior to Giant Ledge's. Panther's "summit" is a very small scenic outcropping beneath the true, viewless, fir-clad summit. The trail, completed in 1936, continues to the north and descends to the Fox Hollow trailhead. Many hikers on GP leave a car at both ends. (Consult AMC's *Catskill Mountain Guide* for details.)

From Giant Ledge, return by the route you came.

DID YOU KNOW?

This area was hit by a meteor 375 million years ago, which left behind a crater and spherules, or tiny iron droplets of condensed gas. Satellite images clearly show the circular crater, defined by the circuitous route of the Esopus Creek.

MORE INFORMATION

Aside from its tremendous appeal as a scenic destination hike, Giant Ledge is an ideal overnight trip for those new to backpacking or wishing to prepare for longer outings. For more information on the Catskill Forest Preserve, visit dec.ny.gov/lands/5265.html. For the DEC Region 3 office in New Paltz, call 845-256-3000.

34

PEEKAMOOSE AND TABLE MOUNTAINS

This remote wilderness hike leads to a pair of quiet boreal summits with southwesterly views.

DIRECTIONS

From NY 28 in Big Indian, go south on CR 47 through Oliverea, Winnisook, and Frost Valley, then turn left in Claryville onto CR 19 (Denning Road) and follow it to the trailhead parking area, about 30 miles from Big Indian.

Alternately, from NY 28 in Boiceville, turn south onto NY 28A and go 3 miles to West Shokan, then turn right onto CR 42 (Peekamoose Road), passing the Peekamoose-Table trailhead 10 miles from West Shokan. Bear right into Grahamsville, Unionville, and Curry on NY 55, turning right at Curry to Claryville, and again right into Denning and to the trailhead, also a total of 30 miles.

From NY 17 (the shortest approach to this area from the south), take NY 55 east from Liberty, turning north onto CR 19 at Curry. Bear right (staying on CR 19) at Claryville, and follow Denning Road to the trailhead. *GPS coordinates:* 41° 57.933′ N, 74° 27.144′ W.

TRAIL DESCRIPTION

What likely will impress you most about Peekamoose and its environs are its storybook forests and the remarkable clarity of the Rondout Creek and Neversink River. The Rondout is conceived on the south- and east-facing watershed of Rocky, Lone, and Peekamoose mountains and is joined by the malachite waters of Peekamoose Lake as it swells through Bull Run and joins its east branch at Sundown. Naturalist John Burroughs loved this flashy, pellucid brook, vowing, "If I were a trout I should ascend every stream till I found the Rondout." If you're coming from the west, you follow the Neversink's east branch from the town of Claryville. The Neversink, too, is famous trout

LOCATION
Denning, NY

RATING
Strenuous

DISTANCE
10 miles

ELEVATION GAIN
2,200 feet

ESTIMATED TIME
5 hours

MAPS
USGS Peekamoose Mountain; AMC Catskill Mountains; NY-NJTC Catskill Trails, Southern Catskills

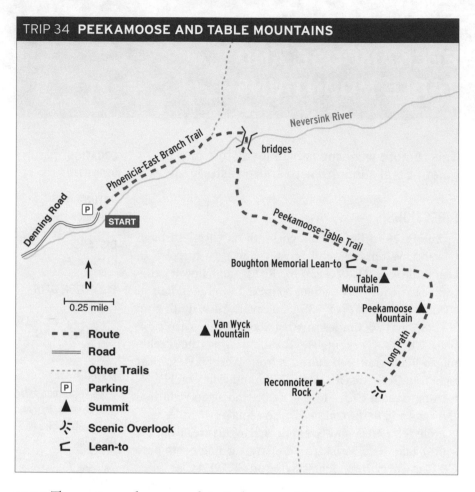

water. The most popular approach to Peekamoose Mountain (3,843 feet) is from the southern trailhead in Sundown Wild Forest along Peekamoose Road and involves a 2,643-foot elevation gain within 3.5 miles. The recommended and more interesting Denning Trail, or Phoenicia–East Branch (PE) Trail, with its crossing at Deer Shanty Brook, is a gentler and more scenic option, and it will save you a few hundred feet of cumulative elevation. If you want only to climb Peekamoose, which these days has a better view than Table's, the trail from Peekamoose Road provides the shortest route. The distances and logistics involved with leaving a car at each trailhead make this an impractical hike to shuttle.

Park at the end of Denning Road where trail signs to Slide Mountain are posted. The setting is a high farming-valley plain with frequent plots of old-growth forest. You may see deer feeding close to the road here, where old apple trees provide them with seasonal treats.

Follow PE through a hemlock woods on an old woods road, crossing a small plank bridge and a seasonal brook. Within 25 minutes, you will reach a trail junction, where you turn right onto the blue-blazed Peekamoose-Table Trail. Go downhill into a wet area (seasonal), watching for the blue blazes and continuing downhill to cross two log stringer bridges, one of which spans a dry bed at various times of year. This is the confluence of Deer Shanty Brook and the Neversink. The bridges are kept simple because these two creeks rise considerably during runoff, and they must be replaced frequently. Be careful crossing the stringers. The lean-to that existed mid-stream here has been removed as a nonconforming structure due to its proximity to the creeks and the difficulty of siting a privy so close to a water source, but there are a few legal, designated campsites in the area. Most of the heavily impacted, old, now-illegal sites along the banks of both Deer Shanty Brook and the Neversink have been closed for recovery.

Continue uphill through a lush forest of fern, oxalis, club moss, and huge birch. Within a half hour, the trail will level somewhat, skirting a ridge exposing Woodhull and Van Wyck mountains to the southwest. The trail varies in pitch, generally gaining elevation as you go through thin stands of hardwood, climbing through broken rock ledges. Within 45 minutes of leaving the confluence, you will reach a ledge among the cherry trees with a view of Peekamoose to the south. Several more spur trails lead to the right 20 or 30 feet off the trail, some with worthwhile views. Beware: These are dangerous ledges. Through the trees to the left (north) as you continue, you may see Slide and its neighboring peaks, and as you gain in elevation, you'll identify Panther, parts of Giant Ledge, Lone, Rocky, Balsam Cap, and Friday mountains. Just below the 3,500-foot mark, and a short way beyond a spur to a piped spring, a spur trail to the right leads to the Boughton Memorial Lean-to.

Hikers enjoy a well-earned rest on the boreal summit of Peekamoose Mountain.

Within two hours of the Neversink, you'll reach Table's summit (3,847 feet). There is no view here. At one time, a herd trail led to an extraordinary north-facing viewpoint, but this location has been lost over time, obscured by heavy spruce-fir growth. Several herd trails appear in the summit area, heading nowhere in particular and creating an undesirable pattern of sustained overuse. Continue on the main trail to Peekamoose; you can see it ahead as you descend. Some faraway views are available along this downhill section of trail, extending beyond the Shawangunks and into the Highlands. Even Anthony's Nose and the deep gulch spanned by the Bear Mountain Bridge can be seen with binoculars or good eyes.

As you drop into the fragrant, balsam saddle between Table and Peekamoose, the trail becomes wet, and within ten minutes you begin climbing again. You may see a vague Y in the trail as you approach the summit of Peekamoose. Go right to reach the summit, where a large boulder sits in a small clearing surrounded by scrub evergreens. This boulder can be climbed for more views, but they are inferior to those ahead.

Continue south another 0.6 mile, going steeply downhill through a series of ledges and overlooks, following the backbone of a long ridge extending south-southwest. Within a half hour of leaving the summit, following frequent blue blazes, you will cross several open areas with interesting ledges and flats to reach an outstanding viewpoint at 3,500 feet. This spot exposes the Rondout, Neversink, and Mongaup valleys; Bangle Hill, Breath Hill, Samson and Little Rocky mountains; and some interesting ridges and peaks to the west, among them Big Indian, Doubletop, and Balsam Lake mountains—the latter with a fire tower (319 degrees). Any additional descent to see the limited, seasonal views from Reconnoiter Rock would be counterproductive. The views are better here on the high southern flanks of Peekamoose.

Return by the route you came.

DID YOU KNOW?

The 358-mile-long Long Path crosses the summits of both Table and Peekamoose mountains. The Romantic-era name of the latter is a shortened version of "Peak of the Moose."

MORE INFORMATION

For more information on the Catskill Forest Preserve, visit dec.ny.gov/lands/5265.html. For the DEC Region 3 office in New Paltz, call 845-256-3000.

35

ASHOKAN RESERVOIR

This flat hike along a popular section of the Ashokan Reservoir—the scenic middle dike— affords the most intimate views of the Catskills from the Hudson Valley lowlands.

DIRECTIONS

From Exit 19 of the NYS Thruway in Kingston, set your trip odometer to zero and travel west on NY 28 toward Phoenicia. At 12 miles, turn left at Winchell's Corners in Ashokan, a small, easily missed intersection. Soon you will recognize the managed forests of the Ashokan's buffer zone. As you cross the dividing weir separating the upper and lower basins, you'll see the Slide Mountain Wilderness area on your right (west), across the upper basin. At 13.8 miles (cumulative from Exit 19), turn left onto Monument Road. Go down the hill and bear left onto NY 28A. At 15.3 miles, turn left into the area known locally as the Frying Pan. The "pan" is formed by Leonard Hill Circle, where you will park. *GPS coordinates:* 41° 56.870′ N, 74° 10.925′ W.

TRAIL DESCRIPTION

Although the Ashokan Reservoir's middle dike has been a well-known hiking and cycling destination for decades, the western section of Reservoir Road, which extends this hike and crosses the dam, was open to vehicular traffic until September 11, 2001, after which it was closed indefinitely. Today hikers can travel these joined sections of the dike and dam (paved), which on clear days are popular with pedestrians and cyclists, as well as with landscape artists who set up their easels before the sweeping panorama of the Catskill High Peaks. The scenic value of this unusual viewshed cannot be overstated. Many of the peaks you will see on this hike have been the subject matter of the

LOCATION
Shokan, NY

RATING
Easy

DISTANCE
4.5 miles

ELEVATION GAIN
150 feet

ESTIMATED TIME
2 hours

MAPS
USGS Ashokan; AMC Catskill Mountains

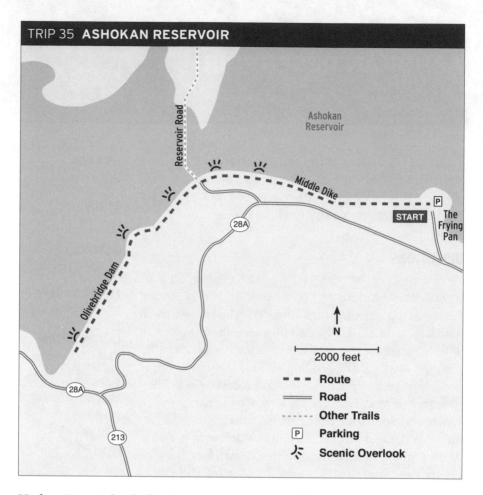

Ashokan
Reservoir

Reservoir Road

Middle Dike

28A

Olivebridge Dam

START

The
Frying
Pan

28A

213

N

2000 feet

- - - **Route**
=== **Road**
----- **Other Trails**
P **Parking**
Scenic Overlook

Hudson River School of landscape painters. Landscapes such as these spawned a new concept of a picturesque and sublime American wilderness, and the values derived from that vision led to the formation of the National Park Service.

From the parking lot, walk west through the barrier gate and onto the paved middle dike. Immediately you are greeted with the extraordinary array of the major Catskill peaks, running from Overlook Mountain in the east to the Sundown Wild Forest in the southwest. Between these two mountainous regions lies the bulk of the Catskill Forest Preserve, where many of the region's finest hiking trails are located. A 26-mile-long trunk trail known as Devil's Path traces the skyline to the north, and the Slide Mountain Wilderness area features the rugged trails of the Burroughs Range. Many of the peaks you see before you, however, are trailless.

Many birds, such as loons, cormorants, diving ducks, ospreys, eagles, and turkeys, make their homes here. Small herds of deer feed off the mowed grass of the dike's steep embankments. As you approach the dividing weir, look for Ashokan High Point in the Sundown Wild Forest to the southwest. Continue along the dike. At 1.3 miles, you will arrive at the intersection of Monument and Reservoir roads. Carefully cross the intersection onto Reservoir Road, continuing west. Down the hill on the left, you will see the aerator (a fountain used for oxygenating water), which is no longer used for the aeration of drinking water but remains as a monument open to the public. At the intersection, a Department of Environmental Protection kiosk stands beside the roadblocks, preventing vehicular access to the main dam. Walk through the blockade and continue west along the dike. This section of the route is popular with photographers and birders. In recent years, it has been the domicile of several families of eagles that maintain nests in the large white pines along the water's edge. Interpretive signs inform the public of the ongoing preservation efforts in the Ashokan buffer zone. It's possible you will see several eagles hunting and nesting in the dense tract of woods ahead. Carrying a camera with a long lens or a small pair of binoculars will add to your enjoyment here, as the eagles have become fairly comfortable with human presence and can be closely observed at times.

Now the road passes through a beautiful section of maturing mixed woods, where planted pines of several varieties and large oaks appear. As the road straightens, you will see Ashokan Dam ahead, where the road narrows. Continue to its center span, your turnaround point (the road does continue a bit farther but there is nothing more of interest to hikers). The dam is fairly inconspicuous as far as dams go. It is not a contemporary poured-concrete and steel-gated dam, but rather an earthen dam, one of the very last to be "hand built" by steam and manual labor. The volume of earthwork composing the dam and its surrounding dikes is astonishing, as is the story of the impoundment's creation.

The Ashokan Reservoir's construction began in 1909, as one of six that were built to supply New York City with drinking water. The city's water system had begun to leak cesspool seepage, and cholera and dysentery were repeatedly breaking out. The wealthy were able to afford kegged water, which at the time was shipped from Staten Island. The city's nearest option for a large water supply was the Ramapo Mountains, but a group of private investors who controlled the water there had anticipated the city's needs and held out at a high price. The city instead turned to the Catskills, and established rights of eminent domain. This resulted in the inundation or relocation of seven towns, the relocation of 2,000 inhabitants, the disinterment of 2,600 graves from 32 cemeteries, and the building of 11 miles of railroad and 64 miles of roads. In 1913, water filled the large excavation that had once been a thriving collection of hamlets. At the time of its construction, the Ashokan Reservoir was the largest impoundment in the world. Today it is one of two reservoirs in the New York City Catskill Water Supply System. The other is the Schoharie Reservoir, located 27 miles to the north, the waters of which join the Esopus Creek and are carried to the Ashokan. The Ashokan supplies about 40 percent of New York City's drinking water supply during non-drought periods. Water from the Ashokan is carried to New York City via the 92-mile Catskill Aqueduct, at one point crossing 1,100

feet beneath the Hudson River into Westchester County's Kensico Reservoir. It enters the city's distribution system at Hillview Reservoir in Yonkers, just outside the city line.

As you emerge from the woods, you will see the dam ahead, where the road narrows. The original channel of the Esopus Creek can be seen below. The creek originally flowed through a natural flat valley that the local Sccpu (of the Delaware Indians) called the Plain of Ashokan, or the "place of fish." The dam and dikes placed around the Esopsus's original course rerouted the creek to the wastewater spillway in Hurley. The impoundment now resembles what the post-glacial lake looked like about 17,000 years ago. Looking across the upper basin, you see the edge of a high glacial cirque formed by Panther Mountain, Giant Ledge, and the Burroughs Range (Slide, Wittenberg, and Cornell mountains). Much earlier in time, as recent research has demonstrated, the Panther Mountain area was the epicenter of a meteor impact that defined the topography of the upper Esopus Valley.

From the dam, retrace your steps back to the Frying Pan and your car.

If you are returning to the NYS Thruway (I-87) from here, detour past the West Hurley Dike and the spillway, which are scenic locations similar to the middle dike though not walking destinations. To see these areas, bear left out of the circle and set your trip odometer to zero at NY 28A. At 0.6 mile, you'll pass over the spillway. This is a spectacular sight in early spring, when, at times, a large volume of wastewater channels its way into the gorge below. At 6.1 miles, leave NY 28A and bear left onto Basin Road. Within 0.2 mile, you will cross the West Hurley Dike and be treated to another fine view of the Indian Head Wilderness area—only you'll be closer this time. At 7.3 miles, turn left in front of the Reservoir Inn restaurant, and at 8 miles, turn right onto NY 28, back toward I-87.

DID YOU KNOW?

During the Ashokan Reservoir's construction in the early 1900s, kegged water in New York City cost more than gin.

MORE INFORMATION

For more information, please see: nyc.gov/html/dep/html/watershed_protection/ashokan.shtml

Facing page: The Catskill High Peaks rise behind the impounded waters of the Ashokan Reservoir.

36

ASHOKAN HIGH POINT

A gradual climb to a scenic and extensive blueberry heath affords intimate views of the high peaks.

DIRECTIONS

Turn south onto NY 28A from NY 28 in Boiceville, west of Kingston. (At this time, automobiles cannot use the Ashokan Reservoir route on Monument Road.) Follow NY 28A for 3 miles to West Shokan, then follow Peekamoose Road (NY 42) west and set your trip odometer to zero. At 4 miles, turn right into the Kanape Brook parking area. Cross the road to the footbridge and the trailhead. *GPS coordinates:* 41° 56.140′ N, 74° 19.685′ W.

TRAIL DESCRIPTION

The trail to Ashokan High Point (3,080 feet) follows an old but very well-built dirt settlement road along hemlock-fringed Kanape Brook. Bluestone walls and ditches constructed by the Civilian Conservation Corps in the 1930s have protected the trail from erosion, and trail maintenance is carried out by a local Boy Scout troop from the Rip Van Winkle Council.

Follow the trail uphill through a slope forest of beech, birch, and maple, gently climbing up and away from Kanape Brook, to your right. Within ten minutes, you'll cross one of several stone culverts running under the trail, draining the northwest watershed of the mountain. These are structures you ordinarily won't see on Catskill trails. Several are entirely handmade; the ditch itself is lined and capped with large, flat stones. You will see some very attractive bluestone walls along this part of the trail, as well as stone bridges spanning seasonal creeks. You'll cross two such bridges and climb gradually but steadily into an area where mountain laurel appears.

LOCATION
West Shokan, NY

RATING
Moderate

DISTANCE
7.5 miles

ELEVATION GAIN
1,980 feet

ESTIMATED TIME
5.5 hours

MAPS
USGS West Shokan; AMC Catskill Mountains; NY–NJTC, Catskill Trails, Southern Catskills

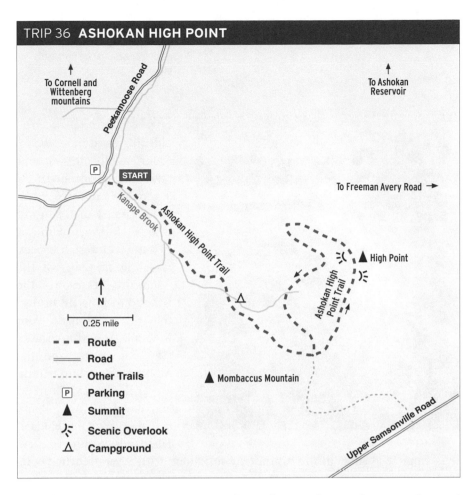

↑
To Cornell and
Wittenberg
mountains

Peekamoose Road

↑
To Ashokan
Reservoir

P
START

To Freeman Avery Road →

Kanape Brook

Ashokan High Point Trail

▲ High Point

Ashokan High Point Trail

⤵ Scenic Overlook

↑
N

0.25 mile

– – – Route
═══ Road
------ Other Trails
P Parking
▲ Summit
⤵ Scenic Overlook
△ Campground

△

▲ Mombaccus Mountain

Upper Samsonville Road

Within 30 minutes or so, at 1.4 miles and 1,600 feet in elevation, the trail crosses Kanape Brook at a clearing with a designated campsite. This is a pretty spot; the brook forms a large pool as it flows from the shady Norway spruce forest upstream. Keep going uphill, never strenuously, for another twenty minutes through a second-growth forest. Curving gradually toward the east, the trail soon reaches higher open forest, becoming level and grassy amid the oak and laurel. Within five minutes, you'll arrive at a T in the airy, forested saddle between High Point and Mombaccus Mountain (trailless) at 2.5 miles and 2,060 feet. This is the border of state land. The adjoining property, south to Freeman Avery Road, is private.

Turn left (north) at the trail junction for the 1-mile, 1,000-foot ascent to Ashokan's summit. Slightly beyond the trail intersection, take note of another red trail marker (this is where you'll come back to the main trail if you choose to complete the loop), but for now continue straight ahead, climbing gradually over broken rock. Views appear as you climb through this hardwood forest over steeper, terraced terrain. The vague side trails you may notice lead to

Once a commercial blueberry heath, Ashokan High Point is now a popular destination for casual pickers.

older, treed-in views. From saddle to summit takes nearly one hour. At 3.5 miles from the trailhead, Ashokan's summit is a rock ledge with an east-to-southwest aspect, revealing the edge of the Ashokan Reservoir; the Kingston-Rhinecliff Bridge; the Shawangunks, from Mohonk to Minnewaska (Sky Top Tower and the Mohonk Mountain House are visible at 165 degrees) and down to Sam's Point; and deep into the Hudson Highlands. Weathered carvings from 1878 show in the summit stones, along with several anchor bolts from an early observation tower and a few benchmarks. There is a shallow overhang just beneath the summit ledge. The best is yet to come.

From the summit, the trail continues to the north, crossing open balds with exciting, close-up views of Slide, Friday, Balsam Cap, Rocky, Lone, Table, and Peekamoose mountains. Most hikers will stray from the trail here to explore the bald and the broken views of the Ashokan Reservoir to the east, through the trees. The popularity of camping (legal) is obvious on the bald, where there are a few large, informal fire rings. Very few places in the Catskills provide such an intimate look at the interior High Peaks area. But what may astonish you the most are the lowbush blueberries, ranking easily as the best in the Catskills. The thick heaths cover the entire unshaded summit.

Many hikers take the short bushwhack to Little High Point (2,800 feet), where herd trails have developed. From Little High Point, you can see almost the entire Ashokan Reservoir, appearing as a long, flat strip of indigo. Spun into the scene are the somber, drab outcrops of rock that pockmark the summits and ranges beyond, and short stilts of wind-battered, nut-brown tree trunks, festooned with the scarlet berry clusters of mountain ash. Looking left (north) from east to west, you observe the Devil's Path range. To the north are Wittenberg and Cornell mountains. To the east and beyond the reservoir are the Taconics and the Berkshires. Moving westward is the long Shawangunk Ridge and the plain of the Neversink, Rondout, and Mongaup valleys. Suddenly Mombaccus Mountain again fills your eye, and you've covered about 270 degrees for what is one of the best overlooks in the Catskill Mountains. Return to Ashokan High Point summit and descend by the route you came.

You can also complete the loop discussed earlier, time allowing. To do so from Ashokan High Point's summit (where the benchmarks are), follow the trail as it skirts the balds on the mountain's northwest side, soon descending through a thick and viewless forest. This is a longer option (add about 2 miles) than returning the way you came; the only advantage is that it's a little easier on the knees. The descent back to the main trail will take more than an hour. The loop is completed near the saddle between Ashokan High Point and Mombaccus, where you turned north for the final ascent. It is much easier to return the way you came—and safer, if your time is running short. It's not a good idea to be caught in low light on the less established, sometimes vague loop connection, which is not as well marked or self-guiding as the main trail. If you plan to spend the day and do both Little Ashokan Point and the loop, it's a good idea to carry a headlamp and extra provisions.

DID YOU KNOW?

Through the early 1900s, Ashokan High Point's summit yielded a commercial blueberry harvest.

MORE INFORMATION

For more information on the Catskill Forest Preserve, visit dec.ny.gov/lands/5265.html. For the DEC Region 3 office in New Paltz, call 845-256-3000.

37

MOUNT TREMPER

An interesting hike leads past a quarry and two lean-tos to the summit fire tower.

DIRECTIONS

Phoenicia Trail begins on the east side of the Esopus Creek, 2.3 miles northwest of Mount Tremper Corners and 1.6 miles southeast of Phoenicia, off CR 40 (Old Plank Road or old NY 28). *GPS coordinates: 42° 3.964' N, 74° 18.190' W.*

TRAIL DESCRIPTION

The hike up Mount Tremper (2,740 feet; named Timothy Berg in Colonial times) is most direct and interesting from the southwest, following the red-blazed Phoenicia Trail. This trail, a longtime favorite of Catskill hikers and backpackers, has become even more popular with the reopening of its now-reconditioned fire tower.

The trailhead lies along the northeastern banks of the Esopus Creek, an important trout fishery and New York City water source. Romer Mountain (2,240 feet) can be seen to the southwest across the Esopus Creek from the trailhead parking area. Follow the trail across two wooden bridges to a flight of stone steps. The trail levels, heading northwest to join an old truck trail at 0.5 mile. Turn right (northeast), passing the trail register.

Several larger feeder streams intersect the trail. Evidence of logging is visible in the abundance of second-growth hardwood. Yellow blazes running north and southwest mark the forest-preserve boundaries. This piece of trail also sports a few of Long Path's aqua blazes.

As the trail steepens to 15 or 20 degrees, you cross an energetic brook that cuts a deep gully into the mountainside as it bursts from an unevenly aged hemlock stand. The large drainage area of Mount Tremper's southwestern slopes crosses the trail here, making it very wet at times.

LOCATION
Mount Tremper, NY

RATING
Strenuous

DISTANCE
5.6 miles

ELEVATION GAIN
1,960 feet

ESTIMATED TIME
4 hours

MAPS
USGS Phoenicia; AMC Catskill Mountains; NY-NJTC Catskill Trails, Northeastern Catskills

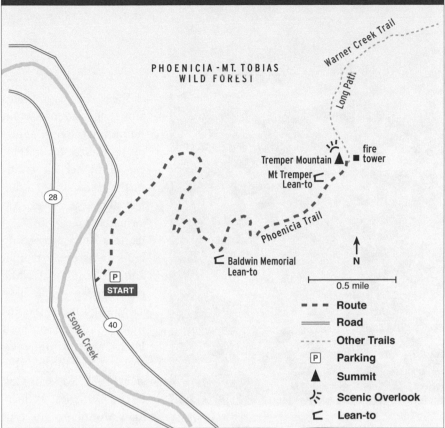

PHOENICIA-MT. TOBIAS
WILD FOREST

Warner Creek Trail

Long Path

fire tower

Tremper Mountain ▲ ■

Mt Tremper ⊏
Lean-to

Phoenicia Trail

28

⊏ Baldwin Memorial
Lean-to

↑
N

Ⓟ
START

0.5 mile

Esopus Creek

40

- - - Route
═══ Road
------- Other Trails
Ⓟ Parking
▲ Summit
⅄ Scenic Overlook
⊏ Lean-to

You will have reached the first switchback when the trail suddenly turns south and uphill, where large maple and ash dominate an understory of young hemlock. To your left (east) and uphill, a long outcrop that has slid in many places begins an interesting visual transition. Water appears from a spring on your left. Fallen rock can be seen below the trail to your right, now heavily covered with moss and accumulated forest litter.

As you turn through the next switchback, you see a huge pile of quarry tailings on the left; the broken stone was shoved aside as longer slabs of bluestone were mined. The pile now forms a sort of manufactured ridge covered with thin soil and vegetation. The quarry itself is accessible from a small, overgrown roadbed on the trail's left that ascends gently into the quarry, covering an acre or two. You can follow it to a high, right-angled face, where the slabs were removed. Other than this vertical stone wall, only a small foundation and a few rusted iron remnants bear testimony to the once-thriving industry. During your exploration, be alert to the possible presence of the quarry-dwelling rattlesnakes, which habitually bask in the warm sun of early spring. (There is a documented den here.)

A highly regarded trout stream, Esopus Creek flows past the trailhead to Mount Tremper.

The trail continues along a flatter section into an oak forest, joined by the laurel cover typical of higher elevations in the Catskills. At 1,800 feet above sea level, you switchback about 120 degrees on a steepening grade, where paper birch and an occasional white pine appear. You'll have a few glimpses southwest toward the southern High Peaks during early spring. Once through the switchback, you can look to the northwest at Sheridan Mountain. The trail steepens, heading directly uphill, nearly due east. Within a few minutes, you'll see the Baldwin Memorial Lean-to on your right. At this point, you are 2 miles from the trailhead, 2,000 feet in elevation. Keep a sharp eye out for this shelter if you intend to use it because it's off-trail, positioned somewhat downhill, and facing south. It is in better condition than the summit lean-to, is more private, and has a water source nearby (uphill 0.1 mile off the trail), but has no summer views. Finally, after one more switchback, you climb slightly and walk a long ridge. Just as you expect the summit to appear, you discover the ridge continues for another 0.5 mile through a canopy of twisted oak, tormented and battered by exposure. After twenty minutes of hiking, you reach a stand of bright-barked beech trees on your left and soon after that the Mount Tremper Lean-to. This hike ends here, but the trail continues to the north, joining Warner Creek Trail to Silver Hollow Trail (Long Path route), and Willow Trail into Hoyt Hollow and the hamlet of Willow.

The fire tower is just ahead and offers a 360-degree view. Plattekill and Indian Head, both summits of Twin Mountain, as well as Plateau Mountain in the Indian Head Wilderness area, are visible to the northeast. You see Blackhead and Black Dome mountains in the far distance; closer are Hunter (looking carefully, you can find Hunter's fire tower with binoculars), Southwest Hunter, West

Kill, and the seemingly endless array of peaks in the central Catskills, including Belleayre and Balsam. To the south are Ashokan High Point, bits and pieces of the Ashokan Reservoir, and several High Peaks, including Wittenberg and Slide. To the right of Slide are Giant Ledge and Panther. To the east, you can see Cooper Lake (Kingston's water supply), as well as Overlook Mountain. You can see Sky Top and Eagle Cliff in the Shawangunks to the south, and the Hudson Highlands beyond.

This fire tower was built to replace the one on Slide, after New York State acquired the Mount Tremper tract between 1906 and 1910. The extractive resource and tourist industries followed the usual patterns here. In addition to intensive quarrying, the area gave heavily of its hemlock stands between 1836 and 1879, with one local tanner recording a total harvest of 170,000 cords of bark. The Tremper House hotel was built in 1879 near the existing railroad bed at the base of the mountain. This was the Catskills' first railroad hotel, built in an era when remoteness was more in fashion, and was visited by so many colorful personalities that it threatened even the popularity of Charles Beach's Catskill Mountain House. Oscar Wilde patronized the hotel (it was on his lecture circuit), assuring its owners that "the top of a mountain is no place for a mountain house . . . it should be put in the valley; there the picturesque and beautiful is ever before you." The hotel was named for its manager, Major Jacob H. Tremper Jr., who renamed the mountain as well.

Return to the parking area by the route you came.

DID YOU KNOW?

Many of the nineteenth-century Catskills hotel owners disliked the imposing quarries. By the early 1880s, Major Jacob H. Tremper's Tremper House was competing for business with the Catskill Mountain House, so it could ill afford the nearby bluestone quarries robbing the hills of their peace and quiet.

The Mount Tremper fire tower has been restored and listed on the National Register of Historic Places.

MORE INFORMATION

Volunteers staff the fire tower on summer weekends, and they can supply information about the tower restoration and history. Mount Tremper is managed by the State of New York. For more information on the Catskill Forest Preserve, visit dec.ny.gov/lands/5265.html. For the DEC Region 3 office in New Paltz, call 845-256-3000.

BLUESTONE

The period of bluestone quarrying in the eastern Catskills lasted from 1840 to 1880, in uneasy partnership with the tanbarking industry. In many cases, quarriers used the same roads the tanners had cut years earlier, and many of the same laborers—most of them Irish—worked for both as the seasons overlapped.

Settlers and tenant farmers recognized immediately that the bluish, fine-grained sandstone was easily worked and made an ideal building material. They used it for their homes, barns, smokehouses, shops, roads, hearths, and lintels; some even ventured into the commercial end of quarrying. But soon the big stone dealers, who shipped their flagstones by sloop and, later, by three-masted schooner and railroad, put the small operators out of business. Bluestone was prized for its ease of handling and shaping. It was used extensively for sidewalks, as it proved durable, attractive, and attainable in volume. As a result, it provided the first pavement for New York City and quickly found its way to St. Louis, San Francisco, and even to Havana, Cuba. Whereas the tanning industry ended as the result of the near deforestation of the hills, the quarrying industry ended with the invention of cement in Rosendale and High Falls, New York, in 1825.

As you hike trails once used by quarriers and their teams, you will see the old quarries and note where some of the stones lying mid-trail bear the century-old mark of a wedge or chisel. On closer examination, you can still find flags and perfect lintels lying neatly stacked, waiting for the teamsters who never came—testimony to a way of life that changed nearly overnight.

38

OVERLOOK MOUNTAIN

This steep hike climbs to old hotel ruins, a fire tower, and Eagle Cliff from Meads Mountain, above the town of Woodstock.

DIRECTIONS

From the Woodstock village green, turn north onto Rock City Road. Continue straight through the intersection with Glasco Turnpike at 0.6 mile and climb Meads Mountain Road to the trailhead parking area at 2.6 miles. *GPS coordinates: 42° 4.215′ N, 74° 7.287′ W.*

TRAIL DESCRIPTION

Overlook Mountain (3,140 feet) is Woodstock's main hiking draw. The trailhead begins at the height of land on Meads Mountain (the high saddle between Overlook and Mount Guardian), opposite the Tibetan Buddhist monastery Karma Triyana Dharmachakra and adjacent to the Magic Meadow of Woodstock Rainbow Tribe fame. The Rainbow Tribe, formed in the late 1960s, still exists, although it bears no resemblance to the original group. The Catholic Church of Christ on the Mount is here, too, made famous in the 1960s by its "hippie priest," Father William Francis. This area is a sort of vortex zone, one that has attracted monks, hikers, and artists for 100 years or more. It was due to the view from Meads that artist Bolton Brown encouraged fellow artist Ralph Whitehead to build his art colony in Woodstock in 1902, based on the utopian ideas of John Ruskin and the poetic vision of Walt Whitman. Whitehead named his art colony Byrdcliffe, after his wife, Jane Byrd McCall, and situated it in the shadow of Overlook Mountain.

At the Overlook Summit trailhead, locate the map kiosk and trail register. The trail is an easy though not dull climb up a consistent grade on a dirt road, all the way to the fire

LOCATION
Woodstock, NY

RATING
Strenuous

DISTANCE
5 miles

ELEVATION GAIN
1,440 feet

ESTIMATED TIME
3 to 4 hours

MAPS
USGS Woodstock; AMC Catskill Mountains; NY-NJTC Catskill Trails, Northeastern Catskills

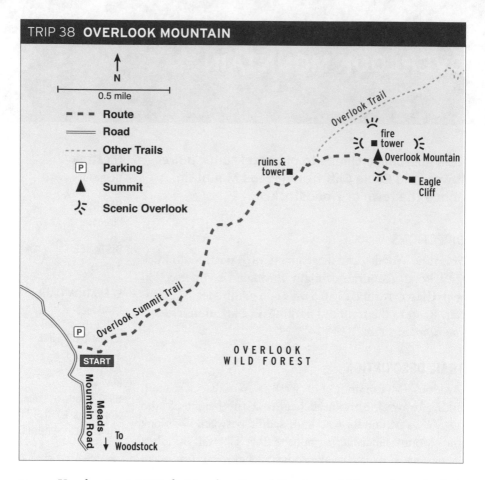

N

0.5 mile

- - - Route
=== Road
----- Other Trails
P Parking
▲ Summit
Scenic Overlook

Overlook Trail

fire tower
■ Overlook Mountain
■ Eagle Cliff

ruins & tower ■

Overlook Summit Trail

P

START

Meads Mountain Road

To Woodstock

OVERLOOK WILD FOREST

tower. You begin at 1,700 feet in elevation, following red blazes through dark hemlock that opens up into hardwoods and mountain laurel as the trail climbs. The forest is strewn with large sedimentary boulders, dragged off the mountaintop by retreating ice some 15,000 years ago. The ascent is consistent and at times monotonous as it follows the TV-tower maintenance road in the presence of electrical wires, having lost the character it certainly had when quarriers and tanners first built it. But soon mountains appear everywhere, and Indian Head, a scant 3 miles distant, comes out of nowhere in the Devil's Path mountains.

Within 45 minutes of hiking, you will come to the somber ruins of the Overlook Mountain House. The Mountain House opened in 1871, but despite its various distinctions, including its status as the highest mountain house in the Catskills, it seemed cursed. It burned completely in 1875, was reconstructed in 1878, and burned again in 1924. In 1928, under new ownership, the existing poured-concrete foundation and walls were erected near the old hotel site. Walls, windows, and plumbing were all that was completed when the stock market crash of 1929 forced the project to be abandoned. Trees now grow in the main hall. In the 1990s, artists pasted biodegradable images and histories to the walls, which have long since disintegrated.

Continue on the trail, rising easily, passing the TV and cell tower on your left. At 2 miles, you'll pass the blue-blazed Overlook Trail on your left. Continue straight, passing several herd trails that lead right (south) to limited views that aren't worth your time. At 2.5 miles, you will arrive at the summit. There's an observer's cabin, open on summer weekends and serving as a museum to the fire tower.

Barry Knight, a local resident and volunteer, has climbed Overlook dozens of times in all weather conditions. A tower enthusiast, he located, restored, and rebuilt a dismantled state fire tower on his property in Hurley. "If it weren't for the efforts of volunteers, these towers would not only be closed to the public, they'd all be dismantled," he says. The view here at Overlook would not be as spectacular without its tower. In 1997, the tower was recognized by the National Historic Lookout Register for its historical and cultural significance. The stewards will be happy to show you around the summit and tower. The tower's cab is locked when no observer is present.

The summit view is among the Catskills' finest and includes the Berkshires and the Taconics, the Hudson River south to the Highlands, the Shawangunks,

Hikers will pass the skeletal ruins of the Overlook Mountain House en route to the summit.

the Ashokan Reservoir, and more Catskill peaks than you can count. (Remember, the Catskills have 100 peaks of more than 3,000 feet in elevation.)

Compasses don't work here due to the steel tower, but a working alidade (a large, circular sight set on a compass rose) and the on-site steward will help you identify the major peaks. Take the time to visit with the volunteer and have a look in the cabin. Follow the trail to the right of the cabin door to a more private view over the immediate valley. (Beware of the vertical drop.) This is Eagle Cliff, named by the landscape painter Charles Lanman, who was inspired by the legend of an American Indian infant who was stolen by an eagle, whereupon the child's heartbroken mother threw herself over the cliff.

Just as inspiring a view is that of Overlook Mountain itself from the valley floor, a sight that merited the brushes of Frederic Church and Thomas Cole and prompted the pen of Charles Herbert Moore. The mountain continues to provide inspiration for aspiring artists from the village of Woodstock below.

Return by the route you came.

DID YOU KNOW?

From the tower, six states are visible: New York, Connecticut, Vermont, Massachusetts, New Jersey, and Pennsylvania. Some argue New Hampshire can also be seen from the top of the fire tower.

MORE INFORMATION

Parts of the Overlook Mountain House building have collapsed, and the New York State Department of Environmental Conservation (DEC) has advised the public not to enter the ruin. The fire tower and the observer's cabin, open on summer weekends and serving as a museum to the fire tower, are staffed by volunteers. For more information on the Catskill Forest Preserve, visit dec.ny.gov/lands/5265.html. For the DEC Region 3 office in New Paltz, call 845-256-3000.

39

CODFISH POINT

This historical hike to an old quarry provides views overlooking the Hudson River, with a spur to Plattekill Falls.

DIRECTIONS

To reach the trailhead, turn south off NY 23A at the (only) light in Tannersville onto CR 16 (Spring Street). At 1.3 miles, this road intersects Bloomer Road, where you bear left. At 1.8 miles, you will reach a Y, where you bear left onto Platte Clove Mountain Road (still CR 16). At 4.6 miles, you pass Dale Lane on the right (trail to Sugarloaf, Twin, and Pecoy Notch mountains). Stay on Platte Clove Mountain Road, and at 5.7 miles, you see Prediger Road on the right. At 6.5 miles from Tannersville, turn left onto the dirt entrance to the Kaaterskill Wild Forest Area parking lot. (See Huckleberry Point for alternate seasonal directions through Platte Clove.) *GPS coordinates: 42° 08.033′ N, 74° 04.918′ W.*

TRAIL DESCRIPTION

This little lookout point, deep within the magical realms of the Platte Clove quarries and tanbark haunts, has never been treated as a destination hike, but it deserves to be. Only a few miles round-trip, the hike can be done in two to three hours, allowing enough time to explore and relax, with a view of the Hudson and its rolling, eastern midlands. Afterward, you can descend the trail from the Platte Clove Preserve to sit in the cooling mists of Plattekill Falls.

Codfish Point is a spur off Overlook Trail. The trailhead for Codfish Point represents the northern portion of the historical Old Overlook Turnpike, often used by hikers as an alternative to reach Devil's Path, which begins 1 mile to the west at the top of Prediger Road. From the forest

LOCATION
Hunter, NY

RATING
Moderate

DISTANCE
3.5 miles

ELEVATION GAIN
680 feet

ESTIMATED TIME
3 hours

MAPS
USGS Kaaterskill; AMC Catskill Mountains; NY-NJTC Catskill Trails, Northeastern Catskills

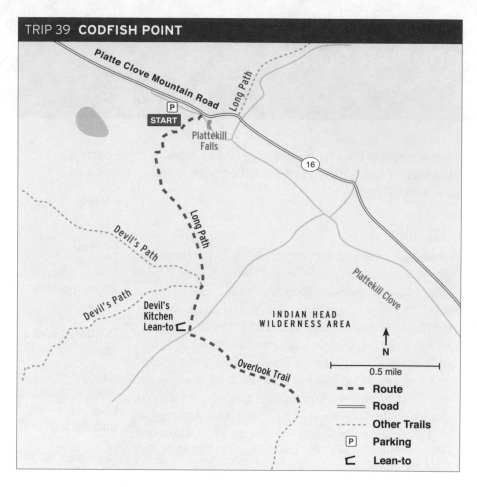

preserve access parking lot, walk to the right (west) along Platte Clove road, 250 yards to the trailhead on your left (south). This is the Catskill Center for Conservation and Development's (CCCD) Platte Clove Preserve, through which you walk to reach Overlook Trail. You'll find trail signs at the roadside. To the left of the trailhead, you will see the CCCD's little red artist-in-residence cabin. Go down the embankment and cross Plattekill Creek on a timber bridge, following green CCCD diamond blazes and aqua Long Path blazes, heading south. There are CCCD interpretive signs posted along the trail. Due to intensive erosion of the original turnpike roadbed, the trail has been rerouted and is not yet entirely self-guiding.

Watch for the blazes. You slowly gain elevation through this pretty hemlock woods until leaving the preserve and entering state land (Indian Head Wilderness area) at around 2,000 feet in elevation.

Soon you arrive at the junction with Devil's Path (red), which comes in on your right from its trailhead at Prediger Road. Just before it, there's a small but interesting quarry on the left (east) of the trail. Continue straight ahead to

Once a noisy bluestone quarry, today's Codfish Point is a quiet outcropping of curious remains on the easterly slopes of Plattekill Mountain.

another junction only a short distance beyond, where Devil's Path departs to the southwest toward Indian Head, and Overlook Trail (blue-blazed) begins. Follow the blue blazes now, and within ten minutes you will arrive at the Devil's Kitchen Lean-to. Here, the trail crosses a wooden bridge above the Cold Kill (folk toponymized from Coal Kiln). This was the site settlement where a coal-fired kiln was used to make charcoal. Extensive quarrying took place here, and widespread talus fields appear off-trail to the west.

Now the trail begins to climb up the eroded roadbed, rising 350 feet in elevation in the next 0.7 mile. After a half hour or so, be aware of the trail changing direction into the south. Just as it does so, it levels off, following even terrain along the east shoulder of Plattekill Mountain. As the trail levels out, watch very carefully to your left (east) for the Codfish Point spur trail. It is not adequately marked at this time—though the trail is well established, if narrow—and there is usually a rock cairn at the intersection and a flat rock with an etched directional arrow lying in the junction. The trail is very short and brings you into an old quarry. Continue until you arrive at an east-facing lookout, poised above the valley. A pioneer stand of white birch has taken hold where the talus was thrown in order to clear the quarry of debris. You can explore this extensive quarry, seeing the face where the stone was mined and areas where the flags were trimmed for shipping. There are a few remaining hut foundations, which were typically covered with hemlock boughs and bark shingling during their operation.

The views are very good, extending east to the Taconic Plateau and lowlands, and south along the Escarpment to the summit of Overlook Mountain. (You'll see the fire tower.) You can see Tivoli Marsh and a good stretch of the Hudson River; points in the Shawangunks, such as Guyot Hill and Bonticou Crag; and the guardian promontories of the Central Hudson Highlands, Storm King and Breakneck Ridge, far to the south.

Retrace the route back down to the CCCD Preserve. If you have the time, take the blue- and green-diamond-blazed trail that leads from the CCCD artist-in-residence cabin driveway down to Plattekill Falls, a high, vertical fall and pool at the head of the Plattekill. (The CCCD has requested that hikers do not disturb the artist-in-residence.) From a point along the trail, you can get a good look out across the top of Platte Clove itself, facing east. But be careful: There are no barriers or restraints, and the trail can be very slippery when wet (not recommended in icy conditions). This 50-foot fall is a vertical plume that runs heavily following rain, but due to its high elevation and its proximity to the watershed of the west-flowing Schoharie River, it runs down quickly. Return the way you came.

DID YOU KNOW?

Codfish Point takes its name from an incident during the late quarrying period of 1890, when a blizzard marooned quarrymen for several days. Having exhausted their food supply, they were left with only salt cod. The workers nailed a cod crate to a tree both in mock protest and as a marker to aid their supply party in locating the snowed-under trail. The crate remained for some time, and the name stuck. Salt cod was a Dutch staple survival food, dating back a millennium. In its salted state, it could last years.

MORE INFORMATION

For more information: dec.ny.gov/about/607.html; catskillcenter.org

40

INDIAN HEAD MOUNTAIN

Featuring an interior forest hike to a boreal summit with exciting views, Indian Head is among the Catskills' most popular peaks.

DIRECTIONS

To reach the trailhead, turn south off NY 23A at the only light in Tannersville onto CR 16 (Spring Street). Set your trip odometer to zero. At 1.3 miles, this road intersects Bloomer Road, where you bear left. At 1.8 miles, you will reach a Y where you bear left onto Platte Clove Road. At 4.6 miles, you pass Dale Lane on the right (the trail to Sugarloaf, Twin, and Pecoy Notch mountains). Stay on Platte Clove Road, and at 5.7 miles, you'll see Prediger Road on the right. Follow it 0.5 mile to the trailhead loop and park. (See Trip 45, Huckleberry Point, for alternate seasonal directions through Platte Clove.) *GPS coordinates: 42° 8.044′ N, 74° 6.260′ W.*

TRAIL DESCRIPTION

Indian Head, a beguiling triad of peaks, forms a profile that from afar looks like a face. It is best seen from the north or east, from the Taconics or from Olana (Frederic Church's Persian castle in Hudson), and from the NYS Thruway and the surrounding valleys.

At the trailhead you will see signs identifying the red-blazed trail to Indian Head Mountain, Jimmy Dolan Notch Trail (blue blazes), and Echo Lake Trail (red blazes). This is the Devil's Path trailhead. You will follow Devil's Path a short distance to Jimmy Dolan Notch Trail and join it again as you turn east on Jimmy Dolan Notch Trail to summit Indian Head and complete the loop.

The foot trail leads you into the forest over a stringer bridge and across one of several lively creeks that will keep you company until you reach higher elevations. Follow the

LOCATION
Hunter, NY

RATING
Strenuous

DISTANCE
6 miles

ELEVATION GAIN
1,573 feet

ESTIMATED TIME
4.5 hours

MAPS
USGS Kaaterskill; AMC Catskill Mountains; NY-NJTC, Catskill Trails, Northeastern Catskills

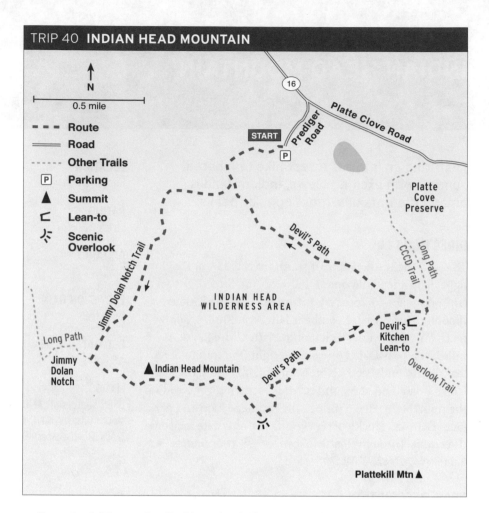

Legend:

- - - Route
——— Road
- - - - - Other Trails
P Parking
▲ Summit
⊏ Lean-to
☇ Scenic Overlook

N
0.5 mile

16
START
P
Prediger Road
Platte Clove Road
Platte Cove Preserve
Devil's Path
Long Path
CCCD Trail
Jimmy Dolan Notch Trail
INDIAN HEAD WILDERNESS AREA
Long Path
Jimmy Dolan Notch
▲ Indian Head Mountain
Devil's Path
Devil's Kitchen Lean-to
Overlook Trail
Plattekill Mtn ▲

well-marked (blue and red) old road uphill, reaching the trail register within 500 feet. Maps are posted here. Within ten minutes you will pass a stream on your right and arrive at a trail junction. Bear right onto the blue-blazed Jimmy Dolan Notch Trail to Jimmy Dolan Notch and Indian Head Mountain.

Jimmy Dolan Notch Trail rises slightly over a rocky footway with exposed tree roots into a pure beech forest. To your right, in a northerly direction, you can see Kaaterskill High Peak and Roundtop Mountain through the trees in springtime. The trail is not strenuous yet, as you slowly bend to the south, getting a view of Twin Mountain's northerly shoulder up to your right.

As you continue along a steeper, eroded section of the trail, you'll have a peek at Indian Head Mountain on your left (southeast) and will see more of Twin to the right. Climbing higher, about 45 minutes into your hike (1.5 miles), you can look back (north) at Kaaterskill High Peak, Roundtop Mountain, and the Blackhead Range. Within ten to fifteen minutes more, you will be happy to arrive in Jimmy Dolan Notch (3,100 feet) for some rest before the steep summit climb.

Indian Head Mountain (left, in midrange) rises behind the weir gatehouse of the Ashokan Reservoir, with Overlook Mountain to the right.

In the notch, Long Path intersects with the Devil's Path, showing Indian Head at (a rugged) 0.5 mile, and Platte Clove Road at 3.9 miles. Jimmy Dolan Notch is in every sense a classic notch: a symmetrical cut through the mountain that is scattered with large boulders and crumbling rock shelves following an ancient river canyon whose waters have long since run away to a dried-up sea.

The trail climbs and eases alternately as you scramble uphill from the notch, heading east. After gaining nearly 400 feet in elevation from the notch, the trail, thick with hemlock and balsam fir, flattens suddenly. This is the only indication you have reached the summit, which is completely surrounded by trees, with no view. Within five minutes, you'll go downhill slightly to another flat area where climax spruce trees soar above.

Continue along through a pure evergreen forest. Some restricted views of the Sawkill valley are available to the south if you want to push your way through the trees and explore a little, but the best views lie ahead.

You are now descending to the middle knoll, from the forehead (summit) to the eyebrow of the Indian's head. On the eastern end of the middle knoll, you'll reach a high overlook that juts out to the east with a vertical, dangerous drop at 3,200 feet above sea level. A nearly 180-degree view reveals Ashokan High Point, the Shawangunks, Overlook Mountain, the Hudson River (part of which is obstructed by the east knoll, or nose), and the Highlands, Taconics, and Berkshires. You are roughly midway through the hike, with 3 miles behind you.

From here, follow cautiously down a very steep section of trail into a shallow saddle separating the eyebrow and nose. Within ten minutes, you'll encounter another thick stand of fir that would be difficult, if not impossible, to walk through without a trail. This is a prime example of "cripplebrush." Going uphill and leveling out onto the nose, in ten minutes you'll reach a spot where views have been maintained by the Department of Environmental Conservation's (DEC) cutting. (Many people disagree with maintaining vista cuts in wilderness areas and have questioned its legality.) The result is an outstanding look at the Catskill High Peaks area, running from Ashokan High Point over to Slide Mountain and beyond. In this collection of peaks are also Peekamoose, Table, Lone, Rocky, Balsam Cap, Samuels, Friday, Wittenberg, Cornell, Giant Ledge, Panther, and many more. You see Overlook's fire tower, the Tibetan Monastery in Meads, the Overlook Mountain House ruin, and as far south as High Point State Park, New Jersey. (With binoculars, you can see 220-foot High Point Monument, built in 1930 as a war memorial, at 219 degrees.)

Within a few minutes of leaving this area, you'll swing toward the north, skirting the nose's easterly rim, which will give you a look at Plattekill's (trailless) western shoulder. With fair views to the east along the trail, you have the opportunity to look deep into Platte Clove, and within five minutes you'll reach Sherman's Lookout, which has also been cut to provide views to the north and a previously unavailable look at the Blackhead Mountains, Kaaterskill High Peak, Roundtop Mountain, and the Hudson River. The ledge was most likely named at the behest of Ulysses S. Grant, under whom Williams Tecumseh Sherman—a brilliant and ruthless strategist—served as a Union general in the Civil War. Looking beyond the deep cut of Platte Clove, you can see Bash Bish Gorge in the Southern Taconics. This is the last scenic overlook before the plunge into the valley.

After approximately twenty minutes of hiking downhill with diminishing views to the east, you may find the trail wet as it terraces down, going level for a way, then steep again. The footing is red shale with broken conglomerate. The majestic stands of large virgin hemlock here, some more than 30 inches in diameter, reflect the magnificent primordial forest before the tanning period. Within 30 to 40 minutes of leaving the nose, you'll reach a trail junction.

To your right is Devil's Kitchen Lean-to (this makes for a pretty, fifteen-minute side trip to the bridge over the Cold Kill), and far beyond it, Echo Lake. Bear left (north), and within 500 feet or so, Devil's Path dodges left (northwest). Watch closely for this turn; it's not obvious. If you go straight (north) on the Catskill Center for Conservation and Development Trail, you'll wind up a mile east of Prediger Road.

Turning left (northwest) and back into deep hemlock woods, the trail takes you uphill slightly. In ten to fifteen minutes, you'll cross a creek continuing through a fern glade then another small stream before reaching the trail junction with

Jimmy Dolan Notch Trail. The 1.5-mile section of trail from Devil's Kitchen will take you about 40 minutes. Turn right and you'll be back at the parking lot in a few minutes.

DID YOU KNOW?

Artist Thomas Cole depicted Indian Head Mountain in his 1843 painting *River in the Catskills*.

MORE INFORMATION

For more information on the Catskill Forest Preserve, visit dec.ny.gov/lands/5265.html. For the DEC Region 4 office in Stamford, call 607-652-7365; catskillcenter.org.

DEVIL'S PATH

Twenty-three miles long, with a cumulative elevation gain approaching 9,000 feet, Devil's Path is one of two long-distance trunk trails in the eastern Catskills, connecting Indian Head Mountain in Platte Clove to West Kill Mountain in the high Spruceton Valley. Crossing six peaks in excess of 3,500 feet (including Southwest Hunter Mountain), this rugged trail, often undertaken as a long weekend backpacking experience, begins on Prediger Road in the town of Hunter. (See Trip 40 [Indian Head Mountain] for directions to the Devil's Path trailhead from the east, and Trip 54 [West Kill Mountain to Buck Ridge Lookout] for directions from the west.) The trail also can be done as a series of day hikes from access points in the north. Hikers looking for more of a challenge can begin at the Overlook Mountain trailhead in Meads (where Devil's Path ought to begin), adding 2 miles and 1,400 feet in elevation. Few trails are so spectacular—or so difficult. Rugged, boreal peaks; deep, weather-ravaged notches; a scarcity of water; and steep, rocky terrain characterize the route. Several lean-tos are conveniently located along the way, on or near the main trunk.

The terrain of Devil's Path inspired fear in early Dutch settlers with its deep, dark cloves (ravines), where the Devil was said to dwell. In the 1940s, the New York Department of Environmental Conservation created Devil's Tombstone State Campground in Stony Clove Notch, putting a symbolic end to the era of superstition and legend for which the Catskills are famous. Today the trail continues beyond Stony Clove, into the west.

41

TWIN MOUNTAIN

Twin is a double-peaked mountain with superior views of the Hudson Valley and the Indian Head Wilderness area.

DIRECTIONS

From Tannersville, turn south at the light (the intersection of CR 23C and Railroad Avenue, CR 16) to join Spring Street (CR 16), bearing right onto Elka Park Road at 1.8 miles. Go over Schoharie Creek, pass the post office, and bear left at 2.8 miles. Go another 1.2 miles to the trailhead and park on the right. The trailhead also can be reached from Platte Clove Road (CR 16) via Dale Lane by bearing right onto Elka Park Road (a.k.a. Roaring Brook Road) at the intersection with Wase Road and going 0.7 mile to the trailhead. *GPS coordinates: 42° 09.068′ N, 74° 07.862′ W.*

TRAIL DESCRIPTION

Twin-peaked Twin Mountain is one of the Devil's Path mountains, those craggy and tempestuous summits you see crowding the western sky as you drive north–south on the New York State Thruway between New Paltz and Catskill. Twin is best hiked from Pecoy Notch Trail, which ascends gradually along Roaring Kill Trail from Elka Park Road (seasonal, unmaintained in winter but accessible by four-wheel-drive vehicles). From the Roaring Kill trailhead on Elka Park Road (2,150 feet elevation), take the yellow-blazed Roaring Kill Trail 0.25 mile to a junction and follow Pecoy Notch Trail to the left (southeast). The trail ascends gradually, passing a few quarry pits where you may notice some large, hand-dressed flagstones. Enter a hemlock woods and descend slightly to the left to arrive at a large, open quarry face over an extensive talus field providing views to the north. Dibble's Quarry is probably the best trailside example of a bluestone quarry in the

LOCATION
Elka Park, NY

RATING
Strenuous

DISTANCE
4.4 miles

ELEVATION GAIN
1,740 feet

ESTIMATED TIME
5 hours

MAPS
USGS Kaaterskill; AMC Catskill Mountains; NY-NJTC, Catskill Trails, Northeastern Catskills

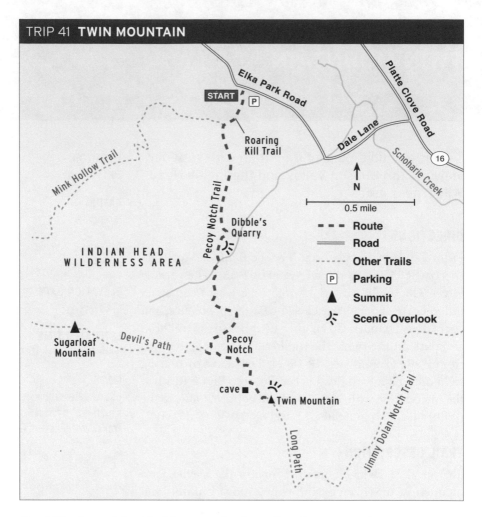

Catskills. Several druidic bluestone "recliners" and an array of intriguing stone sculptures have been constructed to take advantage of the views over the Clove toward Huckleberry Point. You can get a look at Twin Mountain from here, and to the north and downhill, you see the Hutterian Bruderhof, an intentional Christian community that is one of 23 settlements on four continents; they renounce private property and share everything—and love to hike. Kaaterskill High Peak and Roundtop Mountain are in the foreground. After you explore the area, continue along the trail. You'll leave the quarry and enter hardwoods, crossing a bridge and ascending.

Soon you will skirt the outlet of a beaver pond on your right. Beaver activity is spotty in this pond that feeds the high upper Schoharie River, but several dams and lodges have been evident in recent years. The pond, fed by runoff coming down the northeast slopes of Sugarloaf Mountain, attracts wildlife and has a quiet, primordial spirit about it, making a welcome stopover. As you continue, the trail heads uphill, and you begin to get views to the north of the Blackhead

Range. After about an hour's easy hiking, you'll reach Pecoy Notch, and Devil's Path. There is no trail out of Pecoy Notch to the south, only a profusion of tumbledown boulders and twisted logs. This is one of the notches, along with its easterly neighbor Jimmy Dolan Notch, that can be seen as bright bare scrapes from points as far south as the Shawangunks.

Bear left (east) for Twin, following Devil's Path (red) and Long Path trails. Blue and aqua are used interchangeably for Long Path, although the official color is aqua, to distinguish it from state markings. Twin Mountain is 0.5 mile ahead, with an additional 540-foot vertical rise to its first (true) summit.

The incline is steep with a westerly aspect, soon exposing Sugarloaf Mountain and, beyond, Hunter Mountain and its fire tower. You'll pass a large rock overhang that has been heavily used by hikers and is a convenient shelter in the event of rain. The trail is very steep in places. Suddenly, through a balsam-thick shoulder of the mountain, you see views opening up to the south, the vertical ledges of stone on your path finally subsiding to a series of flat outcrops that form the northerly summit of Twin.

From this point, the view is very good, extending as far south and southwest as the eye can see, but it is blocked to the north and east by mountains in the 3,500-foot class. From this southerly exposure you can survey the southern Catskills' high peaks just west of the Ashokan Reservoir. You may recognize Ashokan High Point and Samuels Point; and Friday, Wittenberg, Cornell, Panther, Giant Ledge, Balsam Cap, Balsam Lake, and Graham mountains, with many lower surrounding peaks identifiable with the aid of map and compass. You will also have a close look at the foreground mountains: Tremper, Carl, and Olderbark (west to east).

During runoff, listen closely and you might hear the noisy waters of the Saw

Twin Mountain is the only Catskill peak with two recognized summits.

Kill or Mink Hollow Brook echoing up from below. Cooper Lake, part of the town of Kingston's water supply, is visible 5 miles south-southwest of you, with Mount Tobias on its right. There was once a glass factory below in the Saw Kill Valley, and until recent years hikers were able to see the mirrorlike reflections of the waste glass that was cast aside, giving rise to the name the Glass Plains. The plains have since been reclaimed by nature.

The southerly summit of Twin is an additional (easy) 0.5-mile hike from here through a saddle of dense coniferous forest, bringing you to another flat rock overlook facing south. Views to the east are of the Hudson River valley and much of the river itself. From here, nearly the entire Ashokan Reservoir is visible, as well as the Shawangunks. On a clear day, beyond them you can see the scattered hills of the Hudson Highlands.

You'll want to visit both of Twin's summits to take in the variety of views that each cannot offer individually. If you have a lunch, plan to enjoy it at the more expansive southerly summit, where hikers feel inclined to loaf.

Return by the route you came, and while descending the north summit, about halfway down, you can test your lungs against the echoes from Sugarloaf.

DID YOU KNOW?

Twin is the only Catskill peak with two recognized summits.

MORE INFORMATION

For more information on the Catskill Forest Preserve, visit dec.ny.gov/lands/5265.html. For the DEC Region 4 office in Stamford, call 607-652-7365.

42

PLATEAU MOUNTAIN

A very steep rise out of Stony Clove Notch leads to a long, level plateau with isolated views.

DIRECTIONS

To locate the trailhead, drive south on NY 214 from NY 23A between Hunter and Tannersville and go 3 miles to the south end of Notch Lake. Or from the south at Phoenicia and NY 28, go north 9 miles on NY 214. Park at the trailhead parking area in Devil's Tombstone State Campground day-use area on the west side of NY 214. There is a day-use fee. *GPS coordinates:* 42° 09.564′ N, 74° 12.218′ W.

TRAIL DESCRIPTION

Stony Clove Notch is a narrow mountain pass with rugged visual appeal. It is formed by the long ridge of Plateau Mountain meeting with that of Hunter Mountain and holds at its apex the teardrop of Notch Lake and the Devil's Tombstone State Campground, where the 24-mile-long Devil's Path crosses NY 214. The notch, a major Catskill landmark, can be seen from 50 miles away. From north or south, look at Plateau's western slope, and you'll have an idea of the ascent you're about to make.

Cross the road to the east, where you'll see trail signs and the red blazes of Devil's Path. Plateau Mountain lookout (a.k.a. Orchid or Orchard Point) is indicated at 1.2 miles, but the mountain's true summit is on the east end of the ridge at 3,840 feet, 2.5 miles from the trailhead. What you will witness from the first lookout will please you more than the boreal, viewless summit. Plateau Mountain Lookout is an outstanding viewpoint at 3,600 feet—one that is grossly underrated in the hierarchy of Catskill vistas.

Climb the steps and ascend over rocky terrain into a mature hardwood forest. The trail quickly becomes very steep, with makeshift stone steps to aid your ascent. In ten

LOCATION
Hunter, NY

RATING
Strenuous

DISTANCE
6 miles

ELEVATION GAIN
1,840 feet

ESTIMATED TIME
6 hours

MAPS
USGS Hunter; AMC Catskill Mountains; NY-NJTC Catskill Trails, Northeastern Catskills

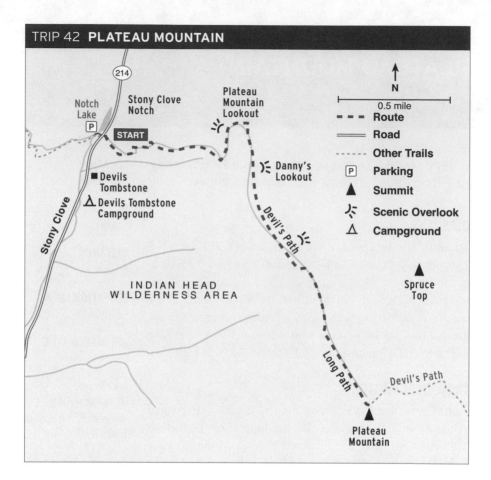

214

Notch Lake
P

Stony Clove Notch

START

Plateau Mountain Lookout

N

0.5 mile

- - - **Route**
═══ **Road**
····· **Other Trails**
P **Parking**
▲ **Summit**
⁆⁅ **Scenic Overlook**
△ **Campground**

Danny's Lookout

■ Devils Tombstone

△ Devils Tombstone Campground

Stony Clove

Devil's Path

▲ Spruce Top

INDIAN HEAD WILDERNESS AREA

Long Path

Devil's Path

▲ Plateau Mountain

minutes or more, as you climb over roots and rocks, you'll encounter extensive talus slides of an old stone quarry to your left and views over your shoulder to the southwest of Slide and Wittenberg in the Slide–Panther Wilderness area, as well as Cornell, Friday, Peekamoose, Table, and Panther mountains, and beyond.

These good views vanish as the trail turns north, with spring beauties and red trillium sprinkled liberally along its edge. If the trillium is in bloom during your visit, you might be surprised at its putrid scent, unbecoming to such a pretty flower. All species of trillium are rare, protected, and may not be picked. In spring you also will see in bloom the very pretty viburnum, or hobblebush, with its large, heart-shaped leaves, a favorite deer food.

On this flat section of trail at 3,400 feet (the first flat stretch since you set out), you can look back west for occasional views of Hunter Mountain. You'll cross the 3,500-foot mark and may see a sign indicating this point. In another ten minutes, you'll traverse ledges that gradually take you up and onto Plateau Mountain lookout. This is a nearly 180-degree view, reaching across the range from Colonel's Chair at Hunter mountain ski area (and its ski trails) to Hunter Mountain's fire tower, Southwest Hunter Mountain, West Kill Mountain, the High Peaks,

Outcroppings en route to Plateau Mountain offer fine views over the northeast Catskills.

and the Ashokan Reservoir. You can see Belleayre, Balsam, Haynes, Eagle, Big Indian (shaped like a molar), Doubletop, and Fir mountains. Giant Ledge looks tiny at 246 degrees; with binoculars, you can make out the cliffs. Slide Mountain is at 220 degrees. Look down into the col and then at Cornell and Wittenberg mountains. You can plainly see the landslide on Slide Mountain; snow helps define it. Wittenberg's steep and sudden dropoff is just above Mount Tremper's fire tower (230 degrees). Peekamoose Mountain is at 228 degrees. Looking to the left of it, you see Ashokan High Point. With binoculars, you can see the Lake Maratanza tower farm in Sam's Point Preserve. Across Stony Clove Notch on the east-facing slope of Hunter Mountain is Becker Hollow, the shortest route to Hunter's summit.

The summit ridge is flat now. Continue following the trail to the east until you reach an unobstructed overlook (Danny's Lookout) on the north side with a large rock on which a crude rising sun is carved. Views include the Blackhead Range, North Point, South Mountain, Roundtop Mountain, Kaaterskill High Peak, and down into Platte Clove. Hard to your right you will see Spruce Top Mountain and then Sugarloaf Mountain, with its long ridgeline plunging into Mink Hollow to meet Roaring Kill and Schoharie Creek. You can see North Lake at 86 degrees. The distant mountain groups to the northeast are the Taconics, including the Greylock range. Continue on the flat ridge over a soft, duff trail—dizzy with trout lilies—for another five minutes until you reach an overlook with the same northerly views. Use caution: This one has a dangerous drop. Many blown-down conifers lie on this exposed ridge like bleached whale-bones against the contrasting verdant life. Continue through a forest of large spruce and fir, where the trail switches to the ridge's south side. You'll begin to go uphill slightly in a few minutes, and within another ten minutes enter a thick understory of balsam, reminiscent of Indian Head's summit but not as enclosed. Whipped winds tear along the thin ridge as you peer through trees into abyssal Silver Hollow and Stony Clove Notch. The forest remains coniferous on this long walk to the cloaked summit; it lends a nostalgic feel, perhaps reminding you of favorite walks in places like the White Mountains or the Maine coast.

In twenty minutes, you'll reach the summit, just beyond a 90-degree left turn where the trail turns south to east. The thick spruce-fir cripplebrush will rub against your shoulders as the trail wanders along the ridge. Follow the trail for another fifteen minutes to your final destination: a rock looking east. Jump across a shallow crevasse and survey Kaaterskill High Peak, and Sugarloaf, Roundtop, North Point, North, Overlook, and part of Twin mountains. The view is limited compared with the ones you had already, but it gives you an intimate feeling for the heart of Devil's Path.

Return the way you came, listening for the *grokk, grokk* of hunting ravens.

DID YOU KNOW?

When trillium blooms in very early spring, its stench attracts pollinating insects in search of decomposing flesh. For this reason, it is called a carrion flower.

MORE INFORMATION

Parking for the trailhead is at the Devil's Tombstone State Campground day-use area at Notch Lake. For more information on the Catskill Forest Preserve, visit dec.ny.gov/lands/5265.html. For the DEC Region 4 office in Stamford, call 607-652-7365.

43

KAATERSKILL HIGH PEAK

A long, remote hike into the isolated Kaaterskill Wild Forest area offers spectacular views from Hurricane Ledge.

DIRECTIONS

To reach the trailhead, turn south off NY 23A at the only light in Tannersville onto CR 16 (Spring Street). Set your trip odometer to zero. At 1.3 miles, this road intersects Bloomer Road, where you'll bear left. At 1.8 miles, you'll reach a Y where you bear left onto Platte Clove Road (still CR 16). At 4.6 miles, you'll pass Dale Lane on the right (the trail to Sugarloaf, Twin, and Pecoy Notch mountains). Stay on Platte Clove Road, and at 5.7 miles, you'll see Prediger Road on the right. At 6.5 miles from Tannersville, turn left onto the dirt entrance to the Kaaterskill Wild Forest area parking lot. (See Trip 45 for alternate seasonal directions through Platte Clove.) *GPS coordinates:* 42° 08.033′ N, 74° 04.918′ W.

TRAIL DESCRIPTION

Kaaterskill High Peak was far more popular 100 years ago during the hotel heyday than it is today. Then, the mountains were defined by hotel magnates who did everything possible to convince visitors their establishments were indeed positioned in the heart of the Catskills. High Peak (contending with Roundtop) was considered the highest mountain in the range until the Princeton geologist and founder of the National Weather Bureau, Arnold Guyot, reduced it to a lowly 23rd on the list of Catskill peaks in 1779. (It's actually 22nd). His authority was considered absolute by many; yet his findings challenged local belief to the point that others claimed he was in scientific error. A veritable empire of tourism had been built on the supposition that High Peak was the very heart and soul of the Catskills, and to question

LOCATION
Platte Clove, NY

RATING
Strenuous

DISTANCE
10 miles

ELEVATION GAIN
1,855 feet

ESTIMATED TIME
6 hours

MAPS
USGS Kaaterskill; AMC Catskill Mountains; NY-NJTC Catskill Trails, Northeastern Catskills

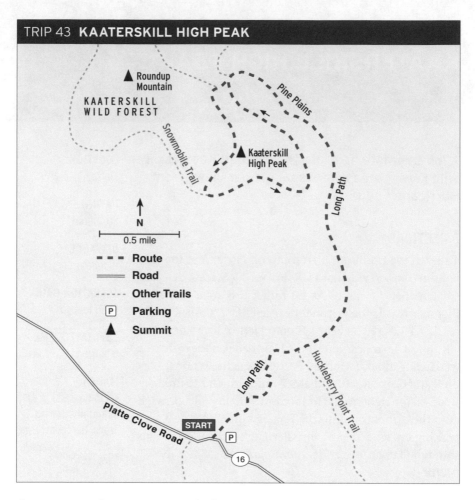

Roundup
Mountain

**KAATERSKILL
WILD FOREST**

Pine Plains

Snowmobile Trail

Kaaterskill
High Peak

Long Path

N

0.5 mile

- - - **Route**
═══ **Road**
- - - **Other Trails**
P **Parking**
▲ **Summit**

Long Path

Huckleberry Point Trail

Long Path

START

P

Platte Clove Road

16

that status was heresy. But science often overrules even the most wishful thinking. From low in the valley, High Peak does appear to be the highest mountain on the skyline. Although it is evident from guidebooks and maps of the golden era that Kaaterskill High Peak was a very popular climbing destination, the mountain has since existed in such anonymity that only an informally marked trail crosses its summit. A snowmobile trail circles both High Peak and Roundtop, providing access to High Peak's summit trail. (Roundtop is trailless.)

At the entrance to the parking area, you will see trailhead signs and orange snowmobile blazes, aqua-colored Long Path blazes, and blue foot-trail blazes. A sign denotes "Junction With Loop Trail, 3.6 Miles"; this is your in-transit destination. Don't be confused by the sign referencing Steenberg Road, a dirt road named for an early quarryman who lived near Huckleberry Point. It is not identified on maps or in the field. Follow the snowmobile trail uphill through a dense forest of hardwood and hemlock, passing old stone walls and listening to a tumbling creek on your right. The trail follows a pleasing old

Facing page: A hiker savors the view
southward from Hurricane Ledge.

dirt road marked as a snowmobile trail that has eroded well below surface grade. Within 25 minutes, you will reach a fork where arrows point to the right. Continue on the well-marked snowmobile trail, and in less than ten minutes you'll reach another Y, where you bear right, passing Huckleberry Point Trail (see Trip 45). Viburnum, yellow and purple violets, and trout lilies (the mottled leaf resembles a trout) form a colorful understory. The trail is relatively level for the next twenty minutes before you cross a pair of short timber bridges between two shallow creeks in a pretty spruce-fir swamp.

The trail then heads uphill and you begin to see beech trees and some remarkably large hemlocks and maples. Wildlife is abundant. Porcupines will scuttle away as you approach; owls will scrutinize you with haunting whispers as you rest. Here, amid the spring beauties, you can look south at Plattekill Mountain and northwest at the shoulder of High Peak. After a fairly stiff ascent, the trail levels out into a birch forest with scattered evergreens, which soon becomes a pure evergreen forest. Curiously, this pure spruce-fir forest is called the Pine Plains.

After 45 minutes of traversing this flat, swampy section of trail (wet and muddy in spring), turn sharply left, still following the snowmobile markers. Avoid the faint trail that leaves to the right (Long Path), which goes to Palenville via Buttermilk Falls, Wildcat ravine, and Poet's Ledge. This sharp left (still the snowmobile trail) heads uphill now, and within a few minutes, you'll reach a T and the start of the loop around Kaaterskill High Peak and Roundtop. Turn right (west), following the snowmobile trail briefly, and look carefully to your left for the blue-blazed trail. There is no sign indicating a trail to High Peak's summit, and marking is poor, so you must be very alert to spy it on your left. Within about 500 feet of turning, at elevation 2,933 feet, an established foot trail can be seen on the left, heading uphill in a southerly direction.

Follow the trail uphill, looking for blazes on rocks and trees (they are scarce), into an area of steep ledges and rock-strewn, moss-cloaked forest.

After about 40 minutes or so of strenuous hiking you cross several ledges and through many tangled blowdowns as you gain the summit, a flat area enclosed by trees. You will get some views to the north of Kaaterskill Clove and the surrounding mountains, but these are mostly obscured.

You will know you've achieved High Peak's summit when you reach a flat area among the evergreens where benchmarks can be studied in the flat stones. Pieces of a wrecked aircraft are strewn about in the woods. Herd trails leading off to the east go nowhere in particular, created by those searching for views and aircraft wreckage. Continue to Hurricane Ledge and its remarkable views by following the trail for another fifteen minutes. This brings you to a large expanse of grassy, open terrain with an east-to-west, south-facing aspect. The view is rare, including a variety of topography from the Hudson River valley, the Shawangunks, the Hudson Highlands, and the immediate Catskills. The ledge is a fine place to snooze, snack, photograph, or bivouac. A crude campsite appears to the right of the trail just uphill of the ledge.

While it is possible to continue following blue blazes heading south off the ledge, the trail is very steep, in poor condition, is hazardous under most conditions, and is especially dangerous when it is wet. For these reasons it is best to turn around here. From Hurricane Ledge, retrace your route back to the snowmobile trail and retrace your steps to the trailhead.

DID YOU KNOW?

High Peak and Roundtop are often present in Hudson River School paintings of the nineteenth century as background or subject matter, particularly in scenes from the Catskill Mountain House area. One of the finest representations of Kaaterskill High Peak appears in Thomas Cole's painting *Sunny Morning on the Hudson*, which depicts a highly romanticized version of High Peak from the vicinity of Roundtop.

MORE INFORMATION

Because the trail crossing Kaaterskill High Peak from the snowmobile trail is remote, you should regard this as a strenuous and challenging hike that requires solid direction-finding skills, a map and compass (and your GPS), and plenty of food and water. Allow plenty of time. The Kaaterskill Wild Forest is a very quiet piece of country, even when the neighboring trails to the south and north (Devil's Path and Escarpment Trail, respectively) are busy. For more information on the Catskill Forest Preserve, visit dec.ny.gov/lands/5265.html. For the DEC Region 4 office in Stamford, call 607-652-7365.

TANBARKING

The tanbark era in the Catskills ran roughly from 1830 to 1870, resulting in the near deforestation of the area's eastern, or Canada, hemlock (*Tsuga canadensis*). The downfall of this romantic symbol of the North Woods was its tannin-rich bark, which was ground for use in the leather-tanning process, mostly for waterproofing boots and equipment for Civil War soldiers. After felling, trees could be peeled profitably only to the first branch, so much of the tree bark was wasted, and perhaps less than 1 percent of the lumber was used. Most of the trees were left to rot because there was no market for sawlogs. Hides were easier to transport than bark, so they were shipped to the Catskills from as far away as Argentina to be tanned.

Tanning was a wasteful process. In the estimation of the early guidebook writer H. A. Haring, "From three to ten hemlocks were felled to obtain a cord of bark [128 cubic feet] . . . probably, in the life of the industry, one hemlock was cut down for each hide tanned into leather." Colonel Zadock Pratt, for whom Prattsville is named, turned out more than 2 million hides during the lifespan of his tannery. Tannersville was previously named Edwardsville by Colonel William Edwards, one of the Catskills' most enduring "tanlords." At least 60 tanneries were running for 40 years, which gives you an idea of the vast number of trees involved.

There are a few virgin tracts of hemlock in the Catskills, most of them positioned on upper-elevation or steep slopes where oxen could not work. Chances are, some of these were in their vigorous youth as the industry waned. In addition to the tanners' hut foundations that can still be found in the hills, other evidence of the ruinous industry remains, including the old roads that many of today's marked trails follow. In a 1984 interview, the legendary forester Ed West (called "Mr. Catskill" by his Adirondack Mountain Club friends) remarked that twenty years earlier he had come across places where hemlock cut in barking days were still hard and firm, noting that "especially where it is damp it will stay like that . . . [it is] one of the most durable and long lived of woods." Hemlock is too slow-growing for plantations and was not considered a viable candidate for reforestation efforts.

44

POET'S LEDGE

This steep hike climbs to a quiet ledge overlooking Kaaterskill Clove, the vantage for Sanford R. Gifford's painting *October in the Catskills* (1845).

DIRECTIONS

From Exit 20 off the NYS Thruway (I-87) in Saugerties, go north on NY 32 for 6 miles and bear left at a light onto NY 32A. At 7.5 miles, bear left at a fork onto Malden Avenue. Proceed another 0.8 mile, crossing Woodstock Avenue, and find the Fernwood Restaurant on your left. (You must ask permission to park here.) To park in the forest-preserve access parking area, continue on NY 32A at the fork, go through Palenville, joining NY 23A at the light, bear left, and continue 0.5 mile. Park on the right and walk back through Palenville, following NY 23A to NY 32A. Go right onto Woodstock Avenue, right onto Mill Road, and right again onto Malden Avenue to the trailhead. *GPS coordinates:* 42° 10.406′ N, 74° 01.668′ W.

TRAIL DESCRIPTION

Poet's Ledge is identified on several very old maps and was accessible by footpath from Haines Falls as early as 1840. It is likely that hunters and surveyors knew of it before then, for by 1820 preparations were being made just a short distance north across the Clove at Pine Orchard to build the Catskill Mountain House (established 1823). Hikers will revel in the magical sense of isolation of this historical destination as they peer over the precipitous cleft and its adjoining, steep ravines. Almost 20,000 years of ice and running water has conspired to create the unforgettable landscape that is Kaaterskill Clove.

This is a strenuous climb. It may look very close to the road on the map, and it is; it's the elevation you need to

LOCATION
Palenville, NY

RATING
Strenuous

DISTANCE
4.4 miles

ELEVATION GAIN
1,780 feet

ESTIMATED TIME
4.5 hours

MAPS
USGS Kaaterskill; AMC Catskill Mountains; NY-NJTC Catskill Trails, Northeastern Catskills

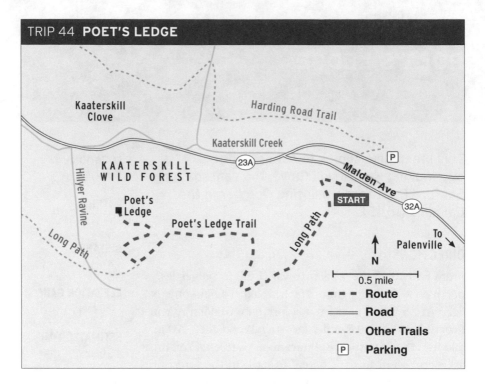

Kaaterskill
Clove

Harding Road Trail

Kaaterskill Creek

K A A T E R S K I L L
W I L D F O R E S T

Hillyer Ravine

23A

Malden Ave

Poet's
Ledge

Poet's Ledge Trail

START

32A

Long Path

Long Path

To
Palenville

N

0.5 mile

- - - **Route**
═══ **Road**
····· **Other Trails**
P **Parking**

consider. Although this can be a hard climb (it will prove to be a very strenuous season opener), finding parking near the trailhead could prove even harder. However, the hiker-friendly owners of the Fernwood Restaurant, located at the trailhead, will allow you to park in their lot if you ask permission. Without doing so, you may have to park on the street in Palenville, adding another mile to the hike. You can also park at the forest-preserve access parking area just west of Palenville on the north side of NY 23A, just before it enters the Catskill Park. But be careful—the traffic is very fast here.

Assuming you've parked at the Fernwood Restaurant, walk east back the way you came on Malden Avenue and look carefully for the trailhead about 200 feet east of the Fernwood. The trail is not immediately identified, but you will see the trusty aqua Long Path blazes on a telephone pole. Turn south on this little dirt road, and walk about 100 feet to a forest-preserve access gate on your right, where you will see blue state trail disks. This is Red Gravel Hill Road. Follow it uphill as it rises behind the Fernwood and switches back once or twice before maintaining a long, fairly steep southerly ascent. The road's surface improves with elevation. By the time you reach the forest-preserve boundary, identified by yellow blazes and wild-forest signage, you'll have worked up a sweat.

Stay alert, as the trail turns off the road to the right, heading west and uphill; Red Gravel Hill Road continues south onto private property. Now you climb on a heavily washed-out 1800s quarry road, hardly recognizable as a road anymore. As this section of trail switches north, it levels and improves. Look on the left now as the forest type changes markedly from second-growth hardwood to the typical oak and laurel cover of the mid-elevations, and you may see the remains of a quarry tucked into the undergrowth along the uphill edge of this terrace. Hand-dressed stone fragments are still found along the trail.

The trail climbs, levels, climbs again, and rises through a series of ledges and natural stone steps to a point where you encounter a fine view upriver. A private party has placed a sign here (Maeli's Lookout). Across the clove, you will see Palenville Overlook and Indian Head (not the mountain by the same name), a pair of high ledges along the southerly flank of South Mountain. You also look out across the Hudson Valley to the vague blue-green hills of the Taconic Plateau, Mount Greylock, and the Green Mountains, far beyond.

Back at it, you will soon be pleased to see the forest type changing again, this time to hemlock, promising a boreal summit-like experience. A frail northern hardwood forest (beech, birch, and maple) has failed to invade this almost pure stand of conifers. Once again, the trail flattens and begins to meander over a delightful and most welcome stretch of flat ground at 1,700 feet. The trail is often wet here on the northern fringes of Deer Laurel Swamp, a small wetland that you will see on the left.

Suddenly you come to Poet's Ledge Trail, a yellow-blazed spur. The sign is wrapped in hardware cloth, or wire, to protect it from porcupines. The distance is marked as 0.47 mile. Descend through an area of primordial texture, past huge boulders heaped with heavy clods of thick moss and detritus. The trail is self-guiding and well marked. Hemlock needles and cones blanket the trail. Patches of fern and laurel, an understory of vigorous red spruce, and maturing hemlocks make up a dense transition zone. Suddenly, the trail flattens

The trail to Poet's Ledge follows a quarry road built in the mid-nineteenth century.

onto a bare bluestone dance floor of sorts hemmed in by pitch pines. Continue, bearing left and southwest and descending through ledgy terrain.

As you approach the open vista of Poet's Ledge, be alert to the existence of a substantial crevice dividing the ledge. Though narrow, this crack is deep enough to be of some consequence, especially if it is hidden by snow. It is large enough to fall into, and children should be carefully supervised.

From this small patch of rocks, you can sit and muse over the deep abysmal clove and lose your thoughts in time while gazing west at Onteora and Parker mountains, the north-draining ravines off Kaaterskill's shoulder, and the enviable, precariously perched houses of Twilight Park at the top of the clove. Both Kaaterskill Falls and Haines Falls, located in the upper elevations of the clove, are hidden behind low ridges. To the north you can see Black Dome and Blackhead mountains in the Windham Blackhead Range Wilderness.

Although not documented, it is possible that William Cullen Bryant, who together with Washington Irving created the first literary allusions to the Catskills, visited Poet's Ledge, thus engendering its name. More than likely, a clever cartographer familiar with the works of James Fenimore Cooper, and Irving, in tune with the Romantic spirit of the times, made it up. There is little doubt, however, that the walkers of the Twilight Park–based Linger Not Society and artists of the time knew about Poet's Ledge. What seems hauntingly apparent (and is a subject of recent interest by the Clark Art Institute) is that Sanford R. Gifford painted his *October in the Catskills* from the vantage of Poet's Ledge (most likely from 1845 field sketches), where the Kaaterskill rises to the south and Haines Falls is seen due west. The work is in the collection of the Los Angeles County Museum of Art and can be viewed online at collections.lacma.org/node/239245.

Return by the route you came.

DID YOU KNOW?

The trail to Poet's Ledge was lost for decades, perhaps even a hundred years. The landmark was rediscovered by the Salvador Dalí scholar Albert "Cap" Field in the early 1980s.

MORE INFORMATION

For more information on the Catskill Forest Preserve, visit dec.ny.gov/lands/5265.html. For the DEC Region 4 office in Stamford, call 607-652-7365.

45

HUCKLEBERRY POINT

A short walk through hemlock and pitch-pine woods leads to a scenic overlook above Platte Clove and the Hudson Valley.

DIRECTIONS

These directions bring you the back way over scenic Platte Clove Road, a seasonal road that should not be attempted unless it is legally open (April 15 to November 15) and clear of ice and snow. When it is closed or when the road conditions are questionable, follow the directions to the Codfish Point trailhead.

From Exit 20 off the NYS Thruway (I-87) in Saugerties (either northbound or southbound), bear left a short distance to the intersection of NY 32 and NY 212. Set your trip odometer to zero and head west on NY 212 toward Woodstock. At 2 miles, watch carefully on your right for CR 35 (Blue Mountain Road). Follow it, bearing left at a Y, through Blue Mountain. At 5.3 miles, pass Woodstock–Saugerties Road on your left, then pass Manorville Road on your right at 5.4 miles. Now you will head straight up the mountain on Platte Clove Road. As the road tops out, look on your right for the Kaaterskill Wild Forest parking area at 7.8 miles. Turn right into the lot. You'll see the trail register and trail signs here for Steenbergh Road (the trail follows this dirt road, named for an early bluestone quarry) and the blue-blazed trail. The trail begins on the northwest side of the lot. *GPS coordinates:* 42° 08.033′ N, 74° 04.918′ W.

TRAIL DESCRIPTION

Huckleberry Point is an ideal picnicking spot, suitable for those sunny, clear days when an easy hike to its quiet, scenic ledges is the goal. Especially on nice weekends, however, expect to see many other hikers. It's no wonder: This pretty

LOCATION
Hunter, NY

RATING
Moderate

DISTANCE
4.4 miles

ELEVATION GAIN
780 feet

ESTIMATED TIME
3.5 hours

MAPS
USGS Kaaterskill; AMC Catskill Mountains; NY-NJTC Catskill Trails, Northeastern Catskills

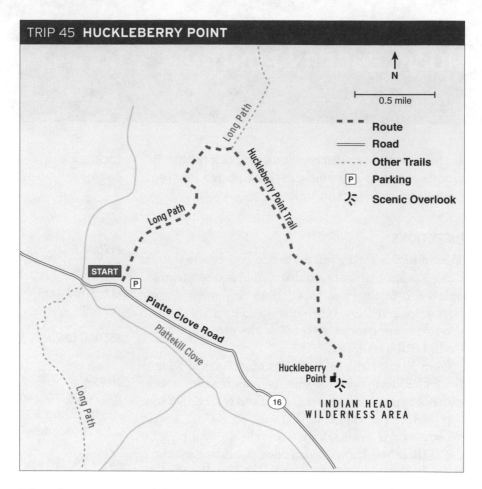

N

0.5 mile

- - - Route
═══ Road
····· Other Trails
P Parking
⅄ Scenic Overlook

Long Path

Huckleberry Point Trail

Long Path

START

P

Platte Clove Road

Plattekill Clove

Long Path

Huckleberry Point

16

INDIAN HEAD
WILDERNESS AREA

hike takes you to one of the Escarpment's most accessible and expansive south-easterly viewsheds on an easy trail with minimal vertical rise. Huckleberry Point Trail is reached via the Kaaterskill High Peak snowmobile trail, which circles Kaaterskill High Peak and Roundtop Mountain and which you follow for 1 mile. From the Kaaterskill Wild Forest parking area, follow the blue foot-trail blazes, red/orange snowmobile trail markers, and aqua Long Path blazes (sparse). The first section of trail rises through a dense hemlock forest over a deeply eroded old quarry road, within audible range of Mossy Brook downhill to the east.

After twenty minutes of hiking uphill, the trail reaches a Y in the hardwoods, where you bear right. Continue for ten minutes to an arrow pointing to the right, following the blue footpath and snowmobile blazes. Another five minutes along, you will leave the blue-blazed trail, bearing right (east) at the yellow-blazed Huckleberry Point Trail. (There's a sign and an arrow.) Travel through a level hardwood forest with a developing hemlock understory, where you will see obscure signs of an early quarrying and subsistence-farming community: stone piles, walls, and an old foundation or two. Within a few minutes, you'll drop slightly downhill into an oak woods, crossing Mossy Brook, which is several feet deep during runoff. Ford cautiously and continue directly on the other side. Don't make the mistake of following one of the old overgrown quarry roads. After the brook, you begin to climb slightly into an oak and beech transitional forest. The trail undulates easily uphill and downhill, yielding early spring views of the Devil's Path peaks, including Overlook, Indian Head, Twin, Sugarloaf, and Plateau mountains.

At this point, you will enjoy the extensive "slicks" (shrub thickets) of mountain laurel (*Kalmia latifolia*), an evergreen named by the biologist Carolus Linnaeus (1707–1778) for his researcher and student Peter Kalm (1716–1779). These bright-leaved members of the heath family are sharply contrasted against a young overstory of paper birch. Laurel blooms here in late spring with large, pink flower clusters. These vigorous but fragile trailside shrubs are easily killed or damaged by overzealous or untrained trail maintainers.

Within a half hour of the Huckleberry Point trailhead, you'll cross the southerly slope of a pitch-pine hillock. This is the prettiest section of trail, where you begin to sense the abyss ahead. The ledgy oak-pine terrain suddenly opens up like a curtain rising onto the blueberry precipices of the point. The views are

The distinct profile of Indian Head Mountain rises above a clutch of wild azaleas on Huckleberry Point.

expansive and the ledges are vertical, so be careful. You'll see the Devil's Path mountains in the Indian Head Wilderness area directly south, only a few miles away across the thousand-foot-deep Platte Clove (the hamlet of West Saugerties, below you, is 500 feet above sea level; you're at 2,200 feet). The north and east slopes are carved deeply by postglacial parallel drainage ravines. Overlook Mountain and its fire tower, as well as the Plattekill ridge, run west into Indian Head, whose profile is very apparent—lying supine with his distinct chin, nose, and eyebrow. Continuing west is Twin, then Sugarloaf and Plateau mountains.

Going east from Overlook, dropping down its slopes to the small, nearly vertical outcrop of Minister's Face, you look south over the east basin of the Ashokan Reservoir to the toothy hills of the Shawangunks. The left edge of the tooth is Sky Top; you can see the Albert K. Smiley Memorial Tower (a.k.a. Sky Top Tower) with binoculars at 203 degrees. To the right is Eagle Cliff. Hidden on the flat space between them are Mohonk Lake and the Mohonk Mountain House. Moving along the descending ridge of the northern Shawangunks is Guyot Hill, and finally, the last bump is Bonticou Crag. Moving east across the rolling expanse of valley above the flatlands of the Esopus and Rondout valleys, you may see the Fishkill Ridge dipping down into the Hudson River at the Highlands, and coming north, you see the city of Kingston, then Saugerties. In the middle of the Hudson's southernmost visible bay is the Esopus Meadows lighthouse at 189 degrees. Above the marshes of Tivoli Bays, just north of the Kingston–Rhinecliff Bridge, are the buildings of Bard College.

With patience, you can find Stissing Mountain at 135 degrees. The long ridge in the east is the Southern Taconic Plateau. The large birds you'll invariably see riding the thermals are not often hawks, but usually turkey vultures and black vultures.

Return by the route you came.

DID YOU KNOW?

This route follows the trail of the Nature Friends, a group that originated among German expatriates who liked to stroll here and, in homage to that spirit, called themselves the *Vanderverder*, or "wandering birds."

MORE INFORMATION

For more information on the Catskill Forest Preserve, visit dec.ny.gov/lands/5265.html. For the DEC Region 4 office in Stamford, call 607-652-7365.

46

NORTH POINT

A popular route along Escarpment Trail's cliffs leads to favorite haunts of the Hudson River School painters.

DIRECTIONS

From NY 23A in Haines Falls, turn north onto CR 18 (a.k.a. North Lake Road/Mountain House Road) and travel 2.3 miles to the North–South Lake Public Campground's main gate. *GPS coordinates:* 42° 12.095′ N, 74° 03.383′ W.

TRAIL DESCRIPTION

This historical and scenic day hike begins along the legendary cliffs of Pine Orchard and reveals the best scenery of the Escarpment. This is the heart of the Catskills, the place that prompted the eloquence of James Fenimore Cooper, the fanciful pen of Washington Irving, and the Romantic vision of Thomas Cole. If you have time for only one hike in the Catskills, make it this one.

The best way to approach this hike is from the beach and picnic area parking lot of the North–South Lake Public Campground and day-use area. Pay the day-use fee and drive through the main gate, bearing left at the Y to the North Lake beach and picnic area. As you approach the bathing beach and picnic area parking lot, note the North Mountain Trails sign on the left. Park, backtrack along the road to the trailhead, and follow the yellow-blazed spur east to the blue-blazed Escarpment Trail (or from the picnic area, simply walk east), toward Artist's and Sunset rocks, Newman's Ledge, and North Point. As you join Escarpment Trail, turn left (north) and follow the edge of some vertical drops as the trail ascends easily in dense evergreen woods.

LOCATION
Haines Falls, NY

RATING
Moderate

DISTANCE
7 miles

ELEVATION GAIN
700 feet

ESTIMATED TIME
4.5 hours

MAPS
USGS Kaaterskill; AMC Catskill Mountains; NY-NJTC Catskill Trails, Northeastern Catskills

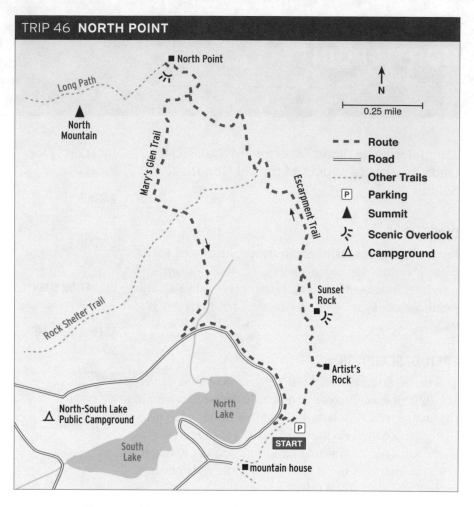

■ North Point

Long Path

▲ North Mountain

Mary's Glen Trail

Escarpment Trail

Rock Shelter Trail

N

0.25 mile

- - - **Route**
── **Road**
⋯ **Other Trails**
P **Parking**
▲ **Summit**
⋏ **Scenic Overlook**
△ **Campground**

Sunset Rock ⋏

■ Artist's Rock

△ North-South Lake Public Campground

North Lake

South Lake

P

START

■ mountain house

A series of historical lookouts begins as scenic vistas, opening up to the east across the Hudson Valley. Identifying the original locations of these lookouts— as they were understood by Mountain House guests—has become a hobby among local toponymists. Few of today's Escarpment place-names accurately match those of the nineteenth century. I'll use the most recent ones.

Climb through broken ledges and along a rocky footway to the first signed lookout, Artist's Rock, which was among the well-loved field studios of Thomas Cole. Cole was fond of pointing out his home—Locust Grove, in Catskill—from this spot, something you can still do today with the aid of binoculars if you know where to look; it's easier to spot Frederic Church's Olana on the eastern banks of the Hudson River, beyond which you see Mount Everett and the long ridge of the Taconics. Continue, and soon you'll arrive at Prospect Rock (2,280 feet), a more expansive version of Artist's Rock. Continue along, passing another little dimple of rock to the right of the trail that was once known as Sunrise Rock. You'll also pass Lake View Pinnacle, recognizable by its old initial carvings and more recent graffiti. Continue along the trail, passing through pitch-pine "orchards," so named for pure stands of the pine whose crooked limbs somewhat resemble a fruit tree. (This was the result of the Romantic imagination at work, remember.) Soon, a large, monolithic rock plateau appears to the right of the trail. This is Sunset Rock, a place that was once called the Bear's Den on account of its deep crevices. As you reach the Sunset Rock Trail junction, bear right and follow the spur trail through the pitch pines to the rock, and you'll agree that either place-name works. The deep fissures and cracks make suitable bear habitat, although the heavy human presence here has likely frightened them off. You will want to be cautious not to slip.

From here, the westerly views are magnificent. You see Kaaterskill High Peak and Roundtop Mountain above the lakes, and the long line of the southerly Escarpment heading for Overlook Mountain. Farther south, you can make out the Shawangunk Ridge, with Sky Top jutting out to the left of Overlook's easterly slopes.

Retrace your steps to the trail junction and continue north, climbing easily to Newman's Ledge, a fine open, vertical cliff looking northeast at 2,500 feet. Judging by its carvings, this was also a popular spot for Mountain House guests. Views expand to the north now to include Albany on a good day and the nearby valley of Rip Van Winkle Hollow (a.k.a. Sleepy Hollow). Look carefully and you might see the Old Mountain Road against the north face of the hollow. The trail continues north over a rocky surface, climbing terraces through hardwood and spruce thickets, and walking the edge of a bog before meeting with Rock Shelter Trail at the site of Badman Cave (2,650 feet). Climb to the

North Point is a popular and highly scenic destination hike along the 23-mile Escarpment Trail.

right, remaining on Escarpment Trail and walking the lip of a scenic, boreal ridge, then soon entering a flat hardwood forest. As you reach the junction with Mary's Glen Trail (your return route), bear right onto Escarpment Trail to begin the only continuously steep section of the trail. After fifteen minutes of strenuous and aerobic effort, you'll pass through a white-birch stand that precedes the large, flat rocks and long views from North Point's summit. Investigate views from various parts of the ledge: Windham High Peak, Burnt Knob, Acra Point, and Blackhead mountains to the north; the broad, flat Hudson Valley toward Albany to the east through the Taconics and Berkshires; and south across the Highlands and into the Escarpment, where North and South lakes lie like spilled quicksilver under the shadows of Kaaterskill High Peak and Roundtop Mountain.

Descend now, retracing your steps to the previous junction, and turn right on the yellow-blazed Mary's Glen Trail. You'll walk through thick spruce-fir forests as you descend to cross Rock Shelter Trail, continuing through a wet area to cross the top of Ashley Falls before descending into the Glen.

Go left when you reach the bottom of Ashley Falls (also called Mary's Glen Falls) on a spur trail to the stone rubble below the cascade. Turn around and follow the trail out to the campground road, turn left, and walk 0.5 mile back to the picnic area and bathing beach parking area.

DID YOU KNOW?

This spot was a favorite of Mary Scribner, the wife of Ira Scribner, who operated a sawmill on Spruce Creek above Kaaterskill Falls.

MORE INFORMATION

You can combine this hike with a picnic or a swim in spring-fed North Lake at the North–South Lake Public Campground. Or you can bring your canoe and paddle North and South lakes, reserve a campsite, and spend the night ($22 camping fee).

If you don't park at the campground, you can park outside the main gate and walk to North Lake beach (a walk-in fee applies), or take the yellow-blazed Rock Shelter Trail (no walk-in fee) to connect with Mary's Glen Trail. To use the latter two options, park outside the main gate in the Scutt Road trailhead parking area. (Two miles of featureless, round-trip hiking applies to either option.) Visit dec.ny.gov/outdoor/24487.html or call 518-589-5058.

47

INSPIRATION POINT

This cliff-edge hike above Kaaterskill Clove to the North–South Lake Public Campground follows a lakeside return route.

DIRECTIONS

From NY 23A in Haines Falls, turn north onto CR 18 (a.k.a. North Lake Road/Mountain House Road) and travel 2.3 miles. Turn right onto Scutt Road, and within 300 feet turn right again into the Escarpment trailhead parking area (a.k.a. Scutt Road Corral). *GPS coordinates:* 42° 12.039′ N, 74° 03.494′ W.

TRAIL DESCRIPTION

The scenic lookouts and labyrinthine footpaths surrounding the old mountain houses of North Lake's Pine Orchard area have been destination hikes since the early 1800s. Detailed in the many guidebooks of the day, the trail system around Pine Orchard was one of America's most popular visual attractions.

Many of the trails emanating from the grounds of the Kaaterskill Hotel and the Catskill Mountain House have since disappeared, leaving only fanciful place-names, such as Fairy Spring, Druid Rocks, and the Sphinx. But the scenery remains, and today's Escarpment Trail highlights the best of it.

Walk east across Scutt Road onto the blue-blazed Escarpment Trail, or ET (also the Sleepy Hollow Horse Trail at this point). Descend, soon crossing two railroad beds. Cross Spruce Creek on a footbridge and ascend slightly, passing an unmarked woods road to the left; this was once the approach to the now derelict but still interesting stone laundry building of the Catskill Mountain House. It is the only standing structure from the era of the great mountain houses. Continue on ET to the trail

LOCATION
Haines Falls, NY

RATING
Moderate

DISTANCE
8 miles

ELEVATION GAIN
500 feet

ESTIMATED TIME
4 hours

MAPS
USGS Kaaterskill; AMC Catskill Mountains; NY–NJTC, Catskill Trails, Northeastern Catskills

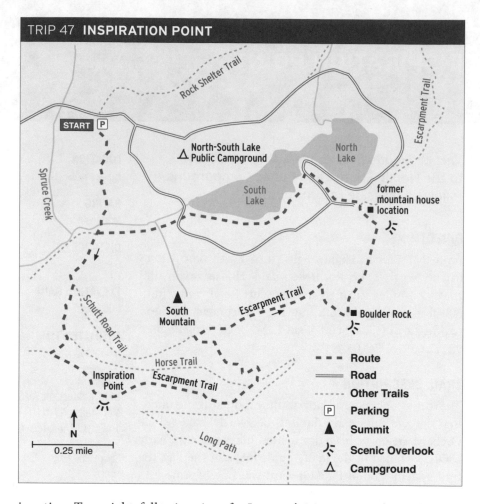

Rock Shelter Trail

Escarpment Trail

START P

North-South Lake
△ Public Campground

North
Lake

Spruce Creek

South
Lake

former
mountain house
■ location

Schutt Road Trail

South
Mountain

Escarpment Trail →

■ Boulder Rock

Horse Trail

Inspiration
Point

Escarpment Trail

↑
N
0.25 mile

Long Path

- - - - **Route**
======== **Road**
· · · · · **Other Trails**
P   **Parking**
▲   **Summit**
)⏑ **Scenic Overlook**
△   **Campground**

junction. Turn right, following signs for Layman's Monument. The trail passes a register and descends through laurels, arriving at the monument to a lost firefighter at 1.2 miles. Now the trail ascends, winding along the Escarpment's edge past steep drops. If you've timed your visit to coincide with the appearance of the pinxter blossoms (mid-May to mid-June), you'll also see swallowtail, bronze copper, and cabbage butterflies alighting on the blooms and on the multicolored hawkweeds and wildflowers clinging to the weather-beaten cliffs along the way. Dodging in and out of oak and laurel woods, at 1.6 miles you'll pass the yellow-blazed connector trail to Scutt Road Trail on the left. Continue straight ahead on the blue-blazed ET, arriving at Sunset Rock at 1.7 miles. The trail descends to Inspiration Point (1.9 miles), a narrow ledge with improved views of Kaaterskill High Peak and Roundtop Mountain across Kaaterskill Clove. This is the spot where Ulysses S. Grant, a regular visitor to the Catskill Mountain House, enjoyed firing a shotgun so he could hear the echoes bouncing back across the ravine.

Continue through the forest for another twenty minutes of easy walking, passing views (and precipitous, dangerous ledges) to the south and east. Note Palenville Overlook, the ragged rock outcropping jutting from the clove's northern flank, down to your right. Here ET joins Sleepy Hollow Horse Trail at a level intersection, where you continue straight ahead. Bear left here on ET toward Boulder Rock (1.3 miles) and North–South Lake Campground (2.0 miles). The trail climbs a bit now, flattening as you approach the Hotel Kaaterskill site on South Mountain. There is another junction here, where the red-blazed Scutt Road Trail goes left (west). The hotel site is neither marked nor obvious from the junction but lies north of it and can be explored on the herd trails that circle and penetrate it. There are few, if any, remains. Continue on ET through a pretty oak-and-laurel forest dotted with single red spruce trees, passing an unmarked trail that descends to the South Lake beach and picnic area road, and within 0.5 mile, you'll reach a trail junction where the red-blazed trail shortcuts off to the left toward the Catskill Mountain House site. Avoid this trail and continue following the blue blazes, bearing right and descending slightly. In a few moments, you'll reach Split Rock, a large, fractured megalith with a deep fissure lying close to the trail. Suddenly, you're at

Boulder Rock's popularity stretches back to the early days of the Catskill Mountain House.

Boulder Rock, a large erratic that sits on a flat ledge with outstanding views. Old photos show an ornate gazebo perched atop the rock.

Vistas of the Hudson Valley here are outstanding, giving an idea of what's to come over at Pine Orchard. You have fine, far-reaching views of the Shawangunks, Taconics, Berkshires, Stissing Mountain, and the Hudson River. A hundred feet farther is Shorey Point. To the south is the Shawangunk Ridge, with the sharp cleft of Sky Top. Farther south still is the long, serpentine ridge of Schunemunk Mountain. Continue on the trail, leaving Boulder Rock at your back and ascending past the red-blazed trail on your left. Ledges, some of them dangerous, continue to appear as you travel north along the Escarpment's edge. At Eagle Rock, where carvings dating to 1850 can be seen in the stone, bear slightly right to avoid dead-ending in a pitch-pine orchard, drop downhill slightly, and after a brief descent and switchback in the trail, arrive at the flat expanse where the Catskill Mountain House stood—the original Pine Orchard. The pines are gone, but the "orchards," as the romantics of the time called them, still exist on the trail to North Point. You can see many carvings in the rock ledge here, including the best of them, the ornate 1866 inscription of the Smiths Cornet Band. Secreted away in a corner to the north are the initials of one C. A. Beach, most likely belonging to Charles Addison Beach, a superintendent of the Rip Van Winkle Railroad and the brother of Charles L. Beach, a president of the railway and the owner of the Catskill Mountain House.

When you've had enough of the views across the valley (similar to those of Boulder Rock), head west with the ledge at your back and watch the blue blazes. Shortly, ET departs to the right (north) and drops downhill to an open area just east of North Lake (visible nearby). You're at the point where the Otis Elevated Railroad rose from the valley floor to the top of the Escarpment. (You can see the cut in the mountain by exploring to the east a little here.)

Leave ET now and bear left, following the road you can see ahead (also marked as a snowmobile trail) and walk along the south shore of North Lake, with the lake on your right. You will also see yellow foot-trail blazes. Follow this road around the peninsula that juts into the narrows between North and South lakes, and at a point where the snowmobile trail turns east, follow the yellow-blazed foot trail into the hemlock woods as it goes south along the lake's edge. Skirt the edge of South Lake and walk past the bathhouse, keeping it to your left. The yellow-blazed trail continues along the edge of South Lake, reentering the woods where the beach and the lake come together. If your feet are sore, you can follow the access road back to the parking area. Otherwise, follow the yellow-blazed trail into the woods. After twenty minutes, the trail ends on the South Lake access road (paved). As you rise to the road, you'll see the lake to your right. Bear left and across the road to the yellow-blazed and well-identified ski trail, a pleasant, nearly flat trail that brings you 0.5 mile to the intersection of ET and Scutt Road Trail. From here, bear right onto ET to return to the trailhead parking area.

DID YOU KNOW?

Today, power lines mark the route of the old funicular railway that took passengers to the Catskill Mountain House. The railway was dismantled, sold as scrap, and recycled for armament during World War II.

MORE INFORMATION

For more information on the Catskill Forest Preserve, visit dec.ny.gov/lands/ 5265.html. For the DEC Region 4 office in Stamford, call 607-652-7365.

48

KAATERSKILL FALLS

This hike to the state's highest waterfall is the most popular short trek in the Catskills.

DIRECTIONS

From Exit 20 off the NYS Thruway (I-87) in Saugerties, take NY 32 for 6 miles to NY 32A, bearing left into Palenville. In 8 miles, bear left again at the light in Palenville onto NY 23A, ascending through Kaaterskill Clove. The trailhead is located at 11.2 miles, at the hairpin turn on NY 23A between the towns of Haines Falls and Palenville. Park at the designated area 0.2 mile west (uphill) of the trailhead. *GPS coordinates: 42° 11.390' N, 74° 04.443' W.*

TRAIL DESCRIPTION

By the mid-nineteenth-century Romantic period, Kaaterskill Falls had become the most popular symbol of the American wilderness, as notions of the "picturesque and sublime" were shifting away from European scenery. The West was still a frontier by the time the Catskill Mountain House was built on the ledges of Pine Orchard in 1823, and Niagara Falls, discovered by travelers as early as 1683, was old news by 1778. The main reasons for Kaaterskill Falls' immense popularity were its proximity to the largest U.S. population center of the time, New York City, and that the rising upper and middle classes now had the time and means for destination travel. Thomas Cole, the founder of the Hudson River School of American landscape painting, brought the falls to the public's attention.

By the late 1800s, the falls were averaging 100 visitors a day, most of them guests of the mountaintop hotels. At the time, people believed nearby Roundtop Mountain (3,804 feet) was the highest of the Catskill peaks and therefore represented the heart of the Catskills. They also believed the Catskills were the embodiment of a new national

LOCATION
Haines Falls, NY

RATING
Easy

DISTANCE
1.4 miles

ELEVATION GAIN
200 feet

ESTIMATED TIME
1.5 hours

MAPS
USGS Kaaterskill; AMC Catskill Mountains; NY-NJTC Catskill Trails, Northeastern Catskills

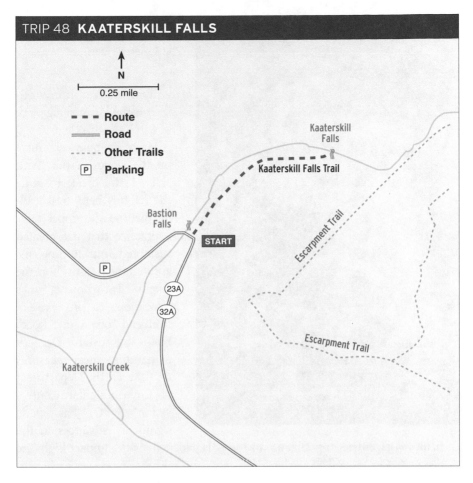

identity, making its definitive case in the art and literature of the times. Today the hotels are gone and the falls enjoy relative obscurity, but you won't think so if you arrive on a sunny weekend, when the parking area is full and hikers of all ages walk single file up the trail.

From the parking lot, descend along the road (NY 23A) cautiously, keeping to the left, where the shoulder is wider. Cross the highway bridge next to Bastion Falls, bear left, and go around the guardrail to begin the climb. There's a trail sign here, indicating the falls at 0.5 mile on the dead-end spur trail. Follow yellow blazes uphill steeply over stone and wooden steps to the trail register. Continue through a small grove of virgin hemlock, one of four such groves in the Kaaterskill Wild Forest, as the trail follows close along the shaded banks of Spruce Creek. Within fifteen to twenty minutes, you'll come upon the falls, hidden from view until you arrive at their base.

Try to time your visit to a period that is not too dry and you'll be treated to the remarkable double-plumed fall; the initial 175-foot drop is the most spectacular. The upper plume fills a huge basin (not seen from below) known as the

A new observation deck on Laurel House Road provides a great view of Kaaterskill Falls.

Amphitheater, immortalized as the slumbering place of Rip Van Winkle.

Many people scramble up the slope on the south side of the creek to scale the narrow herd trail leading behind the upper falls, a practice that has created sustained impact problems and is the reason for the original Escarpment Trail's relocation to its present trailhead on Scutt Road. Following sustained outcry demanding safety measures for the area, the Department of Environmental Conservation (DEC) has made significant advances in the difficult management of public use of the falls. Not only is the impact high; the dangers are, too. Several people have died here, and at least two people barely have survived falls from above. Several dogs also number among the deceased. The most memorable is Vite, a dog who, in the 1800s, had been trained to jump at his master's whistle. A thoughtless whistle caused Vite to jump over the falls. The bereaved master engaged a stonecutter to carve a lavish memorial to "Vite, the Bayard of Dogs" that still can be seen in the ledges on the steep slopes below the falls, where long ago there was once a series of paths, ropes, and ladders leading to the Amphitheater.

The artists, poets, and other writers who focused their creative genius on Kaaterskill Falls are legion. Thomas Cole is credited with the first and most influential painting, *Falls of the Kaaterskill* (1826), which immediately created public interest in the site. Cole's protégés and imitators followed, among them Jasper Cropsey (a late-generation Hudson River School painter), W. H. Bartlett, Winslow Homer, Harry Fenn, Currier and Ives, and countless engravers and illustrators. Poets included William Cullen Bryant, in particular; even Thomas Cole was inspired to write poetry and essays about the falls, as were many writers of the Knickerbocker period, Washington Irving central among them. Henry David Thoreau visited Ira and Mary Scribners' cabin at Kaaterskill Falls in the summer of 1844, during a brief hiatus in the construction of his cabin at Walden Pond, along with William Ellery Channing, another founder of Transcendentalism. For some unknown reason, however, Thoreau deleted references to the Catskills in the first draft of *Walden*.

John Bartram, the chief American horticulturalist of his time, and his son, the naturalist, explorer, and writer William Bartram, visited Kaaterskill Falls in 1753. The latter's book dealing with his explorations, *The Travels of William Bartram* (1791), had a clear impact on both William Wordsworth and Samuel Taylor Coleridge, who would in turn influence the American Romantic imagination. Timothy Dwight, president of Yale College in 1823, contributed his evocative *Description of Kaaterskill Falls, September 28, 1815*. Listings in gazetteers, travel guides, magazines, geographical dictionaries, histories, sketch and art books, pictorial geographies, companion guides, and parlor books further assured the immortalization of Kaaterskill Falls as a household name.

But the most memorable of all the popular literary utterances comes from the American writer James Fenimore Cooper, in a passage that the historian Alf Evers has called "one of the finest pieces of promotional writing to ornament the 19th Century." The reference is from Cooper's *The Pioneers*, published in the same year the Catskill Mountain House opened for business (1823). The protagonist, Natty Bumppo, remarks on the falls to his young companion, Edwards: "To my judgment, lad, it's the best piece of work that I have met with in the woods; and none know how often the hand of God is seen in a wilderness but them that rove it for a man's life."

Significant improvements and infrastructure for public safety have been developed. Road speed has been reduced to 20 MPH between the parking lot and the trailhead, although the shoulders remain narrow due to lack of space and hikers must be very careful. Hazard areas at the falls' base have been marked and cordoned off. A new trail at the end of Laurel House Road leads to an observation deck, from which the plume and plunge pool can be seen. Campers will be interested to find that a free, designated primitive camping area is located a short distance within the red-pine plantation on the west (right) side of the parking area on Laurel House Road. The location is obscure, but a brief investigation will lead to the sites, which are identified by yellow disks.

Return by the route you came.

DID YOU KNOW?

Kaaterskill Falls is higher than Niagara Falls, dropping for a total of 260 feet in two plumes.

MORE INFORMATION

For more information on the Catskill Forest Preserve, visit dec.ny.gov/lands/5265.html. For the DEC Region 4 office in Stamford, call 607-652-7365.

49

BLACKHEAD MOUNTAIN

This steep trail climbs through Lockwood Gap to Escarpment Trail.

DIRECTIONS

From the corners of CR 40 and CR 56 in the village of Maplecrest, follow Big Hollow Road (CR 56) to the north and east, passing Peck Road on your left. Continue 4.5 miles to the end of CR 56, where you will see the red-blazed Black Dome Range trailhead on the left. Park at the dead end just ahead. *GPS coordinates:* 42° 17.355′ N, 74° 06.957′ W.

TRAIL DESCRIPTION

The short but scenic loop trail over Blackhead Mountain (3,940 feet) rewards you with the best scenery of the Windham Blackhead Range Wilderness without the extra work of traversing the entire big three: Blackhead, and to the west, Black Dome and Thomas Cole mountains. The west-lying two peaks of the range, with the exception of a small group of lookouts on the south and east of Black Dome's summit (3,950 feet), offer little to compare with Blackhead's enormous western viewshed. Thomas Cole Mountain, named for the famous landscape painter, ironically is viewless since its single lookout has become overgrown. Despite this, one of the nicest ledges in the Blackheads is the small ledge on Black Dome, so you might want to add extra time to diverge westward when you reach Lockwood Gap, bagging Blackhead on the way out.

Begin at the rustic Batavia Kill trailhead and follow the route of both the yellow-blazed Batavia Kill and red-blazed Black Dome Range trails as they make their way southeast through dense mixed hemlock and hardwoods, crossing a pair of footbridges. The trail follows the washed-out

LOCATION
Maplecrest, NY

RATING
Strenuous

DISTANCE
4.2 miles

ELEVATION GAIN
1,780 feet

ESTIMATED TIME
3 hours

MAP
USGS Freehold, USGS Hensonville; AMC Catskill Mountains; NY-NJTC Catskill Trails, Northeastern Catskills

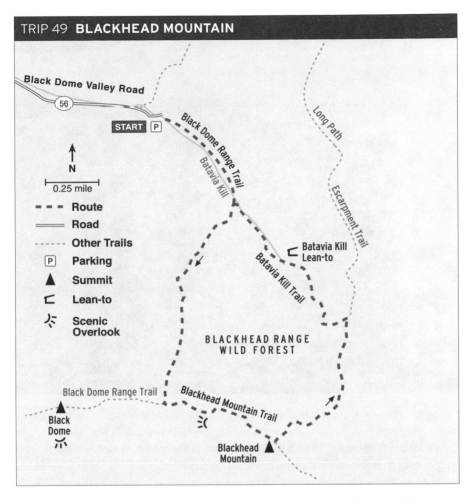

imprint of an old road 0.5 mile to the confluence of two creeks at a trail junction where Black Dome Range Trail bears southwest and where your return route, Batavia Kill Trail, continues east. Turn right onto Black Dome Range Trail, which soon climbs into the gap, becoming very steep. You will pass a reliable spring on the left, unusual for this elevation in the Catskills.

The ascent continues relentlessly through Lockwood Gap (the Gap is rarely spelled out on maps) and levels in the saddle between Black Dome and Blackhead mountains. (The very worthwhile, 0.5-mile ascent of 500 feet to Black Dome's pure fir summit will add another 1.5 hours to your hike, so weigh this side trip against your time and the weather.) The route to Blackhead is to the left (east), following the yellow-blazed Blackhead Mountain Trail, a relatively short connector between Black Dome Range Trail and Escarpment Trail. There is a poorly sited, legal campsite in Lockwood Gap to the northeast of the junction, with very little if any flat ground.

A backpacker pauses on Escarpment Trail, contemplating Blackhead Mountain, in the distance.

Blackhead Mountain Trail ascends immediately into the east, climbing the long westerly slopes of Blackhead. A succession of increasingly scenic terraces leads to a grassy outcropping with broad, penetrating views southwest. These are the hike's best views. You see West Kill over Hunter Mountain's ski slopes, Hunter's fire tower, and the Catskill High Peaks area, including Slide, Table, Cornell, and Wittenberg mountains. East of Hunter are Stony Clove, Plateau, Devil's Path, and Overlook mountains. Kaaterskill High Peak and Roundtop Mountain are due south. The trail climbs steeply ahead, easing up at 3,700 feet. It follows along through balsam and soon arrives at the summit, a bald but viewless dome enclosed in a fir thicket. Escarpment Trail crosses the summit here.

Near this spot in April 2012, Seth Lyon and Alberto Risenberg were trapped by a sudden blizzard. In an attempt to save himself and Risenberg, Lyon set out to get help following a cold and miserable night in an improvised snow shelter. Lyon died of exposure only a short distance from the summit, mired in deep snow. Risenberg survived. Blackhead is a high and exposed peak, so be sure to carry the proper equipment and outerwear. For more information on accidents (and their prevention) in the Northeast, see *Desperate Steps,* published by AMC Books in 2015.

Follow Escarpment Trail to the left (northeast) as it descends steeply, bending into the north and passing a scenic, east-facing overlook on the right. The trail terraces its way down through birch, beech, striped maple, and a ground cover of asters where the sun reaches through the canopy. Canada violets, trout lilies, trillium, bunchberry, spring beauties, and oxalis are seasonal companions along the trail.

Watch carefully now. The well-marked junction of the yellow-blazed Batavia Kill Trail is at 2,850 feet in elevation. Bear left, following the trail downhill and northwest, leaving the lean-to to your right. The contours relax as you descend along the kill, and you'll find yourself back at the junction with Black Dome Range Trail.

Continue straight ahead to arrive at the trailhead parking area.

DID YOU KNOW?

Blackhead and Black Dome get their names from their dark, virgin fir summits, which early lumbermen called "black growth."

MORE INFORMATION

For more information on the Catskill Forest Preserve, visit dec.ny.gov/lands/5265.html. For the DEC Region 4 office in Stamford, call 607-652-7365.

50

WINDHAM HIGH PEAK

Windham High Peak is a charming but strenuous walk through mature spruce plantations to the northern Escarpment, with sweeping views to the north.

DIRECTIONS

From NY 23, turn south onto CR 65 to Hensonville. From there, go 2 miles into the town of Maplecrest on CR 40. Turn left onto CR 56 (Big Hollow Road) and continue until you reach Peck Road at 1.8 miles on your left. The trail begins within a mile, at the end of Peck Road. *GPS coordinates:* 42° 17.848′ N, 74° 10.149′ W.

TRAIL DESCRIPTION

This scenic hike follows the Escarpment's northern shoulder, where the long, western-sloping ridge of Windham High Peak (3,524 feet) reaches in a high arch from Burnt Knob to Elm Ridge. Windham High Peak is the last mountain on the 23-mile Escarpment Trail that begins at Scutt Road Corral in Haines Falls. In 2008 this 4,250-acre wild forest area was annexed to the Blackhead Wild Forest, and the two became the Windham Blackhead Range Wilderness.

Begin on the yellow-blazed trail toward Elm Ridge Lean-to (1 mile). The trail was once a dirt road and climbs through vestigial pasturelands, now grown into a forest of mixed hardwoods. Stone walls mark the field divisions of early settlements. After hiking for a while, you'll see a yellow-blazed trail to your left (west). This trail, signed as Middle Mountain, is called the Cranberry Bog Trail, and is part of a mountain biking trail system that was recently developed in the Elm Ridge Wild Forest (which abuts the Windham Blackhead Range Wilderness area to the west and north). The Elm Ridge system is expanding

LOCATION
Maplecrest, NY

RATING
Strenuous

DISTANCE
6.6 miles

ELEVATION GAIN
1,475 feet

ESTIMATED TIME
5 to 7 hours

MAPS
USGS Hensonville; AMC Catskill Mountains; NY-NJTC Northeastern Catskills

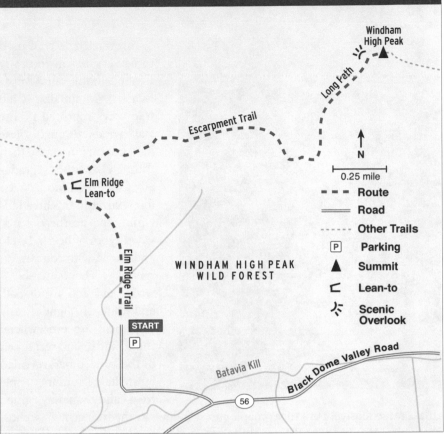

all the time, with a new trails added in summer 2015. In twenty minutes or so, you should reach the trail junction, where you will see additional signage and trailhead blazes for the Elm Ridge trail system. Turn right, following the blue blazes (Escarpment Trail, Long Path) indicating Windham High Peak, Burnt Knob Mountain, and Acra Point. The nicely situated and frequently used Elm Ridge Lean-to will appear on your right as you continue. There are a few primitive, designated campsites to the rear of the lean-to. After a half hour of hiking, you'll pass through dark Norway spruce forests that will spark your imagination. These trees—including the Norway, or red pine—are native to North America and get their name from their nursery of origin in Norway, Maine. The trees were planted throughout the Catskills by the Civilian Conservation Corps in the 1920s and 1930s, mostly in the open fields of abandoned farmlands. Higher-elevation lands in the Catskills were never very good for agriculture, and when farmers "ran out" pasturelands (in this case, for sheep that would be left for the summer and herded out in winter), they often found it more profitable to sell to the state rather than to pay taxes.

Windham High Peak provides a clear view of the Blackhead Range.

This stretch of trail used to be very wet in the early season, until an Appalachian Mountain Club trail crew improved it. The trail winds through these magnificent forests and then through hardwoods, gradually ascending. Most of the forest cover in this area falls within the northern hardwood types of beech, birch, and maple, with companion species of hemlock, basswood, red and white oak, and white ash. Signs of early settlement are everywhere: some hidden and reclaimed by the forest, others revealed by telltale, vagrant apple trees and runaway grape vines. An extensive, pure sugar-maple forest follows as the trail gently ascends. Thick mats of grass cover the rich soils of the western slopes, and you will cross a seasonal creek. (The streams in the Windham Blackhead Range Wilderness Area are high-gradient tributaries of the Batavia Kill and Catskill Creeks, and are dry most of the year.)

When you reach the southerly shoulder of the mountain at 3,000 feet in elevation, you'll get a look at the nearby Blackhead Range and the more westerly East Jewett Range. Blackhead and Black Dome mountains are named for the dark balsam-fir growth you can see on their summits. At this point, you are about 3 miles into the walk; you'll slowly turn northeast for the 0.5-mile, 520-foot climb to the summit. During periods of scanty foliage in this birch, cherry, and maple forest, you will be able to look east at Burnt Knob and Acra Point and the long Escarpment Ridge. The last and steepest incline will take you about 30 minutes. Once on the long, level summit, you'll discover a benchmark and the views that have made Windham such a popular destination hike.

The most imposing of these will be from a small ledge on the right side of the trail facing the Blackhead Range, which feels remarkably close at only 3 miles south across the scenic Black Dome Valley. Down and to your right (southwest) you see the sister peaks of Round Hill and Van Loan Hill. From the left side of the trail, another ledge appears. At this point, you see a long line of lesser peaks disappearing into the Schoharie Valley; a flat stretch of open fields and farms, as well as Ginseng, Zoar, and Cave mountains; and slightly to the north, Richmond and Huntersfield mountains, with Ashland Pinnacle between them.

The most popular view is from beyond the summit (east), where a graffiti-inscribed outcrop hangs above the Hudson Valley. (These inscriptions are not of the same age or quality as the North Lake variety from the Catskill Mountain House era, and the few decent initials have been heavily eroded and defaced.) From here you can see the Helderberg Escarpment and, on a clear day, Albany's Empire Plaza, the Egg Performing Arts Center, and the state university buildings. It is also likely you'll see Vermont's Green Mountains, the Berkshires, and the Taconic Range, including the Greylock massif, a geological member of the Taconics. Looking down over the ridge, you see Burnt Knob (3,180 feet), the second knoll from Windham High Peak. Escarpment Trail goes downhill at this point, to Burnt Knob, Acra Point, Blackhead, and Arizona mountains, and points south.

Some hikers prefer to make a large loop over Windham High Peak, returning via Burnt Knob and Black Dome Range Trail, walking west along Black Dome Valley Road and back to the trailhead on Peck Road for a total distance of more than 13 miles. Rather than walk the road, if possible, spot a shuttle car at the end of Black Dome Valley Road.

DID YOU KNOW?

The gangster Jack "Legs" Diamond (1897–1931) kept a hideout home in the town of Acra, under the shadow of Windham High Peak.

MORE INFORMATION

For more on the Catskill Forest Preserve, visit dec.ny.gov/lands/5265.html. For the DEC Region 4 office in Stamford, call 607-652-7365.

51

ACRA POINT

This short hike to an isolated lookout above Black Dome Valley provides intimate views of the Blackhead Range.

DIRECTIONS

From the intersection of CR 40 and CR 56 in the village of Maplecrest, follow Big Hollow Road (CR 56) to the north and east, passing Peck Road on your left. Continue 4.5 miles to the end of CR 56, where you will see the red-blazed Black Dome Range trailhead on the left, or park at the dead end (Batavia Kill trailhead) just ahead. *GPS coordinates:* 42° 17.848′ N, 74° 10.149′ W.

TRAIL DESCRIPTION

The route to Acra Point uses the northern portion of Black Dome Range Trail, located at the eastern end of Big Hollow Road in Maplecrest. Don't be concerned if the road is washed out along the boisterous Batavia Kill. It often is in early spring. This is a dead end, so you can park almost anywhere if the designated parking area is full. The red-blazed Black Dome Range Trail begins on the left (north) side of the road. It's the first trailhead you see; the next one, a few hundred feet ahead, is the Batavia Kill trailhead (yellow blazes). You can also use Batavia Kill and Escarpment trails to reach Acra Point (or to return from it), more than doubling this hike's distance.

Acra Point is an ideal hike for days when you want a scenic outing that's not an overwhelming workout. This part of Escarpment Trail is also less traveled than the North Lake area trails and the neighboring Windham High Peak or Blackhead Range trails, so you're likely to see fewer hikers. You may encounter Appalachian Trail thru-hikers, however. I enjoy meeting these hikers going the distance on Escarpment Trail (also shared by Long

LOCATION
Maplecrest, NY

RATING
Moderate

DISTANCE
3.4 miles

ELEVATION GAIN
800 feet

ESTIMATED TIME
3 hours

MAPS
USGS Freehold; AMC Catskill Mountains; NY-NJTC Catskill Trails, Northeastern Catskills

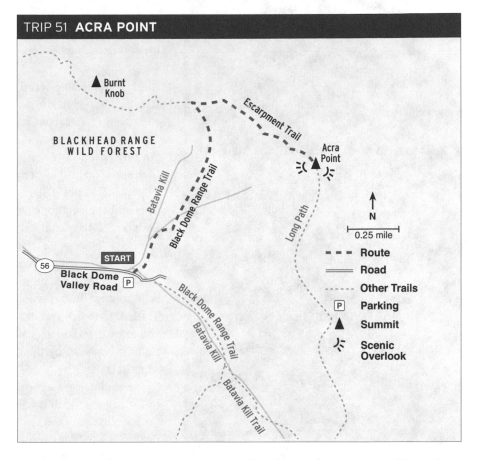

Burnt
Knob

BLACKHEAD RANGE
WILD FOREST

Escarpment Trail

Acra
Point

Batavia Kill

Black Dome Range Trail

Long Path

N

0.25 mile

START

56

Black Dome
Valley Road P

Black Dome Range Trail

Batavia Kill

Batavia Kill Trail

Route
Road
Other Trails
P   Parking
▲   Summit
⅝   Scenic
Overlook

Path); in their floppy hats and rumpled bandanas, they come plodding along with their trekking poles, blending in with the environment. If you meet one here during summer, chances are they may try to "yogi" (a common term of endearment in hiking circles, meaning to "bum" or, less endearingly, beg for) your food, especially your water, in exchange for tales of their adventures. This part of the Catskills is notoriously dry.

Note that the Black Dome Range Trail sign indicates Acra Point at 1.7 miles (3,100 feet). Head north into the woods, following Black Dome Range Trail across Batavia Kill on a wooden bridge. Sign in at the trail register and bear hard right, fording a seasonal tributary. Marking is spotty here, but soon the trail is obvious and remains self-guiding. Climb easily through an attractive stand of large red spruce trees, some snapped in two by high winds. The trail follows the Batavia Kill, passing many pretty spots where the tiny trout stream flows over low, gray ledges into shallow pools. The trail soon recrosses Batavia Kill, turning sharply northwest and north again through a northern hardwood forest. The climb is consistent but never steep. As you gain elevation, there are small pockets of hemlock and a few large, isolated cherry trees, then oaks, providing a good combination of browse for deer, wild turkey, and ruffed grouse. At 2,700 feet, the trail levels out for the last 0.25 mile of

BATAVIA KILL LEAN-TO
JCT. BLACK DOME RANGE TRAIL   .2
BIG HOLLOW ROAD   .9
MILES   1.5

TRAIL TO → MILES

Black Head Mountain   0.9
North Point   7.5
North/South Lake
Campground   10.0
Jct. Route 23A   14.7

NYSDEC

TRAIL TO ← MILES

ACRA POINT
BURNT KNOB   1.8
WINDHAM HIGH PEAK   3.4
RT. 23   5.2
8.5
NYSDEC

A trio of conservation department trail signs points the way to multiple adventures.

Black Dome Range Trail, into a shallow notch on the spine of Escarpment Trail. Trail signs indicate your direction of travel is to the right (south) to Acra Point, 0.7 mile distant. This and the neighboring Dutcher Notch Trail are resupply stations for the college outing clubs and Scout troops that regularly traverse Escarpment Trail. At their drop points, you may see gallon jugs of water brought in by their support staffs.

The following section of Escarpment Trail is flat for a while then rises easily through the remaining 300 feet of ascent to Acra Point. As the trail gains the northwest-facing ridge, boreal forest takes over. Look to your right (west) for an established, unmarked spur trail and follow it 75 feet to a flat sandstone outcropping. Although you are not on Acra Point's summit (3,100 feet), this is the best lookout. The true "summit" lies near the next spur trail to the south. The intimate views of Black Dome/Batavia Kill Valley are the attraction here, where you can lie on the warm, flat rocks off the trail and relax. Seldom are views of such magnitude attained with so little work by the hiker. The rest of the Blackhead Range—Blackhead, Thomas Cole, and Black Dome mountains—slopes downward in a massive ellipsis over Camel's Hump (the westernmost little nub) into a semicolon of Round and Van Loan hills—the latter named for the early Catskill writer and mapmaker Walton Van Loan. To the right (north) of these is Cave Mountain. The large, distant peak with the dorsal profile lying due west (270 degrees magnetic) is Bearpen Mountain, a trailed peak outside the Catskill Park boundary in Delaware County. It is, however, still within the forest preserve, as is Vly Mountain, just south of it, recognizable by its long, flat top.

Looking north, you have Burnt Knob directly in front of you, a sort of mirror to Acra Point, with less interesting views from a small rock ledge on the trail's west side, and better ones in the north; to the right of that, just over 2 miles distant, is Windham High Peak. Looking south past the immense shoulder of Blackhead Mountain (194 degrees) is Arizona Mountain, a high and dry plateau seldom named on maps. Farther south, the Escarpment winds away to Stoppel Point and North Mountain. Views of the Hudson Valley are limited from the east side of the point.

Return by the route you came.

DID YOU KNOW?

Black Dome Range Trail has the advantage of providing the fastest and easiest approach to the top of the northern Catskill Escarpment.

MORE INFORMATION

For more information on the Catskill Forest Preserve, visit dec.ny.gov/lands/5265.html. For the DEC Region 4 office in Stamford, call 607-652-7365.

ESCARPMENT TRAIL

Devil's Path runs east to west, while Escarpment Trail travels south to north along the edge of the Catskills' eastern ledges. This long, north–south-running ridge is known as the Escarpment. The 24-mile Escarpment Trail begins outside the gate of the North–South Lake Public Campground at Scutt Road Corral and is most often hiked from south to north, since many hikers stage their hike from the North Lake camping area. The elevation change and gradient are a bit more forgiving than those of Devil's Path (6,500 cumulative feet), although there are fewer lean-tos on or near Escarpment Trail.

With the exception of the north and south extremes, the views are perhaps not as grand on Escarpment Trail as on Devil's Path's because there are fewer peaks above 3,500 feet, most notably Blackhead Mountain and Windham High Peak. Due to the relative lack of easy and convenient day hikes in this area, with the exception of the trails around North Lake, the sense of solitude is greater once you pass North Point. Long Path uses both Devil's Path and Escarpment Trail as it makes its way northward through the Catskills.

52

HUNTER MOUNTAIN

Hunter Mountain, the Catskills' second-highest peak, demands a long, gradual climb but rewards hikers with a quiet, westerly ledge viewpoint.

DIRECTIONS

From Lexington, 8 miles west of Hunter on NY 23A, travel south on NY 42 for 0.8 mile and turn left (east) onto CR 6 (Spruceton Road). Drive past the West Kill Mountain trailhead, on your right at 3.8 miles, and continue for another 3 miles to the forest-preserve access parking area on the left, where there are trail signs for Hunter Mountain. *GPS coordinates:* 42° 11.050′ N, 74° 16.321′ W.

TRAIL DESCRIPTION

The most interesting and gradual though still challenging climb to Hunter Mountain, the Catskills' second highest (4,040 feet), is by way of Spruceton Trail. The considerable vertical rise of 1,950 feet is distributed evenly over a long western approach beginning at the headwaters of the beautiful West Kill Creek. (Hunter can be climbed in roughly half the time using the steeper Becker Hollow Trail from Stony Clove.)

On the north side of Spruceton Road locate the blue-blazed Spruceton Trail, which leads to the John Robb Lean-to and Hunter Mountain. (There's an overflow parking area 0.2 mile farther ahead on Spruceton Road; Devil's Path is another 0.2 mile past the overflow lot at the dead end of Spruceton Road.)

You'll follow the old Jones Gap Turnpike (a.k.a. Old Hunter Road), built in 1880 and later improved to construct and maintain the present Hunter Mountain fire tower. Also an equestrian route, the truck trail is well defined. After 0.5 mile, the trail turns east and steepens gradually. About 50 minutes into the hike, at 1.7 miles, you'll arrive in the

LOCATION
Hunter, NY

RATING
Strenuous

DISTANCE
7.2 miles

ELEVATION GAIN
1,950 feet

ESTIMATED TIME
7 hours

MAPS
USGS Hunter, USGS Lexington; AMC Catskill Mountains; NY-NJTC Northeastern Catskills

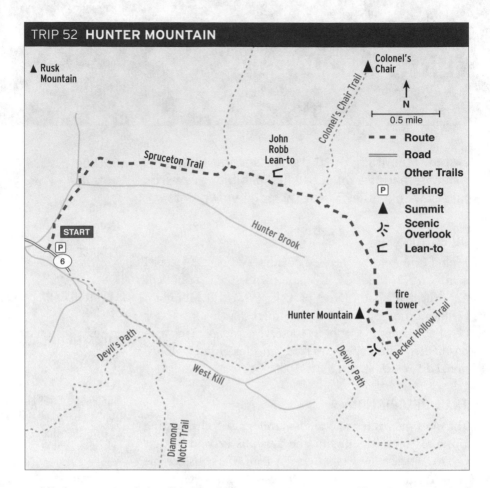

▲ Rusk
Mountain

Colonel's
▲ Chair

John
Robb
Lean-to ⌐

Spruceton Trail

Colonel's Chair Trail

N

0.5 mile

- - - Route
=== Road
···· Other Trails
P Parking
▲ Summit
⽍ Scenic Overlook
⌐ Lean-to

START
P
6

Hunter Brook

fire
■ tower

Hunter Mountain ▲

Becker Hollow Trail

Devil's Path

West Kill

Devil's Path

Diamond Notch Trail

saddle between Rusk (trailless) and Hunter mountains. You'll see an unmarked trail leading north and downhill onto private lands in Taylor Hollow.

The trail continues south-southeast and ascends steeply, reaching a good spring on the right within 0.5 mile. (Be careful: Horses sometimes drink from the pool.) Near the spring are views to the north and southwest with Rusk and West Kill in the foreground. Within 0.1 mile, you'll see the John Robb Lean-to on your left at the 3,500-foot mark.

Continue for another 0.1 mile into a flat area of thick evergreens. Here you come to Colonel's Chair Trail, branching left (north, yellow blazes, easily missed). This is part of the old Shanty Hollow Trail to Colonel's Chair Trail; its last 0.5 mile has been erased by ski-trail construction. The mile-long side trip to Colonel's Chair and the ski lifts and summit lodge (open in summer) of the Hunter Mountain Ski Area is worthwhile if you've allowed the time, but the views are redundant with the fire tower's, and the elevation loss (500 feet) is significant. (See the Appalachian Mountain Club's *Catskill Mountain Guide* for details.)

Soaring hundreds of feet above ground, zipliners have an excellent view of the Northeast Catskills.

Continue on Spruceton Trail. The summit is 1 mile ahead and 450 feet in elevation above you. The heavily rutted, often wet trail leads you through a remarkably dense forest of spruce and fir with isolated ledges to the northeast. From the John Robb Lean-to, it will take you about 45 minutes to reach the summit. Just before the final ascent at approximately 3 miles, a yellow-blazed spur trail leads 1,500 feet to a marginal spring.

Suddenly the fire tower and observer's cabin appear. Once you have enjoyed this rocky peak and the 360-degree view from the fire tower (the highest in the state; it is staffed seasonally, on weekends), continue on the blue-blazed trail to the true summit, where the fire tower and a lean-to were previously located. This additional distance of 0.25 mile through a level spruce-fir wood takes only ten minutes and is well worth the effort. When you reach the small clearing of the old tower site, at the junction where Becker Hollow Trail rises from Stony Clove, you'll see a spur trail to the right (west) leading a short distance to a west-facing ledge with excellent views from the north-northwest to the south-southwest, including West Kill, North Dome, Sherrill, Balsam, Vly, Bearpen, and many other peaks in the southern Catskills and the Shawangunks. When the tower is busy, this is the place to head. In his classic 1918 book *The Catskills*, T. Morris Longstreth sums up Hunter's views: "Hunter is a climb-repaying mountain. From the steel tower on the top the entire Catskill mountainland is visible. Stony Clove . . . is but a gash in mother earth. The mass of the southern Catskills rises in ranged domes . . . dropped into gulfs made pearl gray by the mists of melting snow. Westward the chain that walls the valley toward Lexington wandered away until it grew soft with lilacs and lavendars [sic]."

Your shortest return route (from the Becker Hollow Trail junction) is Spruceton Trail, the way you came (3.6 miles). But if time allows, you can make a loop by continuing ahead on the yellow-blazed Hunter Mountain Trail to Devil's Path, which turns west to join the blue-blazed Diamond Notch Trail at West Kill Falls. This would bring you to a point about 1 mile east of the Spruceton Trail parking area, a total from the Becker Hollow Trail junction of 4.6 miles, or about 2 miles longer than returning the way you came.

DID YOU KNOW?

The Hunter Mountain ski trail called K2 has the steepest vertical rise of any ski trail in the eastern United States.

MORE INFORMATION

For more information on the Catskill Forest Preserve, visit dec.ny.gov/lands/5265.html. For the DEC Region 4 office in Stamford, call 607-652-7365.

53

DIAMOND NOTCH TO WEST KILL FALLS

This trail through a classic mountain notch leads to a secluded waterfall.

DIRECTIONS

From Lanesville on NY 214, drive 5 miles north of Phoenicia and look for Diamond Notch Road on the left, where there are state trail signs. Go up Diamond Notch Road 1.2 miles and into the woods another 0.3 mile to the trailhead parking area. Note that the last 0.5 mile is rocky and may be difficult for all but four-wheel-drive vehicles. A private landowner has posted the area, but it is legal to park on the road as long as you are not blocking traffic. Coming southeast from Hunter, take NY 214 (2 miles east of town), and you'll see the trailhead signs 7 miles into Stony Clove (or 4 miles beyond Devil's Tombstone State Campground) on your right. Turn right onto Diamond Notch Road and follow the above directions to the trailhead. *GPS coordinates:* 42° 8.764′ N, 74° 15.829′ W.

TRAIL DESCRIPTION

This is an easy-to-moderate hike that takes you into Diamond Notch via an old turnpike converted into a ski and hiking trail in 1937. Forest encroachment and landslides have reduced the trail's width considerably, but the footpath remains intact. From the trailhead parking area, follow the blue state trail blazes, climbing next to Hollow Tree Brook. Soon you cross the brook on a flight of stone steps.

   In spring you'll discover a wide variety of wildflowers: Dutchman's breeches, Carolina spring beauties, yellow violets, and purple trillium. After fifteen minutes of hiking, just beyond the bridge, you can make out a high ridge to your left, which is part of West Kill Mountain, the ridge that forms the west side of Diamond Notch in the Hunter

LOCATION
Lanesville, NY

RATING
Moderate

DISTANCE
4.6 miles

ELEVATION GAIN
1,500 feet

ESTIMATED TIME
3.5 hours

MAPS
USGS Lexington; AMC Catskill Mountains; NY-NJTC Catskill Trails, Northeastern Catskills

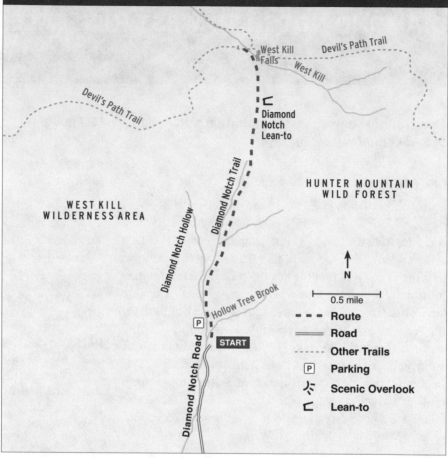

West Kill Wilderness. At this point, hemlock begins to appear, and the trail becomes heavily eroded and gullied. Soon another bridge crosses Hollow Tree Brook, and the trail begins an even ascent, continuing due north into Diamond Notch Hollow. This spot most likely suggested the development of a ski trail through the notch, but you'll probably opt for the novice slopes of a sanctioned ski area after you peer back down from above. Look up to your left (west), and you'll see the rocky, spruce-covered shoulder of West Kill's east ridge jutting out.

About 1.5 miles into the hollow, you'll come across a miniature waterfall on your right and another small kill just beyond it, both running straight down the mountain and crossing the trail. Some outcrops of thinly stratified sandstone lie ahead, hinting that the notch is not far beyond. Within five minutes, there are excellent views to the southwest, highlighting (from right to left) Slide, Table, Lone, Peekamoose, Cornell, and Wittenberg mountains, and Ashokan High Point. Up to the right is a long pile of landslide talus, with birch, cherry, and maple establishing themselves in its thin soil.

An old road descends sharply into the ravine on the trail's west side. Now 1.7 miles into the notch, you approach its highest point. After you have enjoyed the notch and its fine view, follow the trail into an evergreen forest, descending gently to reach Diamond Notch Lean-to. The shelter has a wood floor; its site is cleaner than most and it's in good shape, as far as Catskill lean-tos go. Just below the lean-to is a small wetland that contributes to the upper reaches of West Kill Creek. Follow along on what can be a fairly wet trail, with a view of Rusk Mountain ahead and slightly left. To the west of Rusk Mountain is Evergreen Mountain, and to the east, Hunter Mountain—neither of them visible. Within fifteen minutes of the lean-to, you should reach the junction with the red-blazed Devil's Path and the bridge over West Kill Falls (a.k.a. Buttermilk Falls). Diamond Notch is back the way you came, about 2.3 miles away; the nearest road is ahead on the blue-blazed trail, at 0.5 mile (Spruceton–Old Hunter Road).

The falls here are small but very attractive, with a succession of large pools. Devil's Path (red blazes) runs east and west past the falls. To the west lies West Kill Mountain. Straight ahead, Diamond Notch Trail continues to the Spruceton Road trailhead to Hunter Mountain (see Trip 52).

You will find the falls an ideal place to spend a hot afternoon. Hike out on the route you came in.

A hiker cools off in Diamond Notch's West Kill Falls, a.k.a. Buttermilk Falls.

DID YOU KNOW?

In Diamond Notch, where the mountains of West Kill and Southwest Hunter come very close together, it's theoretically possible to stand on two mountains at the same time.

MORE INFORMATION

Due to its proximity to Spruceton Road, this area was at one time subject to intensive overuse and unregulated camping, but it has since recovered and no camping is permitted. For more information on the Catskill Forest Preserve, visit dec.ny.gov/lands/5265.html. For the DEC Region 4 forestry office in Stamford, call 607-652-7365.

54

WEST KILL MOUNTAIN TO BUCK RIDGE LOOKOUT

This demanding hike crosses the elongated West Kill plateau, taking hikers to the scenic Buck Ridge Lookout.

DIRECTIONS

Turn off NY 23A onto NY 42 South in Lexington, west of Hunter. Follow NY 42 toward Shandaken into West Kill. About 3.8 miles from NY 23A, you will see signs for Spruceton on CR 6. Turn left here and go 3.8 miles to Devil's Path on your right. *GPS coordinates: 42° 11.528′ N, 74° 19.454′ W.*

TRAIL DESCRIPTION

This is the longer but gentler approach to West Kill Mountain from Spruceton, with a slightly greater vertical rise than the approach from the eastern end of Spruceton Road (a 1,780-foot rise). This is the terminus of the red-blazed Devil's Path.

Go immediately uphill through a hardwood and pine forest. The trail levels out shortly, and after ten minutes you'll find you are walking the border of a forest transition, with hemlock on your right and hardwood on your left. To your right are Mink Hollow (not to be confused with the better-known Mink Hollow near Lake Hill) and its brook that joins the West Kill. Large, moss-clad boulders decorate the forest. Grouse may burst from dense cover as you walk along.

After twenty minutes over rocky, root-covered footing, you'll meet the creek that runs into Mink Hollow. The trail then veers left, ascending into a rocky hardwood forest. In ten minutes, you'll hear a spring bubbling downhill from the trail as you look ahead into a gap in the forest where a vernal pond sits between West Kill and

LOCATION
Spruceton, NY

RATING
Strenuous

DISTANCE
9.4 miles

ELEVATION GAIN
2,030 feet

ESTIMATED TIME
6.5 hours

MAPS
USGS Lexington; AMC Catskill Mountains; NY–NJTC Catskill Trails, Northeastern Catskills

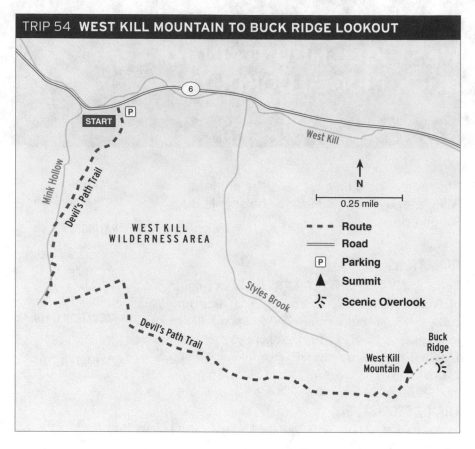

North Dome. The gap runs south, into the head of Broadstreet Hollow and the Timber Lake Camp. There are two signs at this pond section of the trail, one indicating West Kill Mountain summit; the other shows Spruceton Road as back the way you came.

Turn sharply uphill to the north. Continue climbing for twenty minutes or more, over the steepest section of trail you will encounter. The trail eases over grassy, fern-covered flats, through ledges and undulating terrain where beech and cherry appear. This pattern continues for another twenty minutes until you descend steeply. The drop is not severe or prolonged; it flattens out, and the trail climbs again. Be careful here while negotiating slanted slabs of bluestone that are slippery when wet.

As you ascend to a level walk again, it will take you twenty more minutes through winding flats to climb into alpine terrain, where the trail narrows and balsam becomes prolific. A short spur to the north, just before you arrive at the summit, offers excellent views of the Blackhead Range; Huntersfield, Tower, and Cave mountains; and an extensive sprawl of lowlands, with a glimpse of the Schoharie Reservoir. A sign identifying West Kill's summit (3,880 feet) appears just ahead on your right.

Buck Ridge lookout on West Kill Mountain surveys a dramatic Catskill landscape.

Continue for another three to five minutes, to the ledge of Buck Ridge (3,740 feet). This view is on many hikers' list of favorites, and it is impressive. There is enough room for a dozen people to rest here, poised in midair to view a 180-degree collection of peaks. From left to right you can see Windham, Thomas Cole, Black Dome, Blackhead, Hunter West with its ski trails, Hunter and its fire tower, Southwest Hunter, Plateau, Overlook and its fire tower (for hawk eyes only), Slide, Table, Lone, Rocky, Wittenberg, Cornell, Friday, Balsam Cap, Ashokan High Point, the Mohonk Preserve's Sky Top, a piece of the Ashokan Reservoir, and down into Lanesville on NY 214. You can also see a widening in the Hudson River (Vanderberg Cove), as well as Olderbark, Little Rocky, and Carl mountains in the foreground, and Mount Tremper to the right of the Ashokan Reservoir. See if you can find Mount Tremper's fire tower.

On the summit, you will recognize the pungent odor of the balm of Gilead: the pitch of balsam fir, dripping from the blisters on the tree's bark. It is said to have medicinal value, and it does keep bacteria and fungi to a minimum, at least in the tree's case. People once thought it must also do the same for humans, recalling the prophet Jeremiah's reference to the balm that ancient Israelites found on Mount Gilead in the Holy Land. American Indians called the healing balsam salve *cho-koh-tung*, or "blisters." The resin was used commercially to create adhesives for lenses and microscope slides until synthetics were found to be superior.

Retrace your steps to your car.

DID YOU KNOW?

The West Kill Creek was the favorite trout-fishing stream of Art Flick, the grandfather of Catskill fly-fishers.

MORE INFORMATION

For More Information on the Catskill Forest Preserve, visit dec.ny.gov/lands/5265.html. For the DEC Region 4 office in Stamford, call 607-652-7365.

55

BALSAM LAKE MOUNTAIN

This spruce-fir summit would be viewless without its fire tower, which offers a 360-degree panorama of the western Catskills.

DIRECTIONS

From NY 28 in Arkville, go south on CR 49 (Dry Brook Road) for 6 miles, through Mapledale. Turn right onto Millbrook Road and go 2.3 miles to the trailhead parking area on the right. Cross the road and locate the blue-blazed Dry Brook Ridge Trail. Be sure you take this section of the Dry Brook Ridge Trail, not the one on the north (or right) side of the road that crosses northerly Dry Brook Ridge. *GPS coordinates: 42° 4.198′ N, 74° 34.446′ W.*

TRAIL DESCRIPTION

From the trailhead to Balsam Lake Mountain (3,723 feet), you enter a forest of beech, birch, maple, and cherry trees over cinnamon ferns, oxalis, and viburnum. Pass the trail register on your left and follow a flat section of the trail to an ascent that allows occasional views across Mill Brook Hollow to the west. Climb gently through a few switch-backs, where jack-in-the-pulpit, Solomon's seal, wolf's claw club moss, and haircap moss appear. The upright, branched, and densely leaved stems of wolf's claw club moss are used commercially for Christmas decorations. (Picking them here is prohibited.) The moss is widely distributed through the Catskills and northern North America. It can be confused with tree club moss, or ground pine, found in open pine woods and bogs.

In ten minutes or so, you'll pass a spring to the right and downhill (indicated by a sign) among a series of sedimentary boulders, many of them covered with rock tripe. When soaked for several weeks in water, this lichen renders a purple dye that has some popularity among

LOCATION
Arkville, NY

RATING
Strenuous

DISTANCE
6 miles

ELEVATION GAIN
1,123 feet

ESTIMATED TIME
4.5 hours

MAPS
USGS Seager; AMC Catskill Mountains; NY-NJTC Catskill Trails, Central Catskills

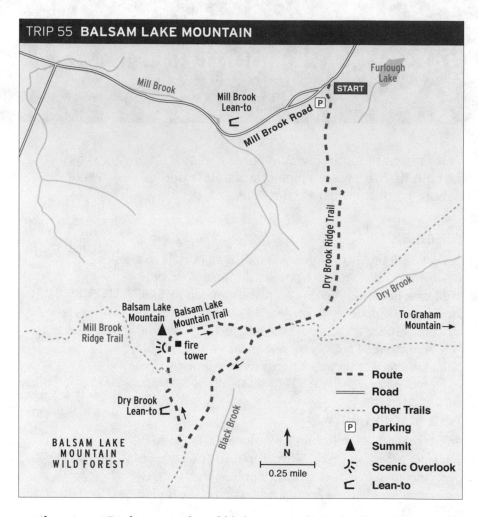

Furlough Lake

Mill Brook

Mill Brook Lean-to

START

Mill Brook Road

P

Dry Brook Ridge Trail

Dry Brook

Balsam Lake Mountain

Balsam Lake Mountain Trail

Mill Brook Ridge Trail

fire tower

To Graham Mountain →

Dry Brook Lean-to

Black Brook

BALSAM LAKE MOUNTAIN WILD FOREST

N

0.25 mile

- - - Route

Road

- - - - Other Trails

P Parking

▲ Summit

Scenic Overlook

Lean-to

textile artisans. Rock tripe is also edible but not at all wholesome. The dried-up, curled disks of lichen resemble moldy potato chips.

In twenty minutes, you'll pass a grass-covered trail on your left that leads to the summit of Graham Mountain (3,868 feet). (Many hikers climb Graham along with Balsam Lake Mountain, but there is no legal public easement for Graham Mountain.)

In a few moments, you encounter several trail signs. Take the red-blazed Balsam Lake Mountain Trail to your right, heading for the fire tower (0.85 mile). Continue uphill over flat rocks with visible glacial scratches. The trail includes vigorous ascents broken up by more-moderate inclines and is hedged in blackberry, bunchberry, and extremely dense spruce-fir thickets.

After twenty minutes, you finally spot the fire tower and the observer's cabin. Climb to the top of the tower, where you can see in all directions (it is staffed on weekends, seasonally). Below the tower and running north is the Dry Brook Ridge. On a clear day, you can see Bearpen Mountain, 15 miles to the northeast. Closer is the ridge on the east side of Dry Brook Valley and its series of peaks. From left to right are Belleayre, Balsam, Haynes, Eagle, and Big Indian. Between the latter two is the summit of Panther. Due east of you is the range that includes Slide and Table mountains. The two neighboring peaks are Graham and Doubletop. To the south and west are the rolling, seemingly endless lower peaks of Delaware County. You can see Red Hill and its fire tower.

Just off the summit, in an impenetrable tangle of fallen trees, is an interesting plant community. This bog contains more sphagnum than others in the Catskill region. A hurricane in 1950 caused extensive blowdown, followed by a heavy second growth of balsam fir. It has been hypothesized that this site may never follow a bog's normal growth pattern due to the infiltration of acid rain, which acts to decompose peat. Water is retained, and the bog remains in its current stage rather than progressing. Balsam Lake's summit recently has been the site of studies into acid rain, a phenomenon that has arisen in the Catskills despite the profusion of limestone, which buffers acids on the earth's surface.

The trail continues downhill past an outbuilding with signs indicating the lean-to at 0.45 mile. Follow downhill, passing Millbrook Ridge Trail, which descends to the west, and farther on, a spur trail to the right (west) that leads to the Eleanor Leavitt Memorial Lean-to.

Within twenty minutes, you intersect with the blue-blazed Dry Brook Ridge Trail once again. Go left (north) and follow this grassy road uphill for twenty

As seen through the fire tower, Balsam Lake Mountain's summit is cloaked in dense spruce-fir forest.

minutes to the junction of Balsam Lake Mountain Trail, which you'll recognize. Descend, retracing your steps to the parking area.

DID YOU KNOW?

Beecher Lake, to the west, once belonged to the family of the American novelist Harriet Beecher Stowe, author of *Uncle Tom's Cabin* (1852).

MORE INFORMATION

For more information on the Catskill Forest Preserve, visit dec.ny.gov/lands/5265.html. For the DEC Region 3 office in New Paltz, call 845-256-3000.

THE *CLEARWATER*: AMERICA'S ENVIRONMENTAL FLAGSHIP

Hikers peering out across the Hudson River may spot the majestic, gaff-rigged sloop, the *Clearwater*, with her tremendous mainsail and her unmistakable topsail with its multicolored compass rose.

The *Clearwater* represents one of the most compelling and successful grass-roots environmental efforts ever undertaken. In 1966, the folk singer and Hudson Valley resident Pete Seeger (1919–2014) became disgusted with the condition of his beloved Hudson River, which was full of raw sewage and unchecked toxic waste. Indigenous fish populations were decreasing, and some had disappeared. Despairing over the Hudson's fate, Seeger brainstormed the idea of building a replica of a Hudson River sloop as a symbol and rallying point in the effort to save the river. He felt the boat would be a cornerstone for concerned citizens, young people, schoolchildren, and educators living in the valley; they could use it to build their own tools and strategies for the protection of their environment.

That dream, though seemingly ambitious and idealistic, was realized. The 106-foot *Clearwater* was built in Maine, launched in 1969, and sailed to the Hudson Valley. The *Clearwater* is identical to the shallow, draft-freighting sloops of the eighteenth century that carried goods up- and downriver between Albany and New York City. Today the ship's home port is in Kingston, New York. Each season since 1969, the *Clearwater* has sailed as a floating classroom, introducing educators and children to a science-based environmental curriculum focusing on the Hudson River estuary. The *Clearwater* organization is credited with creating the first such program in the United States to be held aboard a sailing vessel—a template that has been used worldwide for similar programs. More than a half-million young people have been a part of the *Clearwater*'s onboard environmental program; 15,000 students and 200 teachers participate annually.

Hudson River Sloop Clearwater, Inc., based in Beacon, New York, is a member-supported environmental advocacy group whose mission is to preserve and protect the Hudson River. But it is not simply local. Members take part in supporting the Clean Water Act, the Hudson River Park Act, and the removal of PCBs from the river.

Each year, Clearwater holds a fundraising event at Croton State Park in Croton, New York, called the Great Hudson River Revival.

In 2004, the *Clearwater* was added to the National Register of Historic Places for its part in the American environmental movement. The ship is often joined by its sister vessel, the *Woody Guthrie*, in educational programming. Free sails are provided to the public on a scheduled basis, and anyone with interest can apply to serve as volunteer crew or as an onboard educator.

56

PALENVILLE OVERLOOK

This historical carriage road once led to the Catskill Mountain House and today brings hikers to a pair of peaceful lookouts over lower Kaaterskill Clove and the Hudson Valley.

DIRECTIONS

From NY 23A in Palenville, turn right onto Boggart Road, the first right after the light on NY 23A as you are driving west. Follow Boggart Road for 2.5 miles to a four-way intersection with Mountain Turnpike Road at Pelham's Four Corners (the section to the right is dirt). There are horse trail signs here. Turn left and go 1 mile to the end of Mountain Turnpike Road, where you can legally park along the road. *GPS coordinates:* 42° 12.743′ N, 74° 00.451′ W.

TRAIL DESCRIPTION

To reach this quiet and isolated overlook, you hike the historical Old Mountain Road through Rip Van Winkle Hollow, which, noted the author Roland Van Zandt, became "the classic approach to the great scenic domain of the Catskill Mountain House for almost [all of] the nineteenth century." The road had its beginnings in 1823 as a tannery road and stagecoach route to the Catskill Mountain House. It remained a stage route until the railroad came in the 1880s, causing its eventual abandonment. Yet by 1931, H. A. Haring wrote in *Our Catskill Mountains* that the road "is impassable for any sort of vehicle, but is endlessly charming for the hiker who is equal to an ascent of 2,000 feet within a walking distance of 5 miles." The road has been repaired since, and new bridges are in place for equestrians, snowmobilers, and hikers. This hike follows the Sleepy Hollow Horse Trail to Palenville Overlook.

LOCATION
Palenville, NY

RATING
Strenuous

DISTANCE
8 miles

ELEVATION GAIN
1,300 feet

ESTIMATED TIME
5 hours

MAPS
USGS Kaaterskill; AMC Catskill Mountains; NY-NJTC Catskill Trails, Northeastern Catskills

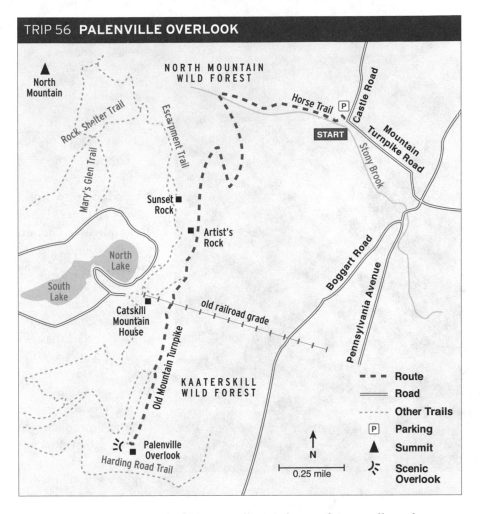

Legend:
- - - - Route
———— Road
· · · · · Other Trails
P Parking
▲ Summit
⅄ Scenic Overlook

0.25 mile

Begin at the western end of Mountain Turnpike Road. You will see the snow-mobile trail markers as the road turns to dirt and curves uphill into Rip Van Winkle Hollow, with Stony Brook on the left. Continuing uphill, you cross Black Snake Bridge within 0.5 mile. A hardwood forest slopes steeply up to your right toward the Escarpment, and a hemlock ravine pitches steeply down to your left. At the horseshoe turn in Sleepy Hollow, you can still see the old stone foundations of the Rip Van Winkle House, a halfway house, or early boarding house and tavern. The 1 mile to this point will take you a half hour of uphill hiking, so you may enjoy a stop here at the traditional resting place for coach travelers to the Catskill Mountain House, who had already traveled 10 rough miles from the wharf at Catskill.

Every effort was made to assure Mountain House guests that this was the spot where Washington Irving's Rip encountered the strange crew of Henry Hudson's *Half Moon*. Nearby was the rock on which he took his famous slumber, and a tree could be pointed out beneath which the bones of his dog Wolf were "discovered."

Once popular with mountain house guests, today's Palenville Overlook is a peaceful, out-of-the-way destination for hikers and equestrians.

It's easy to imagine the Romantics of the time accepting the story as fact. Haring recorded: "Every summer visitors in hundreds scrambled up the perpendicular continuation of Sleepy Hollow in search of the 'flats' where Hendrick Hudson's gnomes thunderously rolled the balls in their game of ninepins." In fact, Irving is not specific as to the location of the events in the legend, which appealed to the Romantic mind for its very vagueness and mystery.

Continue from here on the 0.5-mile-long Dead Ox Hill, going steadily uphill through hardwoods toward Little Pine Orchard and Cape Horn. You reach Cape Horn within 30 minutes of Sleepy Hollow at the site of a stone fireplace and rough campsite. From Cape Horn, views to the east are fair, with the Taconics and the river valley visible. Make a 180-degree right turn here onto what's known as Short Level, a section of trail that takes you up a moderate grade to another horseshoe bend in 0.3 mile, or ten minutes.

Now you turn toward the north, then switch back south to Featherbed Hill. This path is recorded on Walton Van Loan's 1876 *Map of All Points of Interest Within Four Miles of the Catskill Mountain House.* While not entirely reliable for navigation, Van Loan's representation—specifically from the Saxe Farm at the end of Mountain Turnpike Road to Palenville Overlook—fairly accurately shows this section of the trail. From Featherbed Hill, you walk the next 1.5 miles uphill through a hardwood forest until you reach a Y in the trail. Take a left at this Y. This point is known as the Long Level, where the grade becomes flatter.

At the Y, follow a steep downhill grade left (northeast) that switches back almost immediately to the south. In a few minutes, cross the open gash that runs up the mountain: the abandoned Otis Elevated Railroad tracks. Opened in 1892, this incline railway saved three to four hours' stage time on the trip to the Catskill Mountain House during the crucial period when other mountaintop resorts were challenging the supremacy of Charles L. Beach's domain. Lack of patronage and the advent of automobile travel caused the railway to be closed in 1918. Its rails and cables were sold to the government for weapons manufacturing. The bare scrape it left in the Escarpment can be seen for miles.

After crossing the railway clearing, the trail narrows through a forest of mixed hardwoods and continues along, flat and featureless (except for limited views through the trees to the east), until you reach a fork within twenty minutes. Take the left fork, which in twenty minutes or more will take you to Halfway House Lookout (0.45 mile), the location of a ruin that was once a boarding house. All that remains of the house are its bluestone foundation and crumbling walls. Open views to the east appear here, but they improve ahead. Bear right and climb easily to Palenville Overlook. The overlook is not immediately apparent. In the vicinity of a concrete fireplace, follow a faint, very short herd trail through the pines to the south (your left as you're hiking the trail), which will bring you to a long, scenic ledge overlooking Kaaterskill Clove, with the village of Palenville below and remarkable views of Kaaterskill High Peak and Roundtop Mountain to the south. The open ledges of Palenville Overlook are ideal spots for picnicking, sketching, photographing, camping, or simply pondering. The vertical drops are extremely dangerous here, so be cautious. For a more private setting, look for an unmarked herd trail that leaves to the west. The trail will take you to Indian Head, the location of a historic profile rock (not to be confused with Indian Head Mountain).

When you have enjoyed the area to your satisfaction, continue on the trail, which loops back to a Y. (To the left, the Sleepy Hollow Horse Trail heads up the mountain toward North Lake.) Take a right here, and walk about a hundred yards to the Y where you originally turned left. From here, bear left and retrace your route back to your car. Before leaving Palenville Overlook, if you wish to rest in the bewitching silence high above the birthplace of Rip Van Winkle, be careful lest you, too, sleep away a lifetime.

DID YOU KNOW?

Washington Irving did not visit the Catskills until 1832, twelve years after the publication of his short story "Rip Van Winkle"—previously, he had observed the mountains only from the decks of a Hudson River steamboat.

MORE INFORMATION

For more information on the Catskill Forest Preserve, visit dec.ny.gov/lands/5265.html. For the DEC Region 4 office in Stamford, call 607-652-7365.

57
SAUGERTIES LIGHTHOUSE

This easy trail provides beautiful river scenery—
an excellent starter outing for young children.

DIRECTIONS

From either the northbound or the southbound ramp of
Exit 20 off the NYS Thruway (I-87), turn south onto NY
32. (Northbound will turn right onto NY 32; southbound
will turn left onto NY 32 and left again at its intersection
with NY 212. The true heading is easterly.) Head toward
the village of Saugerties on Ulster Avenue. At 0.9 mile
from the northbound entrance/exit to I-87, bear right at
the light on Market Street and go one block. Turn left at
Main Street and go one block. Stay straight to continue
onto US 9W/Main Street. Go 0.4 mile. Where US 9W
curves to the left, turn right onto Mynderse Street. Go 0.3
mile. Take a slight left onto Lighthouse Drive and go 0.4
mile. Turn right into the lighthouse parking lot after the
U.S. Coast Guard station. *GPS coordinates:* 42° 4.334′ N,
73° 56.204′ W.

TRAIL DESCRIPTION

Several lighthouses exist in the Hudson Valley, but only
the Saugerties lighthouse is occupied and accessible by
foot trail. Although the path to this unusual spot is short,
it is fascinating and fun—especially for very young children, for whom it proves an ideal introductory hike.

The brick lighthouse itself (built in 1835, replaced in
1869) and the picnic area and walkway surrounding it are
built on an artificially constructed sandbar jutting into
the river, adjacent to the Esopus Creek. (The Esopus, once
called Sopus, was named for the Delaware word for river,
seepu.) The lighthouse sits on a large granite base, 60 feet in
diameter and supported by 56 wooden pilings driven into
the river bottom. Views up and down the river from this

LOCATION
Saugerties, NY

RATING
Easy

DISTANCE
1.1 miles

ELEVATION GAIN
Minimal

ESTIMATED TIME
40 minutes

MAPS
USGS Saugerties; Ruth
Reynolds Glunt Nature
Preserve; Lighthouse
Trail Map

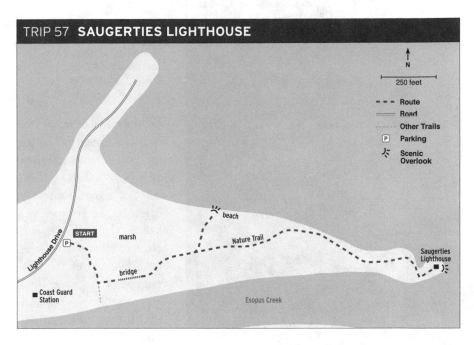

point are uninterrupted for miles. To the east, across the narrow Hudson, are the estates of the rich and famous. To the west, though obstructed, are views of the Indian Head Wilderness area peaks. The tidal wetlands leading to the lighthouse are floristically rich and dense, and the footway is flat and easy to walk.

Take a trail map from the kiosk (though you won't need it for finding your way) and begin at the gated trailhead that leaves from the east edge of the parking area. Immediately you will be struck by several very large eastern cottonwood trees, members of the poplar family. These large trees with their massive trunks grow to 100 feet in height and 3 to 4 feet in diameter; often they are larger still. They typically border streams, appearing in pure stands or mixed among willows, and are the common pioneer species on newly formed sandbars and moist, open floodplains. One of the fastest-growing native trees, they often attain 13 feet of vertical growth annually, making them a prized source of pulpwood. They are named for the cottonlike seeds that you often see blowing around the woods and across roadways.

Pass a private dock to the right and cross a short bridge over a muddy tidal channel. Ahead, a second bridge passes through swamp shrub, and a spur to the left (at the fork), where an interpretive kiosk is located, leads to a sandy beach looking north up the river. Take this spur and enjoy the scenery before returning to the fork and the main trail. Follow the main trail again, crossing a low boardwalk and passing through a swamp forest of mixed hardwood. Ahead is another low boardwalk, at times inundated by the tide. You'll see cables securing the walk, which has a tendency to float away with very high tides. Because there is always the chance you and your party may arrive during such a tide, it is best to come prepared with sandals or boots, depending

on the time of year. Due to the volume and nature of debris that continually washes ashore here, it is not a good idea to go barefoot. Soon you will reach the tall, honey-colored stalks of rushes that have taken over the eastern end of the point. These are members of an invasive species called phragmites, a common reed that grows in alkaline habitats and tolerates brackish water. These reed beds are not affected by frequent inundation from the river.

Hikers will wonder over the oddly shaped, hard-spiked seedpods of the Eurasian (European) water chestnut, another invasive species common to several eastern United States waterways. The Hudson River is among the most problematic areas for this species. Mats of water chestnut severely restrict light and reduce oxygen levels in aquatic habitats. This has contributed to fish kills in some areas and restricts recreational use. In native habitats of Europe, Asia, and Africa, the plants are kept in check by insect parasites that are not indigenous here.

Children will be enchanted by the visage of far-flung shores and the mystery of hidden, watery places as they imagine being marooned in some exotic spot. As they examine bits of flotsam and jetsam washed ashore with the tides, half hidden in the sands, they might even discover a message in a bottle!

Once at the lighthouse, relax on the benches and picnic tables, enjoying the view. The lighthouse beacon is still in operation and aids navigation. It sits very close to the river's channel, which dredging maintains at a minimum 35-foot depth. Large ships and pleasure craft pass close to the lighthouse, making this an interesting and exciting spot. Freighters, tankers, and barges pushed and pulled by tugs come and go between the Port of Albany and points south. Many recreational watercraft pass through here, en route to southern climes from ports in Canada and the Great Lakes via the Erie Canal and the St. Lawrence River. The earliest shipping in these waters was steam powered, and the first steam passenger boat to provide service from New York City to Albany was the *Clermont*, the invention of Robert Fulton. Fulton had financial help from his father-in-law, Robert Livingston, who resided at Clermont, which is the large white mansion seen upriver on the east shore.

The 17-acre nature preserve containing the lighthouse was named for Ruth Reynolds Glunt (1891–1979), who is credited with establishing the Saugerties lighthouse on the National Registry of Historic Places in 1978. Glunt was the author of *Lighthouses and Legends of the Hudson*. She was the widow of Chester B. Glunt, a former U.S. Coast Guard light attendant. Through her preservation efforts, Ruth became the friend of many Hudson River lighthouse keepers.

In 1986, the lighthouse and surrounding preserve were sold to the Saugerties Lighthouse Conservancy (SLC) for one dollar. In 1990, the light was reactivated. With considerable community support, the SLC restored the lighthouse to its present condition.

DID YOU KNOW?

Reeds similar to the ones growing near the Saugerties lighthouse were fashioned into boats and sailed across the Atlantic Ocean from Egypt to South America in ancient times.

MORE INFORMATION

The lighthouse trailhead is located at 168 Lighthouse Drive, Saugerties, NY, 12477. It is open dawn to dusk. Check the tide charts online to time your hike. Avoid periods of extreme high tide. For more information, visit saugertieslighthouse.com or call 845-247-0656. A resident keeper lives at the lighthouse year-round. The keeper conducts tours of the lighthouse interior (weekends Memorial Day through Labor Day, noon to 3 P.M.) and runs a bed-and-breakfast onsite, as well. The B&B, established to support the Saugerties Lighthouse Conservancy's maintenance program, has proven to be very popular. Overnight visitors must book in advance.

To support the continued preservation of this historical landmark, the Saugerties Lighthouse Conservancy offers various levels of membership.

58

KENNETH L. WILSON CAMPGROUND NATURE TRAIL

This easy hike is an ideal first outing for young children, with optional camping, boating, and additional hiking along an interpretive nature trail.

LOCATION
Mount Tremper, NY

RATING
Easy

DISTANCE
1 mile

ELEVATION GAIN
100 feet

ESTIMATED TIME
40 minutes

MAPS
Campsite map

DIRECTIONS

From NYS Thruway (I-87) Exit 19 in Kingston, take the first right from the traffic circle onto NY 28. Go 20 miles west on NY 28 to Mount Tremper, turn right onto NY 212, and continue 0.5 mile to a four-way intersection. Turn right onto Wittenberg Road (CR 40). The campground is approximately 4 miles ahead on the right side of CR 40. From Exit 20 of I-87, follow NY 212 for 8.5 miles to Woodstock then see the following directions from Woodstock.

Alternate route through Woodstock: From Exit 19 (Kingston) off I-87, take NY 28 heading west, go 5.5 miles, then take CR 375 for 2.7 miles into Woodstock. Turn left onto NY 212 and go through Bearsville. Turn left at the Bear Café onto CR 45, and at 2.5 miles go right onto CR 40. Continue 1 mile to the campground on the left. *GPS coordinates:* 42° 1.491′ N, 74° 13.248′ W.

TRAIL DESCRIPTION

This child-friendly, ideal "first hike" is located within a contained and peaceful area that lends itself to the kind of multisport activities young families typically enjoy. Although many state hiking trails begin, end, or pass through public campgrounds in the Catskills, this is one of only a few that have a marked nature trail within the campground itself. This feeling of security, along with the area's diverse activities, makes an ideal setting for the skill- and confidence-building required for more challenging outdoor adventures. The Kenneth L. Wilson

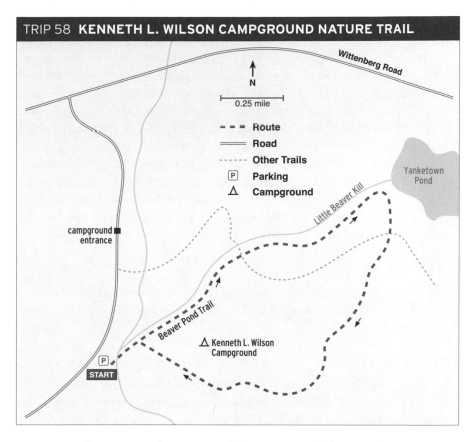

campground is not simply an enjoyable, year-round, day-use destination but also a centrally located staging ground for attractions in the wild forests and wilderness areas of the eastern Catskills.

To find the interpretive nature trail, with numbered stations that describe natural features, proceed to the northwest corner of the parking area next to the lake. There you will find a trail register. Though the trail is short and easy, it's a good idea to sign in at any state trail register. The trail is self-guiding and simple enough that you won't need a map, but try to get one at the entry booth so you can study the interpretive stops along the way. The trail markers feature a beech leaf on a yellow background. You won't see many of them, however.

Cross a small bridge (Station 1) into a beautiful, maturing red- and white-pine forest. A small, seasonal stream flows to your left. Adjacent to Station 2 (Two Pines), the trail forks; bear left. (You'll be returning from the right-hand fork later.) There is no hunting allowed inside the campground, but the adjoining parcels are private, and it is not inconceivable that hunters will position themselves in proximity to the trail. Take the proper precautions and wear bright clothing during hunting season.

At Station 3, the forest type changes to hemlock. Through the woods to the north are open fields. As you reach the beaver meadow at Station 4, the trail splits. The spur to the left leads to private property and is not marked. Continue through the stations, watching for wildlife in the diverse meadow habitat. Bear right and climb gently into a mixed forest of large oaks with a hemlock understory. The trail levels then descends slightly as it curves around, back toward the west. Some large white pines are visible, as well as beech, black birch, and tulip trees (members of the poplar family). Soon you will arrive back in the red-pine forest you entered at the beginning of the hike. Bear left and return to the trailhead.

The final station (Station 10), provides a brief explanation of the Catskills' geological history. It traces time from the Wisconsin Ice Sheet to the streamlined hill, or drumlin, represented by Ticetonyk (Dutch for "steep ladder"), which lies to the south across Little Beaver Kill. The campsite's two narrow lakes were artificially created by the damming of the creek.

DID YOU KNOW?

A small but popular public campground today, this area was once the location of several farms. The land was purchased by the state in the 1960s, and the campground opened in 1979.

MORE INFORMATION

This campground has 76 tent and trailer sites, a lakeside picnic area with tables and grills, flush toilets and hot showers, and is accessible. Bicycles are permitted on the campground roads, but a formerly designated mountain-bike trail no longer exists. Kayaks and canoes are permitted and are available for rent at the site. Rowboats (no motors) are allowed as well. Fishing for bass, pickerel, and sunnies is permitted in the small, sheltered lake. There are baseball and soccer fields. The site is located within view of the rugged Mount Tremper Wild Forest, which you can see to the west. The campsites are large, secluded, and heavily wooded. Dogs are allowed on-leash except in the family picnic and day-use area. (You must have proof of current rabies vaccination.) No untreated firewood may be brought to this campsite from outside of a 50-mile radius. For more information, visit dec.ny.gov/outdoor/24472 .html or call 845-679-7020.

The dog- and family-friendly Wilson campground offers canoeing, hiking, camping, and more.

THE HELDERBERGS

The hikes in the Helderbergs explore two of the state's most striking geological formations. Here, accumulations of sand and lime mud, which had been compressed into rock, uplifted and eroded to form the mountain bastions bordering the plains that much later became the Sea of Albany. These light gray ramparts derive their name from the Dutch *Helder* ("bright" or "light") and *Berg* ("mountain"). The uplift of these hills in the early Tertiary Period and later glacial actions expose a long segment of Earth's history. Views from Vroman's Nose and the cliff face at Indian Ladder are phenomenal. From Vroman's

Nose, perched over the ancient Schoharie floodplain, you look south and east from Grand Gorge to the northern Catskill Escarpment. From Thacher Park and Indian Ladder, the viewshed extends from the southern Adirondacks through Vermont's Green Mountains and across the Taconics.

During the time of the great patroonships, or deeded tracts of land, most of the Helderbergs were owned by the family of Kiliaen van Rensselaer, a major shareholder in the Dutch West India Company and one of the original patentees of the royal land grants of 1629. At the time, Fort Orange (Albany) was the center of the Dutch fur trade, which ultimately proved to be much more profitable than the patroon system. The rich easterly bottomlands would later be populated by the same German Palatines who arrived in the New World at Germantown and were settled in east and west camps in a failed attempt to produce naval stores. A hundred years later, settlers began to arrive from the west to farm the rocky Helderberg escarpment. Many settled along the rich alluvial flats of the Schoharie. Adam Vroman purchased the land in this area from the Mohawks in 1711 but did not receive the official title to it until 1714. He was among the area's earliest farmers.

Vroman's Nose and the acreage surrounding it, now protected for public use, have been in the Vroman family ever since. In 1983, the family formed Vroman's Nose Preservation Corporation (VNPC), which manages the land as forever wild.

59

VROMAN'S NOSE

This beautiful walk offers sweeping views of the Schoharie floodplain and the northern Catskills.

DIRECTIONS

From the intersection of NY 30 and NY 145 just south of Middleburgh, go south on NY 30. Vroman's Nose is obvious; its vertical cliffs rise above NY 30 in front of you. At 0.6 mile, turn right onto Mill Valley Road. Go 0.6 mile on Mill Valley Road and park on your left in the designated lot. *GPS coordinates:* 42° 35.684′ N, 74° 21.500′ W.

TRAIL DESCRIPTION

Vroman's Nose is a trip to save for a lazy afternoon when you'd rather gaze out over the countryside than take a long hike. From this geologically unique, ice-gouged cliff 600 feet above the Schoharie Valley, there are fine views of a vast alluvial farmland floodplain and of the long ridge of the northern Catskills.

At the kiosk, help yourself to a map. A wagon road runs south through a hay field and then through a pair of gates into a forest of large pine and hemlock, turning right as it leaves the field. This trail has been improved with water bars and grading. Follow the green diamond blazes. There are no state trail signs; this is private property belonging to Vroman's Nose Preservation Corporation (VNPC).

The path is self-guiding, and a steady climb over easy terrain (steep in places) continues through mixed hardwoods, pine, and juniper stands. At 1,100 feet or so, the trail turns from southwest to east where Long Path joins it, then swings north as it ascends, yielding fine views of the Schoharie Valley. Twenty-five minutes from the trailhead, you will arrive at the summit, a wooded plateau of roughly 10 acres. The area of flat stone near the precipice is known as the Dance Floor; dances were held here

LOCATION
West Middleburgh, NY

RATING
Moderate

DISTANCE
2 miles

ELEVATION GAIN
480 feet

ESTIMATED TIME
2 hours

MAPS
USGS Middleburgh; Vroman's Nose Preservation Corporation map available at trailhead

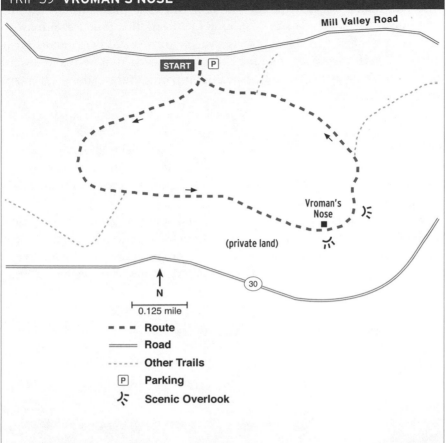

Mill Valley Road

START   P

Vroman's
Nose

(private land)

N
0.125 mile

- - -   Route
=====   Road
······   Other Trails
P   Parking
太   Scenic Overlook

in the early 1900s, during Prohibition. The eastern scarp is vertical and very high. Use caution.

The heavily scored summit of Hamilton sandstone shows evidence of its past in scratches (striae) and chatter marks of a glacier that moved from the northeast beginning about 50,000 years ago, forming the present topography of the Schoharie Valley. The cliff is defaced with engravings and graffiti to such a point that the tagging has had an erosive effect. Several concrete fireplaces have been built to discourage fire-ring assembly by visitors, and impact seems to be under control.

Trees such as oak, hickory, pine, and red cedar thrive on the plateau, which is covered in bearberry (called *kinikinick* by the American Indians). Fringed polygala, an early spring flower, also appears here.

Vincent J. Schaefer, the 1930s founder of Long Path, observed the presence of brachiopods, pelecypods, and trilobites that characterize the Middle Devonian Period's thin sedimentary sheets of Hamilton sandstone. Flagstones from Vroman's Nose were used for the construction of sidewalks in cities such as Troy, Albany, and Schenectady. Schaefer pointed out a curious atmospheric phenomenon that generates a strong thermal updraft against the cliff, noting: "The dark-colored rocks of the cliffs of Hamilton shale and sandstone become quite warm whenever the sun is shining on them. This produces a massive up current of heated air. Light objects such as grass, small twigs, and similar objects when thrown away from the cliff edge are carried upward and toward the north." You may notice birds, especially turkey vultures, taking advantage of this free ride.

The view of Schoharie Creek is striking, and the ancient floodplain is remarkably well defined, with little farms and neatly arranged orchards fringing the creek. Beyond the valley to the east you see the Middleburgh Cliffs. Looking south you will have fine views of Windham High Peak and the Blackhead Range beyond long esplanades of furrowed ground, a geographical contrast that is as distinctive as Vroman's Nose itself.

The long, open fields to the north, east, and south of Vroman's Nose were settled originally by American Indians, who left evidence of campfires under the thin soil. A Schenectady farmer, Adam Vroman, established the first farm here in 1713. He was followed by the German Palatines who originally settled

The Hamilton sandstone of Vroman's Nose generates heat, causing an uplift of warm air against the cliffs. Photo by Jennifer Wehunt.

in the lower Hudson River valley. Crops common to the valley today are corn and carrots. The rich alluvial flats are often flooded by Schoharie Creek, but this usually happens only in early spring and has little effect on existing crops.

If it's icy underfoot, you'll be better off returning the way you came. Otherwise, walk north now and follow the aqua Long Path blazes, passing a few more head-spinning cliffs to your right, then descend steeply. At an intersection with an old woods road, continue following the yellow blazes. (Don't follow right on Long Path.) The yellow-blazed trail comes out in the corner of the field where you began.

DID YOU KNOW?

Early in 1942, Vincent Schaefer visited Vroman's Nose with an employee of the General Electric Research Laboratory to photograph the testing of fog generators. These generators were used to obscure ships, personnel, and cities, preventing air attacks during World War II.

MORE INFORMATION

At the kiosk, you will find the Long Path North Hiking Club's "Hiker's Guide to the Schoharie Valley" as well as information about the Vroman's Nose Preservation Corporation. For more information, visit schoharie-conservation.org/memberclubs/lpn.

LONG PATH

Conceived by the chemist and meteorologist Vincent Schaefer in 1931, Long Path has the same purpose today as it did then: to link the outstanding scenic, geologic, prehistoric, and historic features of the area between New York City and the Adirondacks. Schaefer died in the summer of 1993. He is missed by those who continue to work on the unfinished Long Path as it forges its way north to the Adirondacks, although his memory is inextricably bound to the trail.

Beginning at the George Washington Bridge in New York City, Long Path will eventually end in the northern Adirondacks at Whiteface Mountain. The path's builders intended to construct lean-to shelters a day's hike apart along the trail, but these ambitious plans were interrupted by World War II. Long Path still has its enthusiasts, however, and their mission it is to maintain the trail and continue it to its planned destination.

Those who walk sections of Long Path may be frustrated by the sparingly applied blue blazes that designate the trail. Unlike newer hiking trails, Long Path was meant to be unmarked except for on topographic maps. To quote Schaefer, "Thus a hiker must know how to read a topographic map." Though impractical today, such a route would reduce most of the problems inherent in traditional trail systems, including maintenance, marking, overuse, and litter.

Long Path is managed by the New York–New Jersey Trail Conference and its affiliate clubs.

60

THACHER PARK AND INDIAN LADDER

Indian Ladder Trail follows a narrow catwalk beneath the cliffs of the world's oldest exposed-surface limestone, with extension trails continuing along the Helderberg Escarpment.

DIRECTIONS

The park is 15 miles west of Albany on CR 157. From I-90, take Exit 4 and CR 85 west to CR 157. From the park's entrance sign on CR 157, continue 1.9 miles to the office and the Indian Ladder parking area. *GPS coordinates:* 42° 39.334′ N, 74° 1.174′ W.

TRAIL DESCRIPTION

Indian Ladder and the Thacher Park trail system offer a variety of short walks and activities, best enjoyed along with a picnic at one of Thacher Park's immaculate scenic recreation areas along the Helderberg Escarpment. By far the most interesting of these walks is along the Indian Ladder Trail and its recent extension to the north.

Verplanck Colvin, the surveyor who mapped the wilderness areas of northern New York, wrote about the Helderbergs in 1869, verifying the existence of the so-called Indian Ladder built by American Indians to climb the steep rock wall. The Indian Ladder that Colvin described once leaned against this cliff, but all that exists now are heavy steel staircases that serve a curious public. This first section of trail follows what was originally the Indian Ladder Road, constructed in 1828 from Albany westward into the Schoharie Valley for the conveyance of farm products. At the Indian Ladder trailhead, a second trail goes off to the north and circles around the northern Helderberg Escarpment, which you can hike later. A short distance from the trailhead you will pass the new Thacher Park Center, a visitor center funded by the Open Space Institute's public and private fundraising initiatives

LOCATION
Voorheesville, NY

RATING
Easy

DISTANCE
4 miles

ELEVATION GAIN
200 feet

ESTIMATED TIME
3 hours

MAPS
USGS Altamont; John Boyd Thacher State Park Trail Map

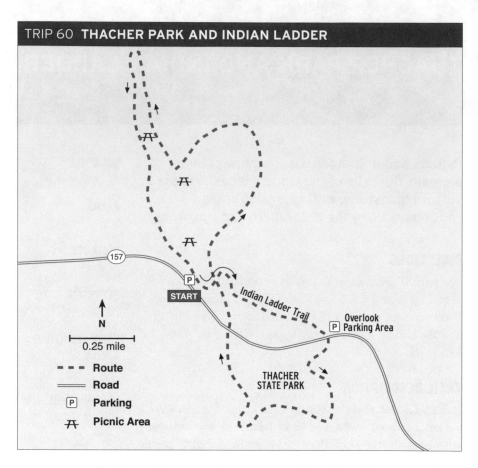

to support and enhance the visitor experience as the park evolves. Descend the stairs and walk beneath the cliffs, heading south.

The upper layers of rock are the youngest, known to geologists as Coeymans limestone. That formation takes its name from the nearby town where it is well exposed. Of the two limestone formations in Thacher Park, Coeymans is the thickest, averaging 50 feet from top to bottom. Look closely here and you may find the preserved remains of small sea creatures: crinoids, brachiopods, and tentaculites. These fossils date from the Late Silurian and Lower Devonian periods, about 415 million years ago.

Continuing down the trail, you'll notice thin layers (2 to 3 inches thick) of alternating light and dark beds of a ribbon limestone that is softer than the Coeymans and recedes beneath it as a result of erosion. This is Manlius limestone, a formation used extensively in the manufacturing of cement in Manlius, near Syracuse. Those thin limestone ribbons form a 50-foot-thick layer that contains the preserved remains of invertebrate sea creatures and algae as well. Part of the formation also contains a 2- to 3-inch layer of water lime, used for making the Portland cement that will set up underwater. This forms a ledge known in the park as Upper Bear Path. At the base of the Manlius Formation is limy mud rock known as the Rondout Formation. This water lime is well exposed near the Ulster County town of Rondout. It was used to produce Rosendale, or natural cement: the invention that brought the Catskills' bluestone quarrying industry to a sudden end. The Rondout Formation is less resistant to erosion but has eroded back to form Lower Bear Path, the ledge you are standing on.

Limestone dissolves in rainwater, causing such phenomena as sinkholes, caves, and disappearing and underground streams. Erosion below ground can form caves that occasionally collapse to form surface depressions, or sinkholes. This phenomenon is known to geologists as karst topography, which denotes any region where bedrock has been dissolved either physically or chemically. It is so named due to its frequent appearance in the Karst region of the Dalmatian Alps.

Once in the large amphitheater, or Indian Ladder Gulf, you will see Outlet and Mine Lot creeks. Together they have been responsible for the erosion of this impressive embayment. When the water table is high, these two creeks form spectacular falls behind which you can walk on the trail. The talus slope beneath the cliff consists of rock that has broken off and fallen from the cliff face. Along Indian Ladder Trail, watch for small, limestone-loving ferns, such as cliff brakes and spleenworts. In the moist spring woods, purple trillium (wake robin) is profuse. Among the endangered species found in the park are the Indiana bat and the spotted salamander. Neotropical magnolia warblers, which winter in the West Indies and Panama, nest in the park's coniferous woods.

At the south end of Indian Ladder Trail, climb the stairs and turn left. (You will see the aqua Long Path blazes along the way now. When Indian Ladder Trail is

The view from the top of Indian Ladder.

open, Long Path follows it. When Indian Ladder Trail closed, Long Path follows along the top, next to the fence.) Within ten minutes, you will arrive at the (auto accessible) Cliff Edge Overlook. Take a minute to enjoy the views of the Green Mountains and the Adirondacks, identifiable with the aid of a large viewshed map.

Continue to the south entrance of the Overlook parking area, cross CR 157, and bear right onto the paved Knowles Flat Picnic Area access road. Watch carefully to the left for Long Path, which you'll see within 400 feet or so after crossing CR 157. Turn left and climb briefly to the Knowles Flat Picnic Area, bear left (south) again along the edge of a field, and enter the woods. Watch for the first junction, a Y, where Long Path and Red Trail go right. (If you've reached the old, rusty water tower, you've gone too far.) Follow the trail through dense, extensive hemlock woods for fifteen minutes.

At a T, take Nature Trail (also marked with white blazes) to your left, ascend, and turn right at a T where you'll see interpretive signpost 13 and signs that read, "To Red Trail." At a four-way junction, bear right at the Nature Trail sign. Follow Red Trail downhill and cross Mine Lot Creek at the head of a tiny gorge. Bear right and descend into the beautiful Paint Mine Picnic Area. Go straight across CR 157, traverse the lawns, and turn left at the fence, following the dirt path back to the Indian Ladder trailhead.

You can finish the hike with a shorter, 2-mile loop on Long Path along the recently designated northern Indian Ladder Trail that follows the Escarpment from this point. From the Indian Ladder trailhead where you originally began, bear left now and follow the trail along the high rim of the Escarpment, passing through the Indian Ladder and Mine Lot picnic areas while threading your way through the woods on Long Path, to the park's northern boundary. Northeasterly views are excellent. Return on the Hailes Cave Picnic Area access road, passing a red-pine plantation and arriving at the Indian Ladder trailhead and parking area in ten or fifteen minutes.

DID YOU KNOW?

The 100-foot-long wooden ladder that Verplanck Colvin described dated to about 1710, when Albany was "a frontier town, a trading post, a place where annuities were paid, and blankets exchanged with Indians for beaver pelts."

MORE INFORMATION

Thacher Park is open year-round from 8 A.M. to dusk. With some allowances made for conditions, Indian Ladder Trail is open from May 1 through November 15. In season, weekend fees apply. Swimming pool season begins June 25, and daily fees apply. There is a 1-hour free-parking limit at Cliff Edge Overlook. A restroom is located at the top of the trailhead. Weekends here can be very crowded. Dogs are allowed on-leash with proof of rabies vaccination. For more information, call the office at 518-872-1237.

APPENDIX
HELPFUL INFORMATION

NYS DEC DIVISION OF LANDS AND FORESTS

Central Office
625 Broadway
Albany, NY 12233
518-402-9405
dec.ny.gov

DEC manages the New York State Forest Preserve lands of the Catskills and detached parcels of state land outside the Catskills. DEC is responsible for search and rescue, planning for management, supervision of campsites, and issuing of camping permits. Because each state region is run independently, it is easiest to obtain local information from one of the regional offices:

NYS DEC Region 3 (Ulster and Sullivan counties)
21 S. Putts Corners Road
New Paltz, NY 12561
845-256-3000

NYS DEC Region 4 Sub Office (Delaware and Greene counties)
65561 State Highway 10
Stamford, NY 12167
607-652-7365

TACONIC STATE PARK AND RECREATION COMMISSION

Mills–Norrie State Parks
P.O. Box 893
Staatsburg, NY 12580
845-889-4646

The Taconic State Park and Recreation Commission manages land assigned to the Office of Parks and Recreation on the east side of the Hudson. It is responsible for state parks and historic sites there, including Hudson Highlands, South Taconic, and Fahnestock state parks.

PALISADES INTERSTATE PARK COMMISSION (PIPC)

Administration Building
Bear Mountain State Park, NY 10911-0427
845-786-2701
nysparks.com
friendsofpalisades.org

The PIPC issues permits and trail information and supervises Harriman and Bear Mountain state parks and the state land of the Shawangunks.

APPALACHIAN MOUNTAIN CLUB (AMC)

5 Joy Street
Boston, MA 02108
617-523-0636
outdoors.org

New York–North Jersey Chapter
New York City Office
5 West 63rd Street, Suite 220
New York, NY 10023
212-986-1430
amc-ny.org

Connecticut Chapter
ct-amc.org

Berkshire Chapter
amcberkshire.org

AMC helps build and maintain trails in southern New York, including some sections of the Appalachian Trail and trails in Harriman, Hudson Highlands, and Catskill state parks. AMC is also a leader in hiking, conservation, canoeing, and bicycling in the metro area. AMC's 12 regional chapters include a New York–North Jersey Chapter, a Connecticut Chapter, and a Berkshire Chapter.

AMC publishes *Catskill Mountain Guide*, also by Peter Kick. The guide can be ordered from the AMC online store, amcstore.outdoors.org, or purchased in many local outdoor shops and bookstores.

THE SIERRA CLUB

Atlantic Chapter
353 Hamilton Street
Albany, NY 12210
518-426-9144
sierraclub.org

Founded in 1892, the Sierra Club works to protect communities, wild places, and the planet itself. The group conducts outings and speaker socials.

THE CATSKILL 3500 CLUB

catskill-3500-club.org

The Catskill 3500 Club is primarily a hiking organization. A membership patch is given for completing climbs of 35 summits of more than 3,500 feet, four of which must be climbed a second time in winter.

NEW YORK-NEW JERSEY TRAIL CONFERENCE (NY-NJTC)

600 Ramapo Valley Rd.
Mahwah, NJ 07430
201-512-9348
www.nynjtc.org

The NY-NJTC coordinates the construction and maintenance of some 1,100 miles of hiking trails, including the Appalachian Trail in New York and New Jersey and Long Path, which connects the metropolitan area with the Catskills and beyond. About 85 hiking clubs and conservation organizations belong to the conference, along with individual members.

ADIRONDACK MOUNTAIN CLUB (ADK)

814 Goggins Rd.
Lake George, NY 12845-4117
518-668-4447
adk.org

ADK has chapters in Ramapo, North Jersey, Mid-Hudson, Long Island, Knickerbocker, New York, Mohican, Albany, and Schenectady, all of which schedule regular hikes in the area described in this guide.

THE CATSKILL CENTER FOR CONSERVATION AND DEVELOPMENT, INC. (CCCD)

P.O. Box 504
Arkville, NY 12406-0504
845-586-2611
www.catskillcenter.org

CCCD is a regional advocate for land-use planning and environmental management, as well as an environmental "watchdog." It is active in natural-area and historic preservation, community revitalization, and public review of regionally significant projects. CCCD owns and manages the 200-acre Platte Clove Preserve, located at the top of Platte Clove in the town of Hunter.

THE CATSKILL MOUNTAIN CLUB

PO Box 404
Margaretville, NY 12455
catskillmountainclub.org

This club offers various hikes and outings for individuals of every ability level. It also conducts stewardship events and volunteer projects dedicated to the preservation of the Catskills.

THE NATURE CONSERVANCY, EASTERN NEW YORK CHAPTER

195 New Karner Rd., Suite 200
Albany, NY 12205
518-690-7850
nature.org

The Nature Conservancy manages and protects natural areas throughout the United States.

INDEX

ABOUT THE AUTHOR

PETER W. KICK is a native of the Catskill Mountains, a New York State licensed guide, and the author of several hiking and cycling guides. His previous books with AMC include *Catskill Mountain Guide, Discover the Adirondacks,* and *Desperate Steps.* Kick's work has also appeared in *Backpacker, Sailing, Cruising World,* and *Adirondack Life.* He is a lifetime member of AMC and lives in St. George, Maine.

AMC IN NEW YORK

The AMC has two active chapters in New York. The New York–North Jersey Chapter offers more than 2,000 trips per year, ranging from canoeing and kayaking, to sailing, hiking, backpacking, and social events. The chapter is also active in trail work and conservation projects and maintains a cabin at Fire Island. The AMC Mohawk-Hudson Chapter serves residents of Albany, Columbia, Fulton, Greene, Montgomery, Rensselaer, Saratoga, Schenectady, Schoharie, Warren, and Washington counties. The chapter offers a variety of outdoor activities for all levels of ability. The Berkshire Chapter has nearly 3,000 members and serves western Massachusetts, maintaining almost 90 miles of the Appalachian Trail. You can learn more by visiting outdoors.org/chapters. To view a list of AMC activities in New York and other parts of the Northeast, visit activities.outdoors.org.

AMC also maintains Harriman Outdoor Center located just 30 miles from Manhattan in Harriman State Park, New York's second largest state park. Harriman Outdoor Center is open to the public, offering common space for outdoor programs, and waterfront access to 64-acre Breakneck Pond. For more information, visit outdoors.org/harriman.

AMC BOOKS UPDATES

AMC Books strives to keep our guidebooks as up-to-date as possible to help you plan safe and enjoyable adventures. If after publishing a book we learn that trails are relocated or route or contact information has changed, we will post the updated information online. Before you hit the trail, check for updates at outdoors.org/publications/books/updates.

While hiking or paddling, if you notice discrepancies with the trail description or map, or if you find any other errors in the book, please let us know by submitting them to amcbookupdates@outdoors.org or in writing to Books Editor, c/o AMC, 5 Joy Street, Boston, MA 02108. We will verify all submissions and post key updates each month. AMC Books is dedicated to being a recognized leader in outdoor publishing.

Thank you for your participation.

APPALACHIAN MOUNTAIN CLUB

At AMC, connecting you to the freedom and exhilaration of the outdoors is our calling. We help people of all ages and abilities to explore and develop a deep appreciation of the natural world.

AMC helps you get outdoors on your own, with family and friends, and through activities close to home and beyond. With chapters from Maine to Washington, D.C., including groups in Boston, New York City, and Philadelphia, you can enjoy activities like hiking, paddling, cycling, and skiing, and learn new outdoor skills. We offer advice, guidebooks, maps, and unique lodges and huts to inspire your next outing. You will also have the opportunity to support conservation advocacy and research, youth programming, and caring for 1,800 miles of trails.

We invite you to join us in the outdoors.

YOUR CONNECTION TO THE OUTDOORS

Catskill Mountain Guide, 3rd Edition

Peter W. Kick

Geared toward intermediate-to-expert hikers, this comprehensive trail guide details every public hiking trail in the Catskill Park. Trek through the area's most scenic destinations with the help of turn-by-turn trail directions, suggested hikes, and a full-color topographic trail map.

$23.95 • 978-1-934028-94-0

Discover the Adirondacks

Peter W. Kick

With so many wilderness opportunities to choose from in the vast Adirondacks, travelers need this concise travel guide. This guidebook invites first-time visitors or seasoned explorers to experience the 50 best multi-sport trips the Adirondacks have to offer.

$18.95 • 978-1-934028-31-5

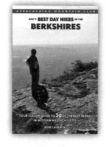

AMC's Best Day Hikes in the Berkshires, 2nd Edition

René Laubach

Discover 50 of the most impressive trails in the Berkshires, home of the Appalachian Trail in Massachusetts. Ideal for families, nature lovers, and hiking enthusiasts, this guide will lead you through the region's spectacular scenic natural areas and up to some of the state's best vistas.

$18.95 • 978-1-62842-012-8

Best Backpacking in the Mid-Atlantic

Michael R. Martin

These 30 overnight trips range in difficulty from intermediate to expert and travel through forests of wild rhododendron at Dolly Sods, across the beaches of Assateague, and over the peaks of New York's Catskill Mountains.

$19.95 • 978-1-934028-86-5

Find these and other AMC titles, as well as ebooks, through ebook stores, booksellers, and outdoor retailers. Or order directly from AMC at outdoors.org/amcstore or call 800-262-4455.